The
I. W. W.

Its First Seventy Years
(1905 – 1975)

The history of an effort to organize the working class

A corrected facsimile of the 1955 volume: *The I.W.W. Its First Fifty Years* by Fred Thompson with new chapter by Patrick Murfin on I.W.W. 1955-1975 and an appendix listing sources on I.W.W. history published since 1955.

Published November 1976

by

Industrial Workers of the World

752 W. Webster Street   Chicago, IL 60614

Glad Day Press
UNION SHOP   I.U. 450
308 Stewart Ave., Ithaca, N.Y. 14850

★ Education

★ Organization   ★ Emancipation

Photo Credits:
Archives of Labor History and Urban Affairs, Wayne State University: Photo section 1, page 1; page 2 bottom; page 3; page 4 top and bottom; Photo section 2, page 2; page 5 top; Photo section 3, page 1 top; page 2; page 3 top.
All others: Industrial Workers of the World.

Library of Congress Catalog Card No. 75-27589

ISBN Paperbound: 0-917124-04-9
ISBN Hardbound: 0-917124-03-0

Set up and printed in the United States of America
by Richard Ellington, Oakland, Calif. and Glad Day Press, Ithaca, N.Y.

CONTENTS

Illustrations are between pages 70-71, 124–125,
200-201.

PREAMBLE TO THE CONSTITUTION OF
THE INDUSTRIAL WORKERS OF THE WORLD

The working class and the employing class have nothing in common. There can be no peace so long as hunger and want are found among millions of the working people and the few, who make up the employing class, have all the good things of life.

Between these two classes a struggle must go on until the workers of the world organize as a class, take possession of the earth and the machinery of production, and abolish the wage system.

We find that the centering of the management of industries into fewer and fewer hands makes the trade unions unable to cope with the ever-growing power of the employing class. The trade unions foster a state of affairs which allows one set of workers to be pitted against another set of workers in the same industry, thereby helping defeat one another in wage wars. Moreover, the trade unions aid the employing class to mislead the workers into the belief that the working class have interests in common with their employers.

These conditions can be changed and the interest of the working class upheld only by an organization formed in such a way that all its members in any one industry, or in all industries if necessary, cease work whenever a strike or lockout is on in any department thereof, thus making an injury to one an injury to all.

Instead of the conservative motto, "A fair day's wage for a fair day's work," we must inscribe on our banner the revolutionary watchword, "Abolition of the wage system."

It is the historic mission of the working class to do away with capitalism. The army of production must be organized, not only for everyday struggle with capitalists, but also to carry on production when capitalism shall have been overthrown. By organizing industrially we are forming the structure of the new society within the shell of the old.

Knowing, therefore, that such an organization is absolutely necessary for emancipation, we unite under the following constitution:

ABOUT THE AUTHORS:

When the greater part of this volume was published in 1955, several reviews expressed surprise that an "official history" should contain such a candid account of ventures that had not worked well. Fred Thompson, who wrote it, likes to quote what Lissagary wrote in his participant history of the Paris Commune, that to glamorize such events and omit what may embarrass is like giving sailors a chart that leaves out the reefs and shoals. Patrick Murfin has acted on that belief in his additions to this book.

Both writers have been active participants in many of the events of which they write, and have talked with participants in events they missed.

Fred Thompson was born in St. John, Canada, in 1900, and became a member of the Socialist Party of Canada in his youth. As secretary of his local, he was in correspondence with radicals on both sides of the border. He worked in a paper box factory, a sugar refinery, the Halifax shipyards where he was involved in his first strike, went west in 1920 and joined the Canadian One Big Union. He came to the United States in 1922, worked in a Hoquiam sawmill, and on various construction projects along the west coast, joining the IWW in San Francisco in September. The following April he was arrested in Marysville and after two trials was convicted as an IWW organizer under the California Criminal Syndicalism law. After his release in 1927 from San Quentin, where he had the company of over a hundred other victims of the same law, he was active in efforts to repair the 1924 "split" in the IWW. He was also elected to the General Executive Board representing Construction Workers Industrial Union 310. At various times he has edited IWW papers, been an instructor at Work Peoples College, an organizer in Detroit and Cleveland in the mid-thirties, secretary of the Cleveland Metal and Machinery Workers Industrial Union 440 branch from 1943-46, and author of several IWW pamphlets.

Patrick Murfin was born in Montana in 1949 and grew up in Cheyenne, Wyoming. He joined the IWW in Chicago in 1969 after being active in student and community organizing, as well as in the peace movement. He has been Chicago Branch Secretary, a member of the General Executive Board, General Secretary-Treasurer in 1972, and currently is editor of the *Industrial Worker.* He has worked at a variety of jobs including labor writer for the Chicago *Seed,* offset pressman, and welder in a bicycle plant. In 1973, he served six months in federal prison at Sandstone, Minnesota, for refusing induction into the armed forces. For the last three years he has worked in a plant manufacturing engineering, drafting, and print-making equipment.

The IWW: Its First 50 Years has been out of print for some time. We are proud to reprint it now as *Its First 70 Years.* We shall keep on trying, for the job the IWW set out to do in 1905 still desperately needs to be done. Are you with us?

General Executive Board, IWW
Terry Dennis, Chairman

I. Why the I.W.W. Was Started

The I.W.W. was started in 1905 by "seasoned old unionists," as Gene Debs called them,[1] who realized that American labor could not win with the sort of labor movement it had. There was too much "organized scabbery" of one union on another, too much jurisdictional squabbling, too much autocracy, and too much hobnobbing between prosperous labor leaders and the millionaires in the National Civic Federation. There was too little solidarity, too little straight labor education, and consequently too little vision of what could be won, and too little will to win it.

Building a new labor movement was not a project to be undertaken lightly. Even to build a new craft union was something then to undertake with great caution and secrecy, but the six men whose meeting in the fall of 1904 gave eventual birth to the I.W.W. aimed at one organization of all labor to replace the existing labor movement. When they met it was only 18 years since the AFL had been set up to rout the Knights of Labor and to protect the craft unions from the inroads that its greater vision of solidarity was making on their vested interests. The Knights had been rendered impotent only ten years earlier, and labor leaders still watched vigilantly lest any similar movement break out. Those who could be counted upon to help were few and were already active in the existing labor movement, its socially-minded or radical minority, and were engaged in vigorous disputes among themselves over theory and policy. To identify themselves with this new effort might mean the loss of their union positions, and worse yet, turning over those positions to reactionaries who wanted, not only the job, but the opportunity to make the unions more acceptable to the plutocrats on the Civic Federation.

The six men who met in Chicago in November of
1904 to consider what might be done to correct the
inadequacies of the labor movement, did so secretly. These six were Clarence Smith, secretary of
the American Labor Union; Thomas Haggerty, editor of that union's paper, "The Voice of Labor";
George Estes and W. L. Hall, president and secretary of the United Brotherhood of Railway Employees; Isaac Cowan, American representative of
the Amalgamated Society of Engineers; and William
E. Trautman, editor of the "Brauer-Zeitung," official organ of the United Brewery Workmen. Involved, but unable to attend, were Gene Debs, long
interested in industrial unionism especially for the
railroad workers, and Charles O. Sherman, secretary of the United Metal Workers. The common
interests of these men perhaps best explain why
the I.W.W. was born; and their discordant interests,
the troubles of the labor movement that the I.W.W.
was to inherit.

The United Brotherhood of Railway Employees
consisted of men mostly in the Chicago and nearby
Indiana yards, and some in Kansas, who had been
with Debs' American Railway Union in 1894, and
who resented the action whereby he "had left them
without a fighting industrial union and forced them
to enter the scab craft movements after he changed
the ARU to a political movement," as one of them
described their situation.[2] Estes had helped organize the Order of Railroad Telegraphers and,
when given the job of revising its constitution, had
urged a federation of all railroad brotherhoods, and
the dropping of the phrase in its statement of purpose, "no quarrel with capital." When the ORT
joined the AFL, Estes and those supporting his program, withdrew and with members from other railroad crafts started the UBRE. However, it felt too
isolated and that year, 1904, it had applied to
the AFL for a charter. This was refused, as the
Scranton Declaration of 1901 restricted industrial
unionism to the coal mines, and to avoid antagoniz-

ing the railroad brotherhoods that the AFL hoped
might join it.[3]

The United Metal Workers had dropped out of
the AFL that year. In 1900 Charles Sherman, with
Gompers' approval, had got the three Chicago locals
of metal workers, which were affiliated directly
with the AFL, to call a convention to launch their
own international. Their originally extensive jurisdiction had been steadily eaten away. After organizing the coppersmiths 95 per cent throughout the
United States, these men were surrendered, against
their own wishes, to the Sheet Metal Workers. A
special charter issued in 1902 lopped off the bridge
and structural iron workers. The expense of efforts
to adjust jurisdictional claims had exceeded $4000,
and the 1904 convention of the AFL ordered the
union broken up into further pieces. On referendum
the United Metal Workers voted 92 per cent to disaffiliate and to adopt an industrial structure.
Though this had meant more opposition and raids,
it grow more rapidly, according to Sherman, after
its separation from the AFL.[4]

The Amalgamated Society of Engineers had been
brought here by skilled machinists coming from
Britain with a strong attachment for the semi-
industrial structure of their union that had been the
model of progressivism from 1851 until the "new
unionism" was born on the docks of Britain in the
1890's.[5] Its American section had just been thrown
out of the AFL on jurisdictional grounds in 1904.

The United Brewery Workmen was fighting for
preservation of its industry-wide jurisdiction. Inside
it a schism had been developing between the previously dominant socialistic old-timers and the rising crop of "major party" labor politicians. It had
been born of America's first "stay-in" strike, in the
Jackson Brewery in Cincinnati in 1884. In those
days to keep the brauerei-knechte or "brewery
peons" at beck and call, management housed them
on the property in a "schalander." They were still
mostly German-speaking in 1904. In this first stay-
in strike, the workers sent management out, barri-

caded themselves with barrels of beer against the
state troopers, and had a food supply to last them
for weeks. Every shot at the barricade poured pre-
cious amber fluid down the streets, unstained by
blood. The employers gave in, and the union was
founded. It declared it would be industrial, and
among its purposes was one of educating its members to make good beer to add to the joy of the Co-
operative Commonwealth.[6]

The Brewery Workmen grew to a national organization, affiliating with the AFL in 1887. Many of
its locals were affiliated with the Knights of Labor.
This was encouraged because of the extra boycott
power it gave, for the union relied heavily upon
this weapon and was engaged for fourteen years
(1888-1902) in a boycott against the National Brewery Owners Association. As a national body it joined
the Knights in 1893; then under penalty of losing
its AFL charter, withdrew in 1896, still urging its
individual members to stay with the badly routed
Knights to build the greater solidarity. That same
year the coopers' union demanded it get the brewery coopers. Then in 1898 came a demand to surrender the engineers. In 1902 the AFL ordered the
firemen and engineers out of it. At the 1904 AFL
convention the teamsters demanded 10,000 beer
truck drivers. The brewery workers voted on referendum 34,612 to 367 not to surrender to these
claims.

At the Brewery Workmen's convention in September 1904 there had been some talk of leaving
the AFL and joining with the American Labor Union, the other major participant in this November
conference; but it was plain that the ALU must become a bigger union to make such a switch possible,
and enable the Brewery Workmen, if so affiliated,
to enforce boycotts and resist jurisdictional raids.
The brewery workers were also held back by an
internal "right-left" schism, born of the political
policy of "reward your friends," and the need of
city central labor bodies for ties with whichever
party got in, ties that were indispensable in the

racketeering in which central labor bodies, especially through their building trades, were at the time heavily involved. Trautman, representing the progressive brewery forces, attended both this and the January conference without notifying his union.[7]

The American Labor Union had been founded by the Western Federation of Miners in 1902 because these metal miners wanted a class-wide labor body with which to affiliate. It had not flourished, and a chief reason for this November conference, and eventually for the determination to launch the I.W.W., was the hope of these western metal miners, and of the men they had rallied to the American Labor Union, and of the progressive forces around Trautman in the Brewery Workmen, that the obvious inadequacy and misdirection of the labor movement might now make it possible, by mergers and re-organization and the organization of the unorganized, to build an organization large enough to give the brewery workers the power to boycott any scab beer, and to provide each affiliate with the unstinted backing of all.

The Western Federation of Miners was frontier unionism, the organization of workers who had become "wage slaves" of mining corporations rather recently acquired by back-east absentee ownership. They built their union when they were not yet "broken in" to the discipline of business management. It had the militancy of the undisciplined recruits who fought for the ten hour day here in the 1830's, or for Chartism in England in the same era, or those who staged the sit-down strikes of France in 1936 and here in 1937. From the founding of the Western Federation in 1893, its story for twelve years is that of a continuous search for solidarity. Metal miners had been organized locally before that time, and formed their federation the better to back each other up in the increasingly hard battles forced upon them by well-heeled big business management. The idea of federating the vari-

ous local unions was said to have been born "in the
Ada County jail" and bull pens where hundreds of
them were herded after the Couer d'Alene strike of
1892. It affiliated with the AFL, but its delegates
to the AFL Cincinnati convention of 1896 came
away not only disappointed with the refusal to aid
their big fight in Leadville, but with a feeling that
they had not been associating with union men, or
with men possessing the moral or intellectual fibre
ever to become good union men.[8]

They left the AFL and launched the Western Labor Union. The miners had reasons for building
unions for non-miners. The mining territory was,
apart from the miners, unorganized; the AFL outside of Denver and a few cities had done little western organizing except on the coast. Workers outside
the miners wanted a union, and the Western Federation either had to take them in or build them
one, for it needed to have them organized and on
their side. How their strikes went depended largely
on how the rest of the community that didn't work
in the mines stood. Their strike experience had
shown it made a substantial difference whether
state politics was under labor-Populist influence or
not. In the Cripple Creek strike of 1891-94 the Populist Governor had used the National Guard to re-
strain the private armies recruited by mine management. In the Leadville strike two years later the
Governor swore the scabs into the National Guard
and deputized the business element to give the miners a hard time. Gene Debs was on hand to help
them organize the Western Labor Union and teach
them socialism and solidarity. In the second battle
of the Coeur d'Alene 1899-1901 Federal troops dem-
onstrated the power of the back east owners, com-
pelling some miners to work at gun point, others
to build their own bull-pens, inventing the rustling
card system so no man could hunt a job without the
sheriff's approval, and using Governor Steunenberg,
whom the miners had helped elect as a Populist, to
oust the elected local authorities who might have
some sympathy with the strikers.

The miners wanted a nationwide labor movement that would not only help provide beans and bacon when long strikes had drained their own treasuries, but would exert some pressure to expose the daily press that lied about them and that thereby laid the carpet for atrocities by Federal troops. Class-wide solidarity was not only an ideal with them; it was a bread-and-butter necessity, the only conceivable means to protect their wives against the atrocities of Federal troops, and their children from the hunger imposed by absentee owners.

The Western Labor Union worried the Washington, D.C., heads of the AFL. Frank Morrison, secretary of the AFL, came to Salt Lake City in 1902 to attend the conventions of the Western Federation and its projection, the Western Labor Union. He threatened that if they did not re-affiliate, he would build a rival union. The delegates knew what that would mean: their dismemberment by crafts in an industry that made industrial unionism a matter of necessity, not one of choice. They feared too it would crush the spirit of their union, and they sensed that the anti-capitalist spirit that they cultivated in themselves and the community was an essential part of the defense of their bread and butter. Mark Hanna had launched the National Civic Federation in 1900 to housebreak unionism, to confine its growth to those fields where management could use it, and to emasculate it by a united front of labor leaders and captains of industry against all socialistic and insurgent elements. Miners knew that this growth of what was called "responsible unionism," in which the members were responsible to the leaders whom Mark Hanna called "the labor lieutenants of the captains of industry," meant more "sell-outs" of the sort imposed on the steel workers in 1901. So they met Morrison's threat by changing the name of the Western Labor Union to American Labor Union, a challenge to the AFL in its back east empire. To spice the retort they endorsed Debs' new Socialist Party, partly because it was an antidote to Morrison's and Gompers' and Mark Hanna's poison, partly because they thought socialism might be a good idea, and partly because they liked Debs who had been around in their strikes making speeches to help their families keep a stiff upper lip.[9]

Between then and this November 1904 conference they had fought a two year war in Colorado. The union had spent over $400,000 in this struggle against the companies, the militia and the Citizens' Alliance. Its members had been put in bull-pens, its officers repeatedly indicted. White-capped vigilantes had invaded its members' homes to deport them; the right of habeas corpus had vanished; the miners' wives were subjcted to outrages and terrorism. As the secretary of the Western Federation, Bill Haywood, told the January conference: "The miners of Colorado fought alone the capitalist class of the United States; we don't want to fight that way again."

The American Labor Union had grown only to about 16,000 members, not counting the 27,000 in its chief affiliate the Western Federation. But these included the two thousand or more in the UBRE which was affiliated with ALU and those in Amalgamated Society.[10] It's paper "The Voice of Labor" edited by a left-wing socialist, Thomas J. Haggerty, often called Father Haggerty, was an effective challenge to craft unionism, organized scabbery, and the Gompers-Hanna unholy alliance. It seemed plain that unless the progressive forces in the labor movement could be rallied to build something new, the metal miners would have to fight that way again, the brewery workers would be dismembered, and that an unbridled and reactionary autocracy would stifle these progressive forces that could be found to some degree in all unions. This is the chief explanation why these six men met in November 1904, to consider whether there was any chance of building a labor movement in which unions would support each other and not, in the name of sacred contracts, scab on each other.

As these six men met it was plain their combined mass lacked the gravitational pull necessary to start

a new movement which it would seem prudent for
progressive forces to join. The labor history of the
last few years made them reckon, however, that a
sufficient mass could be rallied. There had been
great recent changes in the environment of the labor
movement: first "the Morganization of industry" or
mushrooming of great trusts starting with U.S. Steel
in 1900; growth in the size of factories and consequent interdependence of crafts; the open shop
campaign of the Citizens' Alliances from 1902 on
a nation-wide scale with backing of National Association of Manufacturers. The new model for capital
organization, U.S. Steel, had promptly broken the
old Amalgamated steel union in the strike of 1901
and had locked unions out of the nation's basic metal
industry by lulling Gompers into inaction in the
belief that Morgan was a "friend of labor." On the
Great Lakes the Lake Carriers was organizing to
drive off unionism. In the then very important
molding trade, a much prized national agreement
had given way to a current attempt of the employers' association to rout the Molders throughout the
nation. The Machinists similarly after the Murray
Hill Truce now found themselves for several years
in ceaseless conflict with the National Metal Trades
Association. In the building trades, the racketeer
unionism of Skinny Madden and Parks had played
out; AFL unions had been compelled to merge with
dual company unions; their sympathetic strike machinery was disrupted, and a most unpalatable arbitration scheme imposed in major cities. On the railroads the unions existed only for such crafts as the
owners let organize; Clerks were not allowed a union. On the Louisville & Nashville and other roads
the shop crafts were engaged in long and unsupported strikes for survival. On New York's Inter-
borough Transit, as these six men met, August Belmont, bell-wether of the National Civic Federation,
was using the ace strike-breaker James Farley to
build up an army of scabs should the men dare
strike. The Butcher Workmen had just collapsed
before the onslaughts of the Beef Trust in the strike

(made famous by Sinclair's "Jungle") that ended
with unconditional surrender in September 1904.

Could a labor union of the sort needed for this
new industrial situation be built by the re-organization of the crafts and the enrollment of millions
of unorganized? The six men decided there might
be a chance, and invited 36 of those they figured
best able to help to attend a secret conference to
be held January 2, 1905.

The six men were all in the general sense of the
term, socialist as, in that age, were most staunch
unionists, either espousing some specific socialist
program or expressing a general faith in some vague
"Co-operative Commonwealth" as the solution to
the "labor question." Even most old line union Pre-
ambles expressed such ideas, and rather unavoid-
ably, since the reason for their formation was to
win quarrels with employers, and these quarrels
would arise no matter what they won so long as the
employer-employee relation continued. Consequently to contemplate final or complete victory for labor
had for decades been recognized as the contempla-
tion of some social order successor to capitalism in
which workers owned their jobs and the equipment
with which they worked either individually or collectively. While the practical reason for their meeting was the need for greater labor union solidarity,
it was plain to them that the solution of this practical problem would assure the solution of the larger
"labor question," and this was emphasized in their
invitation:

"Asserting our confidence in the ability of the
working class, if correctly organized on both pol-
litical and industrial lines, to take possession of
and operate successfully . . . the industries of the
country;

"Believing that working-class political expression,
through the Socialist ballot, in order to be sound,
must have its economic counterpart in a labor organization builded as the structure of socialist society, embracing within itself the working class in

approximately the same groups and departments and industries that the workers would assume in the working-class administration of the Co-operative Commonwealth;

"We invite you to meet us at Chicago, Monday, Jan. 2, 1905, in secret conference to discuss ways and means of uniting the working people of America on correct revolutionary principles, regardless of any general labor organization of past or present, and only restricted by such basic principles as will insure its integrity as a real protector of the interests of the workers."

Size was important for solving the practical problems that had brought these six men together. In retrospect it appears that they erected a barrier to size by this pre-natal injection of revolutionary theory. While the January conference in Wostas Hall was attended by 23 persons, representing nine organizations, it represented very little more union force than the November conference. Of them 18 came from these same unions, though now Moyer, Haywood and O'Neil represented the Western Federation directly; Sherman and Kirkpatrick came from the United Metal Workers; Trautman had brought along Frank Kraft of the Brewery Workmen. New participants were "Mother" Jones of the United Mine Workers, Shurtleff of the International Musical Union, Schmitt and Guild from the Bakers, the former the editor of its Journal, and W. J. Pinkerton of the Switchmen. Debs was prevented from attending by illness. Though representing no union, A. M. Simons, editor of the International Socialist Review, was present, and though not originally invited, Frank Bohn, national organizer for the Socialist Trade & Labor Alliance, who happened to be passing through Chicago, was asked to participate, and did. This brought the gathering to 25. They decided to go through with the attempt, and issued a Manifesto calling for an Industrial Union Congress in Chicago on June 27. When this met, it became the Industrial Workers of the World.[11]

This Manifesto called for "the economic organization of the working class without affiliation with any political party"; industrial organization, with "industrial autonomy internationally"; transfers between local or national or international unions to be universal; a central defense or strike fund to which all members were to contribute equally; its general administration to be conducted "in harmony with the recognition of the irrepressible conflict between the capitalist class and the working class." It argued for the need for such an organization from the technological changes in industry, the organization of capital, and recent bitter experience in strikes.

The proposals of this Manifesto came however to be considered less on their obvious union merits than on the suspicion what political motives might lie behind them. The Manifesto was much more a union document than the letter of Nov. 29. It went into the socialist issue only by including in its criticism of the craft union movement the comment that "it is blind to the possibility of establishing an industrial democracy, wherein there shall be no wage slavery, but where the workers will own the tools which they operate, and the product which they alone will enjoy." The committee circulated 180,000 copies of the Manifesto, and the reaction was largely the question, what were the bifurcated socialists planning to do to the unions now? One good indirect result: the industrial jurisdiction of the Brewery Workmen was temporarily restored.

To make at all clear the reception of this Manifesto it is necessary to consider at least briefly the past relations of the unions and the American socialist movement. Immigrants, especially Germans, had brought over the controversies of Marx, Lassalle and Bernstein; such books as Bellamy's "Looking Backward" had made a strong impression on American labor; the old Greenback and Populist movements had become impregnated with some of this more systematic socialist theory; the fact that the major labor movements of most other countries

gave at least lip service to socialist ideals, had its
influence; both the immigrant and native socialist
movements had carried on propaganda and sought
converts and positions in the unions. A major argument within socialist ranks was over the role of
unions in relation to their program. Complete Marx-
ists said that not only was the will to build a new
social order an outgrowth of the daily union struggle, but that the unions themselves were the "cells
of the future society." They felt union activity was
part of the work of a socialist. Complete Lassalleans
said workers could gain nothing by unions, that the
unions diverted the efforts of labor into futile channels from the building of a party by which to triumph. But all were sympathetic toward unionism
and strikers. Some of both these divisions said that
the future was one of increasing misery for labor
until it reached the intolerable point where labor
woke up and somehow made itself supreme; others
of both these divisions held that either by union or
legislative gains labor would steadily improve its
lot as it increased its competence to run the world.
Some said victory would be by ballots; some that
it would come only by violent revolution. Some felt
the way to win was to start colonies to practice socialism; some that it required the growth of select
groups studying and agreeing upon fine points of
doctrine; others that it was by building reform
parties with a mass appeal, even if this involved
slogans in which the leaders themselves could not
believe. Socialism was far from a uniform body of
thought, but most socialists felt that it was good to
"bore from within" the unions, to seek converts,
votes, and positions.

Marx's First International, the IWMA, mortally
wounded by the affright of British labor after the
Paris Commune of 1871, and by schisms between
himself and Bakunin, moved to New York in 1872,
and was dissolved at a convention in Philadelphia,
July 15, 1876. Four days later the delegates merged
with a few American labor political groups to found
the Workingmen's Party of the United States which

bore the brunt of agitation in the spontaneous strike movement of 1877, and at the close of the next year changed its name to Socialistic Labor Party of North America. It sought friendly relations with the unions, particularly with those of the Gompers persuasion until 1890 when it began its quarrel with the AFL, and, with the final "ic" off the first term in its name, began its re-shaping under Daniel De Leon. For five years it gave its attention to the Knights of Labor, then losing out in that venture, De Leon grabbed what he could to form the Socialist Trade & Labor Alliance, a union completely dominated by SLP. This body started out with 20,000 but dwindled rapidly though 228 charters were issued prior to its Buffalo convention in 1898; after that convention the Central Federated Union in New York with its locals quit, leaving the ST&LA little more than a "paper" union in which the members of the SLP doubled as union members. It reported 1450 members in 1905 and entered about 1200 into IWW.

One circumstance that shaped its character was the "violence" mania of the mid-eighties. Largely under the influence of Johann Most, a large section of the then appreciable anarchist movement and of those socialists who placed little hope in the election process, adopted the Pittsburgh program of physical force in 1883 and pushed the dynamite philosophy that made the conviction of the Haymarket anarchists easy despite their obvious innocence. The aftermath was a strong employer offensive (the more effective as neither AFL nor K of L had defended the Haymarket victims) and the first clear triumph of conservative bureaucracy in the unions, denouncing all radicalism as tainted with this violence. This was the easier as the dynamite enthusiasts had scorned the union movement and its 8 hour campaign. De Leon, appealing to leftists who tended to assume that the plutocrats would yield to nothing short of a triumph of arms, preached the doctrine as "unquestionable" laws of society, that in election the workers must establish their right to rule, but that "right without might is illusory; in other words,

the field of physical force is the unavoidable court
of second and last resort," and thirdly "He who cannot vote right, ever will shoot wrong."[12] This he
termed putting the class struggle "on the civilized
plane," and jumped to the conclusion that for any
group to advocate a major social change without en-
dorsing a political party and program to legislate it,
implied "physical forcism."

From the 1890 breach with the AFL and the 1898
breach with the Knights, the De Leon group reached
the further conclusion that the labor union movement was a corrupt mobilization of labor for the
defense and perpetuation of capitalism, and that
workers alike for everyday struggles and ultimate
emancipation must build socialist industrial unionism. The possibilities of such unionism as visualized
in the ST&LA and more clearly yet with the launching of the IWW, so long as the De Leonites could
exert a substantial influence in it, tended to replace
the prospect of "physical force" as the field of last
encounter with the prospect of a lockout of employers by an organized working class, to supply might
to the revolutionary SLP ballot.

Though the ST&LA had dwindled instead of
growing, the De Leon movement was an irritant to
the AFL leadership. The presence of Bohn, national
organizer of the ST&LA, at the January conference
and his signature to the Manifesto, was taken by
most union organs as evidence that De Leon was
attempting to use this need of metal miners, brewery
and other workers for a class-wide industrial union
movement, to build a bigger ST&LA which he could
dominate. The discussion on the Manifesto running
for months in the columns of De Leon's Daily People
clearly showed that this was the hope and plan of
those SLP members who favored participation.[13]
This hurt the chances for the new movement the
more because of recent splits in the socialist movement.

Since most socialists felt it necessary somehow to
get along with the unions, even when they were

hostile to socialist ideals, and since the interest in
the labor movement that led a worker to become a
socialist often led him to be active enough in his
union to become an officer of it, the switch of the
only socialist party in the country to a policy of
devoting most of its effort to an attack on the existing unions, created a demand for a socialist movement less doctrinaire than De Leon's and able to get
along with the unions as they were. Debs' conversion to socialism after the Pullman strike provided
this movement with its most popular and effective
exponent. He turned the remnants of his American
Railway Union into the Social Democracy of America,
which by merger with defections from the SLP, in
1901 became the Socialist Party of America. Between the two parties raged such a war as can be
found only between competing radicals. The more
Marxian and "class struggle" tendencies in the
young Socialist Party were focused around the International Socialist Review, a monthly magazine
issued in Chicago and edited by Simons, who also
attended the January conference and signed the
Manifesto. All this put the proposal for a new union movement to end organized scabbery and Civic
Federation hobnobbing, in the middle of vociferous
arguments between different schools of socialists.
Most socialist papers condemned the new effort then
and throughout its formative years, chiefly, as Debs
repeatedly insisted, not because of any principle or
sound argument, but out of personal hostility toward De Leon.[14]

These circumstances not only prevented the proposals of the Manifesto from being considered on
their merits, but beset the new union with internal
quarrels that almost killed it in its infancy. From
the advantaged view of hindsight it seems plain that
had neither Simons nor Bohn attended that January
conference, and had these extraneous political quarrels been sidetracked, it would have been much
better for the IWW and the labor movement.

An indirect good was the preservation of the industrial jurisdiction of the Brewery Workmen.

Trautman, editor of their paper, was deposed for his participation in this new venture; the issue went to referendum of the brewery workers, so that according to Trautman, with 10,481 votes cast for him and only 9,157 against, the AFL Executive counsel bought his ouster by restoring the charter revoked in 1904 in turn for counting out enough of these votes. The threat of the IWW was again to preserve industrial union jurisdiction for the brewery workers in 1908 and 1912.[15]

To the Industrial Union Congress June 27, 1905 came 70 delegates empowered to install the Western Federation, the American Labor Union, the United Brotherhood of Railway Employees, and the Socialist Trade and Labor Alliance, a total membership of 50,827 according to the memberships claimed by each. Also came 72 delegates without power to install, and 61 individual delegates able to install only themselves. With great oratory and repeated assurances by Debs and De Leon that here was common grounds for all socialists to meet, they launched the Industrial Workers of the World, with little more actual backing than at that November conference of six men, minus the hopes then held of including the Brewery Workmen. There could be no blindness to the difficulties ahead; it was started because there was obvious need for a union of, by, and for the working class, and hopes that it might so conduct its affairs that locals and internationals would join, and great masses of unorganized workers become organized through its efforts.

General Sources: Brissenden's "IWW" is the best work available as yet, but covers the story with fullness only up to 1913, and sketchily to 1918. Gambs' "Decline of the IWW" purportedly taking up where Brissenden left off, indicates no such familiarity with the subject as Brissenden had. The story of the IWW in short is given rather well in several chapters of Vol. IV of the History of Labor in the United States, that volume being written by Perlman and Taft. For the Western Federation of Miners, see Jensen's "Heritage of Conflict" which is a detailed history of that union, but takes a rather hostile attitude toward IWW from the year 1906 on. "Bill Haywood's Book" contains much information. Bound copies of the Proceedings of the First Convention of the IWW are available from the SWP. A series in the *Industrial Worker* in 1950, entitled "Hard Rock Miner," considers the relations of the IWW and the WFM and SLP in great detail. Another series, "The I.W.W. Tells Its

Own Story," starting in *Industrial Solidarity* December 23, 1930, and continuing in *Industrial Worker* to August 2, 1932, gives the story in much more detail than it is given in this book up to 1919. In 1945, to mark the 40th anniversary, the *Industrial Worker* ran a series, "The First Forty Years," and much other commemorative material, largely written by those who had participated in the making of the IWW's history, in issues from June to September. Because of space limitations, this booklet has avoided detail on those aspects where detail is readily available; and in these footnotes confines reference usually to items not included in the already published accounts.

1. In article Aug. 1906 in *The Worker,* a Socialist publication, reprinted in *Daily People,* Aug. 12, 1906.

2. Quoted from Pinkerton, one of its delegates to 2nd Convention, in *Daily People,* Nov. 4, 1906.

3. Re Estes, *Daily People,* Feb. 23, 1905.

4. Re Sherman and United Metal Workers, *Daily People,* June 3, 1905.

5. Barou: "British Trade Unions," p. 15.

6. Trautman in *OBU Monthly,* October, 1937.

7. Sources: *Daily People,* March 9 and April 30, 1905, and Perlman & Taft, Vol. IV, pp. 363-365.

8. See Jensen, "Heritage of Conflict," p. 60.

9. All was not friendly between ALU and WFM, according to Trautman in *IUB,* Feb. 22, 1908.

10. Membership of American section of the ASE seems about 4,000; Trautman reported to 2nd convention that for one year its tax to ALU had been $2,688.13.

11. The Manifesto has been frequently republished, as in Brissenden's "Launching," in "Bill Haywood's Book," as a separate leaflet on several occasions, and is currently available as first item in Kornbluh's "Rebel Voices."

12. Editorial, *Daily People,* Feb. 3, 1905. For the general history of American radicalism in 19th century see both Vols. II and IV of the "History of Labor in the United States," and David's "The Haymarket Affair."

13. Examples: *Daily People,* Jan. 26: "With the conception of a Socialist Union comes the cessation of the struggle for higher wages and shorter hours, and the struggle for working class supremacy begins." Feb. 3, W. Cox argued, "The new economic organization must be affiliated with SLP or party must fight it." March 19 issue showed how completely SLP dominated ST&LA. March 31, Olive M. Johnson writes: "It is impossible that the ST&LA can desire a separation of the political and economic organization of labor... or even passively submit to it." April 1 issue, H.J. Schade proposed that the initiation fee of the new union be used for subscription to *Weekly People,* and E.J. Rounier argues: "The Constitution of the SLP designates any union not under the control of the party as pure and simple. The SLP insists that the economic organization be controlled by the political one."

14. Debs wrote in *Worker,* Aug. 1906 (reprinted *People,* Aug. 12, 1906): "It may be that De Leon has designs upon the Socialist Party and expects to use the I.W.W. as a means of disrupting it ... if he succeeds, it will be because his enemies in the Socialist Party, in their bitter personal hostility to him, denounce the revolutionary IWW and support the reactionary AFL and thereby play directly into his hands."

15. Same sources as Footnote 7.

II. Getting Started — 1905-1908

Though the founding convention of the IWW ended with declarations of affiliation by bodies that
gave it a claimed membership of about 52,000 to
start with, it did not start with this membership.
Apart from the individuals who had joined, it
started out with the 1100 members the American
Labor Union entered on August 1, and the $817.59
that John Riordan of the ALU had left after wind-
ing up the affairs of the ALU. This was a substantial let-down from the 16,750 that ALU had reported to first convention. Sherman's United Metal
Workers entered 700 members, not the 3,000 it had
claimed. When the Socialist Trade & Labor Alliance entered 1200 members, this with the UBRE
and individuals and miscellaneous groups brought
the membership for September to 4,247. By that
time individual recruiting was under way and raised
the membership to 5078 in early October and by
Nov. 1, to 7,800. It stayed at about that level until
the membership of the Metal Department doubled
in February and again in March to 3000 bringing the
total on April 1 to 13,266.

This growth in the Metal Department was almost
entirely in Schenectady among General Electric
workers. Punch Press Operators Union No. 224 of
that city was one of the bodies represented at the
first convention. Now with the aid of an SLP group
and others in a Workmen's Sick & Death Benefit
Society, it promoted the IWW idea in this plant
employing 17,000, some two thirds of whom were
under various AFL contracts. The IWW in the summer of 1906 built up a membership of about 2,500
among these workers, taking over some craft locals
intact, and keeping them as 17 craft affiliates of
its Industrial Council of Metal and Machinery Workers. The favorite method used in this first auspi-
cious organizing campaign of the new union was to
sit down until grievances in a department got ad-

justed. This tactic was devised to end the run-
around that management and business agents had
been giving the men on their grievances, and it was
practiced also by the AFL union members in the
plant. On hourly rates they drew their pay while
staging sitdowns lasting from a few minutes in some
cases to most of a shift in others.[1]

Strikes, almost entirely in the east, steadily drained the organization's resources, with no promising
development outside of this in Schenectady, which
led to the first stay-in of the century in December,
noted later. In some of these the AFL sent in scabs.
In Youngstown the tinners and slaters, previously
divided in four crafts, joined the IWW and struck;
the employer wired the AFL for scabs, and these
were sent despite the protest of the local Painters.
The AFL replaced IWW strikers in Yonkers and
San Pedro. In contrast the IWW bricklayers in
Cleveland walked out in sympathy with the building laborers of the AFL and refused to desert them
even when offered a pay boost and a closed shop
contract. In St. Louis and Butte an AFL boycott
was put on IWW products. The Machinists, the Hat
& Cap Makers, the Leather Workers, and the Carpenters all decreed no IWW could belong to their
organization or work on jobs that they controlled.

On February 7, 1906, Moyer and Haywood, president and secretary of the Western Federation, were
kidnaped, along with a friendly non-member, Pettibone, by government officers and taken to Idaho,
charged with the murder of former governor Steunenberg. From that date to their trials in the summer of 1907 the IWW was preoccupied with agitation on their behalf and with raising funds for their
defense. It raised $10,982.51 and secured the serv-
ices of Clarence Darrow. Meanwhile the Western
Federation was for the first time in its history free
from strikes, and the new IWW beset with them,
yet concentrating on this defense case which, while
it got much newspaper space, called no attention to
the new union, but only to the Western Federation

and its past struggles. The WFM was not actually a part of the IWW until after its convention in June of 1906, when it entered 22,000 members. Haywood's imprisonment gave the right wing in the Federation control of its offices and a deal was worked out between these right wing forces, commonly called the "Denver Triumvirate," and Charles Sherman, President of the IWW, aiming to make the forthcoming second convention, in Sherman's phrase, "the Waterloo of the revolutionists." Sherman, the first and only president of the IWW, nominated by Moyer, had been elected at the first convention, chiefly because he stood nowhere, while all those who had taken definite positions felt it would be in the interests of harmony to decline the nomination.

The founding convention, amid its radical oratory, had elected an administration predominantly on the more conservative side, and provided for a system of departmental autonomy that entrenched the position of these conservatives. Simons warned at the first convention: "The men in one of those departments where we have a union today may go in there and adopt the name of that department and seize its machinery. . . . A little handful of men can control the machinery of that department and keep up such a hubbub as to keep all opposition out." Sherman's United Metal Workers, which proved to have only one executive beside himself, did that with the Metal Department and kept out the Amalgamated Society of Engineers. Dictatorship developed in the Transportation Department whittling it down to almost nothing by the second convention, through refusal to furnish dues stamps to those opposing the departmental heads; these ousted men sought a hearing and Sherman refused to do anything on the grounds of departmental autonomy. The only friends of the rebel railroaders were the two radicals in the administration, Trautman, the secretary who weakened his position by traveling, and "Honest John" Riordan, the one rebel on the Executive Board, who stayed in the office but had to content himself with

writing "graft" across the checks drawn for the
junketing trips of those who acted the customary
role of labor leader.[2]

The second convention was supposed to have been
held in May; then it was postponed so that the Western Federation could convene first and be duly installed. Had it been held then it might perhaps have
ironed out these growing headaches but on the urging of Debs and his Terre Haute local, it was further
postponed in the hopes of early trials for Moyer,
Haywood and Pettibone, both to conserve funds for
their defense and to make it a victory celebration
for their acquittal.[3] When it was seen that their
trial could not come until after Supreme Court had
ruled on the kidnaping and related issues, it was
called for Sept. 17, 1906. The delegates assembled
expecting it to be a short affair, and after ten days
spent in wrangles over the seating of delegates from
these dictator-ridden departments, many of them
were out of funds. Sherman later explained in the
Chicago Record-Herald of October 7 how he had
planned to handle the "revolutionists":

"We believed we could starve them out by ob-
structive tactics, but at the end of the tenth day,
De Leon had a resolution passed that they be allowed $1.50 per day as salary and expenses while
attending the convention. That was more money
than any of them had earned in their lives and they
were ready to stay with him until Christmas."

These remarks came rather poorly from one who
in addition to his salary of $150 per month, turned
in expense accounts that even his cronies on the
Denver Triumvirate could not swallow, and who, it
later developed, was planning to make a fortune
from control of the Fraternal Supply Company fur-
nishing badges, buttons, etc. to WFM and IWW.
Providing expenses for the delegates cost the IWW
$450, and won by a vote of 380½ to 251. The Sher-
man group argued this clearly violated the provisional constitution's provision that delegates
should bear their own expenses, and the socialist

and general labor press denounced it as the "coup
of the proletarian rabble," and pictured it as a De
Leon victory over the socialists. Actually SLP followers had only 60 votes at the convention while
followers of the Socialist Party had 158, and the
division was not between these two parties but between those who wanted to make a union in the
accepted patterns and those who wanted to build
an instrument for the emancipation of the working
class. Of the five delegates from Western Federation, two, Vincent St. John and Albert Ryan, were
consistently with the rebels.

With "starve out" tactics foiled, the convention
soon attended to its business and ended Sherman's
position by abolishing the office of president. When
the new executive board went to the offices at 146
W. Madison they found that Sherman and his allies
had hired the Mooney-Bohlen Detective Agency to
hold it against all comers. As Trautman reported to
the 1907 convention:

"With no records or documents left, without addresses of unions or individuals, scarcely in possession of enough cash to communicate the outrageous
proceedings to those who were expected to rush to
the organization in its hour of need, with the whole
press controlled by socialist party individuals, with
one notable exception, as well as the capitalist
mouthpieces, hurling their invectives against the
'tramps and beggars' and the 'proletarian rabble,' it
certainly was a hard task to carry on the work and
duties mapped out by the convention, which had
adjourned a few hours earlier under the most favorable auspices."

St. John got an injunction against Sherman, but
the funds were tied up. After long delays Sherman
allowed the portion that had been raised for the
defense of the Idaho cases to go to the Western Federation, and when the settlement was reached on
Sept. 27, 1907, most of the rest of the funds went
to the two lawyers. The "St. John-Trautman-De
Leon faction" opened offices at 212 Bush Temple
and won in the courts. Soon nothing was left of the

Sherman faction which held the old address until June 1908 and then sold its assets to the Socialist Party for $250, while Sherman and Kilpatrick went on pay as speakers for the Hearst Independent League. Later Sherman was given a job with the Western Federation and still later a clerical job for the Socialist Party.[4]

Though the rebels won in the convention and in the courts and among the scattered locals, they lost the promising start in Schenectady and also the Western Federation.

In November 1906 some draftsmen at General Electric asked to join the IWW and were provided with a circular to solicit members in their department. They organized three dozen and then the three most active were fired. The IWW decided reinstatement or no production. On December 10 their 3000 fellow workers folded arms and stayed in without working. The next morning the draftsmen walked out followed by five thousand including many who belonged to AFL or to no union. Soon antagonisms between pro-Sherman and anti-Sherman forces, between radicals and conservatives, between supporters and opponents of De Leon, between the AFL and the new union broke up the early solidarity. The new draftsmen local withdrew on the 14th, the electrical workers on the 18th. GE was much concerned over invasion of its white collar force and threat of IWW to organize other GE plants. By December 20th when 200 new employees had been hired, the IWW called the strike off.

The craft structure of the industrial council and the dissension over the rift at the second convention wrecked the local organization. For a while there were two IWW bodies competing at the plant, the pro-Sherman Industrial Council, and its ousted locals 1, 34, 50, 55, 58, 76 and 77, which James P. Thompson, organizer for the rebel majority, reorganized in General Electric Workers Industrial Union No. 1. While some IWW support has existed among workers at this plant to this day, the IWW has not since then made any notable local history, despite the IWW sympathies frankly expressed for many years by General Electric's colorful "wizard," Charles P. Steinmetz.

The Executive Board of the Western Federation promptly issued a referendum after the 1906 convention asking: "Shall the acts of the 2nd annual convention of the IWW be held as unconstitutional and illegal?" This carried and the WFM refused to pay per capita to "either faction," even though the Sherman faction existed only on paper and could be given life—and pay its debts—only with WFM per capita. The 1907 convention of the Western Federation by majority supported this position, but manifested the enduring need for a class-wide union that had led it to bring on the scene in succession the Western Labor Union, the American Labor Union and then the IWW, by adopting a new preamble (by 283 to 66 votes) re-stating the same principles as were in the IWW preamble, and concluding, "Therefore, we the wage slaves employed in and around the mines, mills and smelters of the world, have associated in the Western Federation of Miners, Mining Department of the Industrial Workers of the World."[5] It issued at the same time a call for a conference of "the contending factions of the IWW, the United Brewery Workers, and all other labor unions ready to accept the principles of industrial unionism as formulated in the Manifesto issued at Chicago, June 2, 1905, to convene Oct. 1, 1907." The instructions to the delegates for the proposed conference included that the joint body assume no debts of either faction, for Sherman's debts were extensive; that no officer of either side could become an officer of the new body; that departmental autonomy was to be preserved, for the provisional constitution adopted in 1905 gave the GEB the power to pull out all members in support of any group on strike, and the miners needed to protect themselves against this, though the experience with the Metal and Transportation departments had shown the need of some right of appeal to the general organization. It was felt that this proposal was an idle gesture, and it was almost impossible to get any to accept as delegates to the conference. It was repeatedly postponed. Haywood was acquitted a few weeks after this convention, and on Dec. 17, along with the other members of the Executive Board of the Western Federation sent an invitation addressed "To the Officers of Both Factions of the I.W.W." reading in part:

"As executive officers of the Western Federation of Miners we are determined to demonstrate to our membership, the membership of both factions of the I.W.W., and the working class generally, that we are not responsible for the continued dismemberment of the Industrial Workers of the World."

This call for a conference to be held April 6, 1908 was printed in full in the IWW paper, the Industrial Union Bulletin for Jan. 25, 1908, and flatly rejected. In rejecting it, the IWW, though its coming break with De Leon was already quite clear, evidently agreed with the arguments he was making in speeches and in his paper that ever since the founding of the IWW there had been a conspiracy to put it in the hands of those who would tame it and turn it from its declared purpose, and that this was the latest effort in this scheme.[6]

This decision ended the long struggle of the Western Federation to build a class-wide union. Thereafter it rapidly grew tame, futilely trying the approach of not antagonizing the employer in an industrial situation where that approach could not work, and steadily became more innocuous until the re-awakening of American labor in the mid-thirties. Having gone back into the AFL in 1911, after invitations as early as 1907, it changed its name to International Mine, Mill & Smelter Workers. Already in 1908, two days after the April conference that never conferred, the Denver Triumvirate fired Bill Haywood. He had had no connection with the IWW other than as chairman of its first convention, and now went speaking for the Socialist Party, and in 1910 represented it at the International Socialist Congress in Copenhagen, toured Europe lecturing, and joined the IWW upon his return to America in the fall of that year.

Goldfield, 30 miles from Tonapah, in the silver region of Nevada had its 1500 gold miners solidly organized in Local 220 WFM—a progressive local built largely of active unionists deported from the Federation's battles in Colorado and Idaho. In February, 1906, an IWW local of newsboys was formed. Local 70 gradually organized the miscellaneous workers in the town, winning a strike of the Western Union messenger boys in May. In August, the Tonapah Sun declared war on the IWW, and the miners boycotted the paper so that it sold out to the Goldfield Tribune. Following the battle with Sherman at the September convention, these locals steadfastly supported the St. John faction.

In mid-December Local 220 tried to get $5.00 established as low for all work in and around mines. The small leasers, largely former members of the Western Federation, were already paying this scale. They wanted to get all the ore out they could before their leases expired on Jan. 7; but the Florence and Mohawk Combination, owned back east, did not want this scale established and threatened to attack the small operators on the stock markets if they did not play ball. Thus work was stopped until two days after Jan. 7, when the scale was set at $5 minimum below ground and $4.50 minimum on surface.[7]

Once the big operators won out over the smaller, there was a more controlled production and many miners were laid off. They wanted to get some work out of the building boom, but the AFL carpenters objected to miners working even on the Miners Union Hospital. The Miners then demanded that carpenters working at mines carry WFM cards. The Mine Owners, recently re-organized on a straight anti-labor basis sided with the AFL, and locked the miners out March 10 to April 21. AFL organizers with sawed-off shotguns vainly tried to get miners to sign up for working the mines under AFL charters.

On the second day of the lockout, Silva, a restaurant proprietor, refused to pay a waitress her wages,
and the IWW local struck his place. As M. R. Preston was picketing it in the evening, turning away
prospective customers, Silva grew enraged and
came out brandishing a gun. According to the
parole board seven years later, Silva advanced on
Preston for twenty-five feet, threatening to shoot,
before Preston drew and shot in self-defense. (It
was the custom to go armed.) Many were arrested,
including St. John. Preston and Smith, the IWW
delegate, were convicted on a conspiracy charge,
though the parole board belatedly said there was
no evidence of conspiracy. The Socialist Labor Party
made Preston its vice-presidential candidate that
year, over his objections, and though he was not
a member of their party.[8] About a week before
St. John's arrest, the Chicago Journal of Finance
forecast that soon he and other radicals in Goldfield would be arrested. The intent seems to have
been to prevent this camp from sending radical
delegates to the WFM convention; this miscarried,
and also a plot to lynch the victims, to prevent
which miners stood guard around the jail house.

After the lockout had been on 10 days it was
decided to have the miners and the IWW local of
town workers meet separately. They had been
merged early that year in what seems to have been
an effort to submerge a radical minority. Though
now separated they stuck together. Mahoney, acting president of the Western Federation, came to
settle the dispute. He found three-fourths of the
businessmen in town had locked out the IWW, and
that the AFL had sent in scabs. His concern was
the miners, where the mine owners took the stand
that they would not deal with a miners union connected in any way with the IWW, or that got involved in the troubles of the town workers. Mahoney
evidently convinced them that the Western Federation would win out against the IWW. The lockout
was settled, recognizing Local 220, affiliated with

both WFM and IWW, at the mines and with wages and other terms the same as before the lockout.

Throughout the summer the IWW step by step got rid of most of the AFL scabs around the town, and the amicable Third IWW Convention increased respect for the IWW. In October both Tonapah and Goldfield Locals of the WFM—along with various others—passed resolutions in favor of continuing support for the St. John-Trautmann IWW.[9] How the WFM had been working meanwhile to undermine the IWW was explained in the following statement made by the Federation's counsel, Judge O. N. Hilton (later retained by IWW on Joe Hill appeal and in Mesaba Range cases), to the Goldfield Chronicle during the Federation's last unsuccessful bid for the good graces of the Mine Owners Association there:

"Already we have accomplished much along the line of weeding out the undesirable trouble breeders, and we propose to continue the work until such time as there remains only a hard working force of good miners who will not be interfered with or led by undesirables. Last summer when I was in Goldfield, I spent $1200 on transportation for a number of members of the organization whom I thought it was best to send away from camp. These men are now away from here and there remain but a small number who, we believe, should have no hand in affairs here. If our proposition is received and accepted, I dare say that there will be no more trouble and that Goldfield will remain a union camp and a camp only of good well-intending miners."[10]

In October the big nation-wide financial crisis had hit. The Mine Owners asked Local 220 to permit part of the wages to be paid in checks drawn against ore in transit. The union was willing if the owners would guarantee eventual payment. While this was being negotiated with the mines in operation, an effort was made to kill St. John on Nov. 5, but the bullets hit another. When Mine Owners refused to guarantee payment to miners digging gold, the miners struck, Nov. 27. The Mine Owners got the Governor to ask Theodore Roosevelt for Federal troops. There was no National Guard as the top layers feared that if one were formed it would consist largely of union men. The Legislature was not called as required for a request for Federal aid, as it was felt the Legislature would not make such a request. Roosevelt sent in troops, and on the day they arrived, the Mine Owners cut wages and announced a policy of yellow dog contract. A Commission investigated and reported there was no need for Federal troops, but Roosevelt kept them there until Jan. 29, when the legislature enacted a state police bill. On the same day the Mine Owners announced the mines would run open shop.[11] WFM job control was over. Soon the rich ore played out; Goldfield eventually became a ghost town, but with Metal Mine Workers Industrial Union 353 of the IWW holding out and keeping some spark of unionism alive until the First World War.

A sawmill strike in Portland, Ore., starting March 1, 1907 and involving 3,000 men for 40 days, marked the first west coast progress of the IWW. There was a general public sympathy and a favorable press treatment of the demand for shorter hours and a minimum of $2.50 a day. A feature article on the strike, "The Story of a New Labor Union," by John Kenneth Turner in the Sunday Oregon Journal, was reprinted as a leaflet.[11a] A quickie strike pulled at a busy time swamped the IWW hall at 298 Burnside with a demand for union cards. In two weeks 1300 had enrolled. Soon the mill owners made a closed shop contract with the AFL, but the AFL managed to get no men past the picket line. Turner wrote of it: "Absolutely no violence, no lawbreaking, and no crying of 'scab.' Just one man was arrested for trespassing, and he imagined that he was standing in a public street. Other strange features were the red ribbons, the daily speech-making, and the night and day shifts of organizers who received not a red cent for their services." The AFL issued public statements denouncing the strike and the

IWW, and quoting extensively from the WFM Miners' Magazine in their attacks; yet WFM locals sent in over a thousand dollars. The strike committee had to send wires to send no more funds as their conduct of the strike kept expenses down: those not needed for picket duty were urged to go out and spread union doctrine on the various lumbering and construction jobs then in full swing. This was the seed from which sprang the IWW of the northwest.

As sideshoots grew a local of workers building a sewer and another local of harborcraft workers. In Tacoma the IWW smeltermen struck, and despite dissension over the WFM split, they won the 8 hour day and a 15% wage boost, but left the IWW. IWW lumberjacks struck in Humboldt County, Calif., and IWW bakers in San Francisco about the same time. In Montana the IWW had started organizing lumber workers and struck; the AFL gave them opposition, and as most of the logging was on Indian reservations, the bureau agents kept IWW organizers out.

In the east the IWW made progress prior to the panic in the fall of 1907 at American Tube in Bridgeport and in the textile industry, laying the foundations for its phenomenal victories five years later. In Bridgeport organizer French had started a local in June 1907, and when on July 15 the American Tube refused to alternate shifts, the local was ready to organize this indignation into an effective strike, with speakers in the various languages used, and a committee that rode bicycles up and down the parades of strikers around the two plants of the company. There the Machinists co-operated, happy to do so as these unorganized workers had helped them win a short time before. Victory in August came to a local that had enrolled 700 skilled and 1,000 unskilled among these workers.[12]

The IWW got its start in textiles in Skowhegan, Maine. The local there of Marston Mills workers demanded a 10% boost to be effective New Years 1906, but settled for 5% then and 5% in July if

conditions warranted. The manager tried to get rid
of the active unionists. The entire force had met
and decided upon policy; when fifty were put on
notice by the manager, all walked out, including
the boiler room crew who blew off steam and pulled
their fires. This was Jan. 21. President Golden of
the United Textile Workers offered "union scabs,"
and inserted his endorsement in ads through New
England press for other scabs. IWW won on April 23
with re-instatement of all, abolition of fining system, day's pay instead of piece rates for poor work,
shop committee to meet with management twice a
month on all grievances.[13]

In Paterson, N. J., scene of a more noted strike
in 1913, the IWW struck a number of silk dye-
houses in March 1907, over the discharge of members. Private detectives, uniformed police threatened
and arrested the strikers, but after a short time
the local press announced a "pleasant surprise" for
the 6,000 dye-house workers of a dollar a week pay
boost, without mention of the strike or union.[14]
The union grew during the strike to a thousand
members and in the fall tried to organize the American Locomotive plant there, resulting in a short
strike of 300 workers. In November the IWW struck
the international Stehli concern at Lancaster, Pa.,
and despite police interference came through the
strike intact.

As a result of these activities in textiles, the
General Executive Board called a convention in
Paterson, May 1, 1908, to found the National Industrial Union of Textile Workers, the first industrial union, not a local, that the IWW had built.
Progress was also made in the garment industry,
with a local of cloakmakers in Chicago, a strike
of 200 pressers in St. Louis, and a 12-week strike
against Ratner Brothers in New York, white goods,
which cost $2,012 but was defrayed locally by pic-
nics, vaudevilles and other benefit affairs.

This eastern organizing—including a charter to
the already striking flint glass workers of Marion,

Ind., and a strike of 200 car foundry workers in Detroit — was in territory where De Leon held strategic advantages, and it was plain shortly after the peaceful third convention that a fight must be made to keep the IWW from becoming a tail to De Leon's kite. The decision to launch the National Industrial Union of Textile Workers, with James P. Thompson, an able exponent of non-political industrial unionism, as organizer, was shaped by a desire to keep this development out of De Leon's hands. From even before its first convention the IWW had faced an opposition based largely on hostility to De Leon and his record of disruption in the labor movement. Its Industrial Union Bulletin had printed each week in large type across the front page that it was independent of any political party; but its readers could find in the Daily People discussion of its internal affairs and advice how to vote on its referenda.

The conflict grew hotter in the fall of 1907 over a question in economic theory: Does a rise in wages cause a rise in price such that workers achieve no real gain? De Leon said it did. In common with many radical politicians he was inclined toward such a conclusion as it focused attention on the abolition of the wage system rather than on union demands, and support for the conclusion can be obtained by misinterpreting the experience that in periods of rising prices workers are most moved to demand wage boosts and find it easiest to obtain them. The argument to the contrary by James P. Thompson and James Connelly, who was here from Ireland and helping the IWW, appeared in the Industrial Union Bulletin. It followed the Ricardo-Marx analysis that price is a monetary expression of value; that value is not altered by how it is distributed among wage earners and others, but it is determined by the real or labor cost of production; that it can be changed only by changes in the amount of labor required for production. They supported their position by the practical consideration

that employers oppose wage boosts, while they
would profit by them if De Leon's position were
correct. It may have been theory, but it probed deeply into the question whether workers should consider unions worthwhile or concentrate on political
activity.

The General Executive Board met in New York
Dec. 22, 1907. Ever since the 1906 convention the
rule had been that no GEB action was to be kept
secret from the membership. Connelly appeared
before it with a plan that, if acted upon promptly,
might have brought 12,000 New York longshoremen,
then independent, into the IWW. Action was hampered when De Leon induced the Board to go into
secret session to try Connelly on his charge that
his articles on economics constituted heresy. Even
the SLP members of the Board felt all this was
ridiculous, but indignantly rallied to their leader
when the Board, in accordance with the rules, published its proceedings in Industrial Union Bulletin
No. 49.

This brought the quarrel with De Leon to a head
all over the country—and for that matter in the
industrial union clubs that had been formed in
Britain and Australia. Among the western membership there was a hearty disrespect for politicians,
and the hard times starting in October 1907 had
not abated IWW agitation in the west. An exceptionally enterprising organizer in that field was J.
H. Walsh. In July 1907 he got enough support in
Alaska to start the Nome Industrial Worker.[15]
Coming down coast he found that the employment
sharks provided a major grievance about which
something might be done. They had tie-ins with
bosses on out-of-town work to fire the men they
furnished after they had worked a week so that
they were back to buy another job. To reach these
workers and build a concerted refusal to patronize
the "shark" and thus force the employers to hire
directly, street meetings in the skidroads were necessary. The Salvation Army ran interference with

these meetings, and IWW speakers could not speak louder than the big bass drum. Walsh and his fellow workers hit upon the device of making parodies to be sung to the music furnished free by the Army. Thus the tradition of the "singing IWW" grew out of this conflict with the employment sharks. One satiric refrain, "Hallelujah, I'm a Bum" was particularly popular as its music was the customary "theme song" for the Army meetings.[16] Walsh headed a group of delegates to the fourth convention, who traveled by box car, stopping at division points to soap-box and sing and sell the song cards preceding the IWW song book. Their most popular ditty led the unappreciative De Leonites to call them "the Bummery."

The convention met Oct. 1. De Leon's credentials were challenged on the ground that he represented a Store and Office Workers Union instead of belonging to the Printing and Publishing Local that as an editor he should have joined. De Leon argued for his seat on the contention that workers should be organized according to the tool each worked with, and he worked with a pen as did office workers. This was not accepted as sound industrial unionism. The convention then proceeded to recommend a change in the Preamble to the membership. Its second paragraph then read, as De Leon had insisted as a condition for co-operating in the first convention:

"Between these two classes a struggle must go on until all the toilers come together on the political, as well as on the industrial field, and take and hold that which they produce by their labor, through an economic organization of the working class, without affiliation with any political party."

When the present form of Preamble was accepted by the convention, the De Leon followers bolted, held a convention of a few eastern locals at Paterson, and founded what was known as "the Detroit IWW." De Leon followed up with attacks on the IWW as "slum proletarians" for which the GEB formally expelled him. The "Detroit IWW," like the

ST&LA of earlier days, carried on chiefly as a union duplication of SLP membership, changed its name in 1915 to Workers International Industrial Union, and gave up the ghost in 1925.

In one sense this is the launching of the IWW. It is from here on that it exists as an organization with its own distinctive character. The Brewery workers were not in it or likely to be; the Sherman tendency was out; the Western Federation was gone, and now the De Leon forces that had alienated so many unionists. The five thousand members it had after this 1908 convention were no longer divergent groups trying to live together but a compact organization of men attached to the IWW rather than to something else, largely rebels who had been organized by the new union, but who had long experience in the struggle with the employer, and many of whom were very familiar with all the fine points that radicals argue about. This was the IWW that was to add something new to the American labor movement.

1. On Schenectady see Trautman's report to 1907 convention; *Industrial Worker*, Vol. 1, No. 7—Chicago, 1906 series; *Solidarity*, Feb. 17, 1931, and *Industrial Worker* summary, Aug. 18, 1945.

2. *Industrial Union Bulletin* reports of 2nd convention; see also Hardrock Miner series, *Industrial Worker*, July 1950.

3. *Daily People*, May 26, 1906.

4. *I.U. Bulletin* editorial, June 27, 1908.

5. Jensen: "Heritage of Conflict," chapter 11; WFM Preamble, quoted p. 189.

6. For details of conspiracy charge see Hardrock series, July 21, 1950 and for their substance, July 28.

7. To Goldfield, Brissenden and Jensen each devote a chapter; see also *Harper's Weekly* of June 22, 1907; St. John's account in *I.U.B.* No. 6.

8. Parole account, *Solidarity*, June 6, 1914.

9. *I.U.B.* No. 35 and 37.

10. Quoted *I.U.B.* No. 45, Jan. 4, 1908.

11. Details in Jensen's "Heritage of Conflict." 11a. Reprinted *I.U.B.*, April 13, 1907, in full.

12. Detailed accounts in *I.U.B.* Nos. 22, 23 and 27, quoted in *Solidarity*, March 3, 1931.

13. *I.U.B.* No. 1, March 2, 1907, quoted extensively in *Solidarity*, March 10, 1931.

14. *I.U.B.* No. 2, quoted *Solidarity*, ibid.

15. *I.U.B.* No. 32.

16. There are conflicting claims to authorship of "Halleluja." Walsh in *I.U.B.*, April 4, 1908, says it was made up in Spokane hall, and is quoted *OBU Monthly*, March 1938; various other claims to prior authorship in sundry versions exist; one in pocket edition "Treasury of American Folklore," p. 386.

III. Big Fights of a Small Union—1909-1911

The hard times following the financial crisis of
October 1907, the conversion of the previous SLP
support into open enmity, added to the definite loss
of the Western Federation and the collapse of the
promising campaign in Schenectady, all put the
I.W.W. in a tough spot. Yet it grew and its secretary, Vincent St. John, figured a total membership
of 9,100 in 1910 and 12,834 in 1911. Of these, 4,397
were in the textile industry, 2,000 were metal
workers, 1,800 were engaged in railroad construction and 800 in lumbering.[1] It is possible that to
avoid embarrassment he may have about doubled
these figures. In any case the IWW of these years
was a small union, yet it put up some memorable
fights, winning free speech in Spokane and elsewhere, defeating the big steel companies in McKees
Rocks and in the Chicago area, prodding the AFL
into action in many places, and yet with enough
surplus energy to take on a civil war in Mexico.
During these two years, the distinguishing characteristics of the IWW were definitely developed, perhaps most clearly in the argument with W. Z. Foster
over his proposal to "bore from within."

The I.W.W. was small, but widely spread. A list
of locals[2] in January 1910 shows 11 locals scattered through California; 3 in Oregon, all in Portland; in Washington besides locals in Aberdeen,
Bellingham and Anacortes, four each in Spokane
and Seattle; in British Columbia, four. In Montana
there were locals at Anaconda, Butte, Great Falls,
Kalispell, Billings and Missoula; in Wyoming at
Cheyenne; one in Denver, one each at Globe and
Phoenix, Arizona — these locals all showing that
some hold had been maintained in Western Federation territory. There were three in Minnesota, and
one each at Omaha, Kansas City, St. Louis and New
Orleans. East of the Mississippi there were locals

in Chicago, Muncie, three in Ohio, 12 scattered through Pennsylvania; three in New Jersey; five in New York City and one each in Buffalo, Yonkers and Brooklyn; two in Rhode Island and three in Vermont.

Thus over the map it had local organizations agitating, looking for opportunities and spreading its literature. Its official organ, the Industrial Union Bulletin, ceased in March 1909, but the membership in Spokane began at the same time to issue the Industrial Worker. With only one major break, 1913-1916, it continued there, or in Seattle, or in Chicago to the present time. On Dec. 18, 1909 Solidarity, also a weekly, appeared at first as the official organ of the Pittsburgh District Council, but issued at Newcastle, Pa. Later it moved to Cleveland, and in 1916 was brought to Chicago as official organ of the I.W.W., appearing with minor breaks and changes of name, until it was merged with the Industrial Worker when it too was moved to Chicago in 1931.

The strike at McKees Rocks (Pittsburgh suburb) got the IWW started in steel. It started June 28, 1909, as an unorganized protest against a pool system of payment at the Pressed Steel Car Company, U.S. Steel subsidiary, by which the foreman got the pay for his gang and distributed as he saw fit, which meant with considerable favoritism. That day 50 riveters walked out; half returned and the other half got fired. A third of the passenger car department staged a protest, and most of them were fired. On July 1, some of the porch department walked out and united with the discharged workers to picket the works. All came out except the tool and crane departments which were under Machinist contract. AFL policy in the industry was against organizing the "unskilled foreigners"; Secretary Morrison of the AFL passed through town and turned them down. Among these foreigners, however, were men who had been in the Russian Duma in 1905, some who had been members of the Metall-arbeiter-Verband, and Italians who had been in the great resistance strikes.[3] Some of these asked Trautman for help.

In their own preliminary organization two committees developed. One, called the "Big Six," was elected to take charge of the strike. The other developed of itself from among those previously active in the radical movement of Europe, and was referred to as the "Unknown Committee." This committee is credited with taming the Cossacks and with sending 60 strikers inside to bring out the 350 scabs who were living in the plant, and thus winning the strike.

Two troops of State Constabulary, commonly called Steel Cossacks, had treated the strikers with customary brutality, seriously wounding 76 by the end of July. On Aug. 12 when they killed Steven Horvath, one of the strikers, this "Unknown Committee" is reported to have written them: " For every striker's life you take, a trooper's life will be taken." One can neither verify nor refute this much-told story. Ten days later as strikers returning home from their meeting were crossing the O'Donovan Bridge, the constabulary attacked them. Four strikers and three troopers were killed. Secretary Trautman reported in the first issue of Solidarity: "Then the chief of the cossacks called off his bloodhounds. After that no striker or deputy was killed. Organized and disciplined 'physical force' checked the violence and wanton destruction of life." Following victory in the strike, six men, charged with participating in this riot, received sentences of 60 days in the workhouse. These light sentences may indicate that many in the community shared the view expressed by Trautman. The socialist press of the area, heartily supporting the strike, contributed to this favorable attitude. Now that the I.W.W. was definitely non-political, relations with the socialists were sporadically more friendly.

The McKees Rocks strike ended the "pool system," improved the shop rules, secured a 5% wage increase with another 10% to be paid 60 days later.

Its indirect results were much greater. Steel depended on a supply of labor from Europe, much of it obtained by glowing misrepresentation. The IWW gave the facts of life as encountered by steel labor to the European labor press, and this diffusion of information became a major factor to raise wages. Trautman reported to the Fifth Convention: "From data collected in several mills, the statement of a general increase of 15% and a reduction of five hours of working time per week for 350,000 workers would in sum total about express the results of the upheaval of workers in McKees Rocks." At the same time the AFL, appealing only to the skilled and preferably the Americanized workers in the industry, was losing strike after strike.

The IWW continued to win in steel, with victories against Inland Steel and Republic Steel, both at East Chicago, Ind., and another against Standard Steel Car in East Hammond.[4] At Standard the IWW had been organizing quietly, but when the committee representing the riveters got thrown out of the place for presenting a grievance, a strike was called. Special deputies, recruited from the red-light district in West Hammond, began an orgy of brutalities on Jan. 24, 1910, when the strike had been on a week. Resenting abusiveness, the strikers' wives formed a league for self-defense, and effectively stopped scabbing despite the arrest of 12 of the women. On the 24th, all officers were jailed early in the morning, but the picketing became even more effective, and at ten the company sent word to the committee in jail that it would accept all demands except immediate increases. Next day the strikers marched back to work in a body to make sure of no discrimination.[5]

The Pittsburgh District Council grew. It held its second convention in McKees Rocks Jan. 8, 1910, with 26 delegates from five locals, electing Joe Schmidt to assist Joe Ettor as organizer. Its organ, Solidarity, was edited for 90 days from jail, since it had neglected to specify its ownership, but it missed no issues while edited by men enjoying free board and room. It weathered efforts through that spring and summer to take away conditions won at Pressed Steel Car, including an attempted strike by company pets.

Organizers were kept there, and organization developed in other local industries, yet they were unable to keep the union among these victorious strikers more than a year. There are at least two explanations for this. One is that the growth of unionism is a widening of the occupational area in which unionism comes to be taken for granted; unionism first appears as organizing for immediate grievances, usually to strike, and only gradually among the workers lacking a skill that they might monopolize, has the feeling developed that organization should continue between strikes. The IWW has always had to do its organizing on the periphery of the occupational area in which unionism has become an accepted practice; and its "failure to achieve stability" there has also been experienced by all other unions in the same field at the same time. It was not until the mid-thirties that permanent organization of all occupations came to be taken for granted widely throughout industry.

Another factor was pointed out by Secretary Trautman to the Fifth Convention. Referring to a 10% increase just obtained at Republic Steel, he said:

"While we cannot oppose too much the time-contract system of the craft union movement, in this instance and in others that cannot all be recounted, all of the enemies of the IWW used the fact of our not having anything 'black on white' as an entering wedge to pull the workers away from the organization through which they had been able to win the strike."

Originally the IWW had put no restrictions, except requiring G.E.B. approval on contracts, and much of the discussion at the founding convention as to what constituted an industry proceeded on

the assumption that industry-wide action would
depend on the structure of the industrial union
making contracts. The tradition of no contracts
with specified duration had come from the Western
Federation, and persisted until changed in 1938 to
permit each Industrial Union to make its own regulations on this matter. Some Industrial Unions have
persistently forbidden such agreements. Provisions
adopted in 1946 ended the requirement of GEB
approval, but stipulated that no agreement should
provide for a check-off or obligate members covered
by it to do any work that would aid in breaking
any union's strike.

A strike of inside fabricators at Hansel & Elcock
Construction, Chicago, on May 8, 1910, won 8%
increase and Saturday half holidays, after the
crowd, first fed with speeches in Polish, Lithuanian
and other languages, while AFL organizers looked
on in bewilderment, turned down the AFL proposition to divide the 46 craftsmen away from the
246 lesser skilled that it was willing for the IWW
to have. Trautman's report of the victory stated:
"The strike-breakers that came back with the strikers dismissed themselves within 24 hours when
direct action methods were applied by the victorious
strikers."[6]

This is the earliest instance noted in IWW publications of the term "direct action." Its meaning
here may have been either ostracism or fisticuffs, as
no further details are given. About this time the
terms "sabotage" and "passive resistance" appear
in the IWW press for the first time, in reporting
an IWW strike of 580 men and girls against Lamm
& Co., Chicago clothiers. There the IWW had been
asked to aid an unorganized strike, and when scabs
were brought in, "workers in other firms where
the material for the strike-bound firm was made,
'sabotaged' their work to such perfection," to quote
Solidarity of June 4, 1910, that the company yielded
to all demands except that for the reinstatement of
the man whose discharge had led to the walkout
in the first place. Trautman advised them to go

back to work and use "passive resistance" methods to get the man back too. Here this meant putting so little heart in the work, out of regret for the absence of this fellow worker, that the employer decided to cheer them up by re-instating him. (For subsequent twists given to these words, see below Chapter VI.)

In Pittsburgh the district council set out to organize the meat packing plants. First it won gains from the big outside packers who wished to avoid a strike there. Later a general walkout was forced on the union and it struck all plants in the area, winning a reduction to 10 hours with an 8% pay boost, and shop control for a while in six plants. A less successful strike of the period was its first venture into the auto industry with a walkout against Parish, auto frame makers, in Reading, Pa. The men went to work in other shops and the strike petered out.[7]

Out west the IWW grew chiefly among out-of-town construction workers and lumberjacks, men on whom the employment sharks preyed. They worked on jobs with "one gang coming, one gang working and one gang going," and the more rapid the turnover, speeded up by firings, the more fees there were for the shark to split with the boss-man who did the hiring and firing. The IWW urged that the men should collectively refuse to patronize the shark and thus force direct hiring by the employers or through agencies that charged no fee. There were 31 employment sharks operating in Spokane in 1909, and occasionally, against IWW advice, the fleeced men set out to wreck the employment shark's office for he sometimes took a man's last dollar for jobs that did not exist. The Spokesman-Review of Jan. 18, 1909, gives this picture:

"Hurling rocks and chunks of ice through the windows of the Red Cross Employment Agency, 224 Stevens St., several members of a noisy mob of between 2,000 and 3,000 idle men were about to attempt to wreck the place about 6 o'clock last evening, when James H. Walsh, organizer of the IWW, mounted a chair in the street, stemmed the rising tide of riot and pacified the multitude. In the opinion of the police had it not been for the intervention of Walsh, a riot would surely have followed, as the rabble was worked up to such a pitch that its members would have readily attempted violence. Walsh discouraged violence and summoned all members of the IWW to their hall at the rear of 312 Front Ave. The police dispersed the rest. . . . At the hall Walsh warned the crowd against an outbreak. 'There were a lot of hired Pinkertons in that crowd,' he said. 'All they wanted you fellows to do was to start something and then they would have an excuse for shooting you down or smashing your heads in. . . . You can gain nothing by resorting to mob rule.' "[8]

Throughout that summer as employment picked up, IWW street meetings, with the songs that had been born for this special purpose, turned the fury of more and more fleeced men into the constructive channels of building One Big Union. The sharks got the City Council to forbid street meetings in the area they infested, despite the several occasions on which these meetings had prevented riots. The IWW approached the City Council and leading citizens, pointing out the unconstitutionality of this ordinance, and that it would mean worse operation by the sharks and possible riots. Still meetings were forbidden, and the Industrial Worker of October 28 sent out the call: "Wanted—Men to Fill the Jails of Spokane." A communication to all IWW locals stated: "Nov. 2, Free Speech Day—IWW locals will be notified by wire how many men to send if any. . . . Meetings will be orderly and no irregularities of any kind will be tolerated." The City Council arranged for a large rock pile on which to put the free speech fighters to work.[9]

The first day of the fight for free speech, man after man mounted the box to say, "Friends and Fellow Workers" and be yanked down, until 103 had been arrested, beaten and lodged in jail. A legend runs that one man, unaccustomed to public speaking, uttered the customary salutation, and still unarrested, and with no police by the box, paused, with nothing more to say, and in all the horrors of stage fright, hollered: "Where are the cops?" In a month over 500 were in jail on bread and water. The Franklin School was used for overflow, and the War Department helped subvert the Constitution by letting the city use Fort Wright to imprison those upholding the First Amendment.

In succession, eight editors of the local Industrial Worker got out an issue and went to jail. The police tried to destroy all copies of the Dec. 10th issue in which Elizabeth Gurley Flynn, who had delayed her arrest by chaining herself to a lamppost while she spoke, charged that the sheriff was using the women's section of the jail as a profitable brothel, with the police soliciting customers. The Industrial Worker was moved to the quieter city of Seattle, until May 1910 then back to Spokane.

The constant arrests; the police brutalities; the appearance of men in court matted with blood; the disrepute into which Spokane had fallen in the more enlightened portion of the nation's press; the widely-known evil practices of the employment sharks; the mounting cost to tax-payers; the boycott on Spokane merchants by men in many camps—all these made it harder for the city fathers to continue. Feeling was for the prisoners. On the rare occasion when they were marched through the streets to where they could get a bath, citizens showered them with Bull Durham, apples and oranges. On March 4 came victory—the release of the prisoners and the right to speak. Soon the licenses of 19 of the more offensive sharks were revoked, and the practice of direct hiring of men grew rapidly. IWW reputation boomed.

On the heels of this free-speech fight came another in Fresno, Calif. There the IWW was organizing agricultural workers, Frank Little in charge, and the police, to oppose the policy of holding out for higher bidders, forbade three or more workers to talk together on the streets. Street meetings had not been part of the organizing campaign, but now there was a free speech fight. An influx of IWW's camped on land furnished by a friendly socialist—until the camp was burned one night by the vigilantes—and held surprise meetings to get some of their case to the public before each speaker was arrested. The jail was a forerunner of Hitlerian horrors, but this fight, too, was won.

Since IWW advocates frequently used the soapbox to spread their ideas, even where no definite organization campaign was afoot, these successes tended for a while to sidetrack the IWW into fighting for free speech on its own account. The 1912 fight in San Diego, where there was almost nothing to organize, is a case in point.[10] Similar enthusiasm took many members into the army supporting Magon in the civil war in Mexico. On Jan. 29, 1912, what is described as "an IWW army" took Mexicali and later Tia Juana, opening the jails as first order of business. They lost the war, but in July a number of Mexican unions confederated and adopted the IWW preamble.[11]

Elsewhere the IWW was trying to build up the global jurisdiction that its name implied; Tom Mann organized branches in South Africa; it was growing in Australia and New Zealand. James Roe, a one-armed telegrapher, attempted to launch it in Hawaii, but died or was killed in jail. In England a number of clubs, termed the Advocates of Industrial Unionism, formed a movement around the paper, The Industrialist. In the American melting pot, the IWW issued papers in various languages that were mailed to kindred spirits in mother-countries: La Union Industriale (Spanish) at Phoenix, Arizona; Solidarnosc, in Polish, at Buffalo; Emancipation, organ of the Franco-Belgian Federation which consisted chiefly of textile workers; and the friendly Proletarian in Japanese, in San Francisco. On the international field, the IWW had challenged the AFL as a body denying the basic union principle

of class struggle, indirectly at the International
Socialist and Labor Congress at Stuttgart in 1907,
and again through Wm. Z. Foster, its credentialed
delegate, with the backing of the French CGT, at
Budapest in 1910.

On Foster's return he urged a switch in policy
to "boring from within" the AFL. The proposal
was debated in the press and definitely turned
down.[12] Arguments ran that the IWW could
busy itself with the 9/10 of the working class that
the AFL had not organized; that to bore was to get
kicked out; that the rebels in the AFL stood a better
chance if outside it, there was the IWW to point to,
to get into if they got kicked out or left in disgust,
and to maintain a press promoting their ideas; that
vested interests and basic structure of the AFL
would make the IWW impotent inside it; and that
many of the IWW had occupations for which the
AFL had no unions in which to bore. The few who
supported Foster withdrew with him to found the
Syndicalist League of North America, a very small
propagandist society.

IWW relations with other unions formed a varied
pattern. In San Diego, AFL carpenters refused to
build a stockade to imprison free speech fighters.
In Detroit the IWW did much of the work in the
AFL's 8-Hour League and the McNamara Defense.
In Philadelphia, where the AFL divided the men
at the locomotive works into 17 different crafts,
they struck, and the small IWW local, No. 11, went
out with them, June 8, 1911. Through dual membership in other unions the IWW had a majority on
the joint committee, had access to various unions
to seek support, and wound up reporting: "Instead
of driving the men to use different tactics, we were
showing them how to finance their fight, and this
will not win." In New York the IWW organized the
Western Union messengers, then the local organizers
turned them over to the AFL on the grounds they
could provide better halls and more help, but that
strike flopped. In Brooklyn the IWW organized a

number of shoe factories, enhanced their prestige after winning several victories by refusing to go back until the cutters, organized in a Knights of Labor local, had won too. This was a revolt against the policy of Tobin's Boot and Shoe Workers, who peddled the union label to employers in return for a check-off even with wages lower than in non-union shops. In this fight many AFL bodies supported the IWW instead of the AFL affiliate. The IWW ended 1910 with a large number of shoe shops on strike, but settled these strikes one after another from Jan. 22 on, until at end of February only four plants were struck, involving 800, with 2,200 organized back at work. One reason for this was to use available funds for the defense of Buccafori, a striker who had killed his employer after the latter had knocked him down on the floor and kicked him. Bill Haywood, also returning from Europe at this time, renewed his interest in the IWW at this time and spoke for the Buccafori Defense. His talk, "The General Strike," was issued as a pamphlet.

These big fights of a little union 1909 to 1911 laid the foundation for its substantial growth and bigger battles of 1912.

1. From table furnished Brissenden, p. 70, op. cit.
2. List from *Industrial Worker*, Jan. 15, 1920.
3. Duchez in *International Socialist Review*, October, 1909. A more detailed account of McKees Rocks is given in Perlman & Taft, "History of Labor in U.S.," Chapter XXIII.
4. *Solidarity*, issue No. 52, Vol. I.
5. *Solidarity*, Jan. 29, 1910 et seq.
6. *Solidarity*, issue No. 25.
7. *Solidarity*, issue No. 51 et seq., and more detailed summary in series, "IWW Tells Own Story," *Solidarity*, May 26, 1931.
8. Quoted *Industrial Union Bulletin*, Feb. 7, 1909.
9. Story of Spokane free speech fight from IWW papers, Spokane papers and *International Socialist Review* of the period.
10. See detailed series in *Industrial Worker*, July 16-Aug. 9, 1947.
11. Lorwin: "Labor and Internationalism," chapter 12.
12. Discussion starts *Solidarity*, Nov. 4, 1911.

IV. The Textile Workers

Between January 1912 and the tough times that set in again toward the end of 1913, the IWW, with a series of good fights and substantial victories, won widespread recognition as the most forward thrust of the American labor movement. These were the years of victories in Lawrence, Lowell, New Bedford, Little Falls and other textile centers, ending in the hopeless fight at Paterson; of lumber battles in Louisiana and Gray's Harbor, Washington; of railroad construction strikes with thousand mile picket lines; of expansion into auto and other metal working industries; of fighting for the Pittsburgh stogie makers and the rubber workers of Akron; of the accession of longshoremen and seamen to start its Marine Transport Workers; and of sensational trials arising from its fight in Lawrence, Louisiana and the hopfields of California—trials that added to its fame as much as did the strikes that generated them.

A persistent myth about the IWW is that it plunged into strikes without previous organization, bringing out contented workers with spell-binding oratory, won great victories, then deserted the workers to repeat the process elsewhere. The myth is groundless.

Prior to its fame at Lawrence the IWW had been organizing textile workers for seven years, and these constituted roughly half of its membership. It had followed up its initial victory in Skowhegan, Maine, with organization and a victorious three month strike at Mapleville, R. I., in 1907. By next year it had eight textile locals and these were formed into its first national industrial union with James P. Thompson as organizer. These withstood the depression, and in 1910 were all in good standing, and during the years in which strikes had been opportune, had added three more locals.[1]

This stability and steady growth of the IWW textile workers is the more remarkable since few of these workers could bargain through their union, and nowhere did it have "union security" in any form. They were men and women who had been educated into unionism with lectures on the history of the labor movement, with study classes in economics, with union fundamentals handed them in leaflets and strike talks. Social activities and dramatic clubs, for most of their halls had stages, helped cement them. The National Industrial Union of Textile Workers of the IWW was held together by an understanding of what industrial unionism could accomplish, and its members were willing to transmit this vision to their fellow workers as volunteer organizers and leaflet peddlers. They aided various strikes of the small independent unions in their field and steadily built the reputation of the IWW.

Lawrence local 20 had been formed in 1906. It almost died in 1907 but was brought to life again with aid from the National Industrial Union formed in 1908 and from a more thriving local nine miles away in Lowell. By 1910 it owned its own hall, and there the third convention of the Industrial Union was held over Labor Day. In January 1911, on invitation, it joined a newly formed Alliance of Textile Workers Unions of Lawrence with the reservation that it would not be bound to any action contrary to IWW principles. That summer the companies started changing the production system from one in which weavers ran 7 looms at 79 cents a cut to one in which they ran 12 at 49 cents a cut, giving them an average boost in weekly wages from $11.06 to $11.76 for almost double production. The IWW called a strike of the weavers against Atlantic Mills. It won, and the independent Lawrence Weavers Protective Association brought its 500 members into Local 20 on October 1.[2] On November 2 organizer J. P. Thompson was brought back to Lawrence for a two month campaign, and throughout November expounded union fundamentals to enthusiastic

noon-day meetings. Stickers and circulars were issued in support of various small strikes called by
other organizations, all urging a shorter workday
and the One Big Union idea. Plainly the IWW was
no flash in the pan when the big strike broke upon
Lawrence in January 1912.[3]

Lawrence had a population of 85,892 of whom
at least 60,000 depended upon mill wages. Almost
everyone over 14 worked in its textile mills. The
average wage was 16 cents an hour. About 15,000
got only 12 cents. With lost time the prevailing work
week of 56 hours yielded an average pay of only
about $7. Their labor had yielded such profits that
they had more than paid for the mills in which they
worked: Pacific Mills inside ten years had paid divi-
dends alone amounting to 148 per cent of its invest-
ment.[4]

Jan. 1, 1912 a state law became effective reducing
the work week to 54 hours. Without a pay boost
this meant 32 cents less a week for those working
56 hours, and 32 cents then bought 10 loaves of
bread. For some with still longer hours it meant
a still bigger reduction. Wages were so close to
starvation that many expected the weekly pay
would not be cut. When the first pay envelopes for
the year were distributed on January 11, some
workers in the Washington Mills went through the
plant calling their fellow workers to walk out with
them. The strike was on.

Local 20 had not planned for a strike until summer, but seeing how feeling ran it called the entire
local textile industry on strike the following day,
and sent for Haywood, Ettor, J. P. Thompson and
others to come in. By the middle of January 16,000
were out, and by the 27th 25,000, headed by a strike
committee of 60 elected from the ranks of the strikers to represent both each major occupational group
and each of the 16 major languages spoken. From
these 60 various detail committees were elected.

The first few unorganized days of the strike were
disorderly. On the 15th militia and pickets clashed

at the Pacific Mills. Once the IWW organized the strike it amazed all observers by the orderliness with which it was conducted, the only violence that of the police and National Guard who were there at a cost of $4,000 a day, or almost four times what it would have cost the companies not to have cut the weekly pay.

Golden of the United Textile Workers came at once to break the strike, but failed completely. The rather diminutive AFL Central Labor Council refused to recognize the 25,000 textile workers striking under the banner of the IWW, with the result that the Molders Union withdrew in disgust leaving that sedate body without a presiding officer.[5]

On Jan. 20 a plant of dynamite was discovered. Strikers were accused, but soon it was shown that it had been planted by a John A. Breen, member of the Board of Education. On conviction he was fined $500. On Jan. 29 a peaceful parade of the strikers was charged by the militia, and officer Oscar Benoit firing into the crowd, hit striker Annie Lo Pezza, killing her. At once three organizers, Ettor, Giovannitti and Caruso, were arrested as accessories to murder, and held without bail to keep them from strike activity. They were acquitted Nov. 26 after a three week trial. Nothing was done to Benoit or those who had ordered the vicious and needless attack on the parading strikers.

The view of the militia is disclosed by the remarks of an officer to a writer for Outlook: "Our company of militia went down to Lawrence during the first days of the strike. Most of them had to leave Harvard to do it; but they rather enjoyed going down there to have their fling at those people."[6] Harry Emerson Fosdick quotes a Boston lawyer: "Any man who pays more for labor than the lowest sum he can get them for is robbing his stockholders. . . . The strike should have been stopped in the first 24 hours. The militia should have been instructed to shoot. That is the way Napoleon did it."[7] During the nine week conflict 335 strikers were arrested, of whom 320 were sentenced on minor charges most of their convictions being reversed on appeal.

Feeding these impoverished people for 9 weeks would have been an impossible task if it had not been for the help of the Franco-Belgian Co-operative that had its own bakery, and donated its services and also much material. Appeals to labor at large brought in donations totaling $74,011.39, but this figures out to only 33 cents per week per striker. A cotton broker, James Prendergast, connived with a minister and judge to tie the strike relief up by alleging donations made without a name or address to which to send a receipt, and the contention that the strike funds were not properly handled. At the time the funds amounted to about $8000, but these were withdrawn all but 48 cents to save them from seizure. Later an accountant appointed by the court certified that the IWW had spent some $3000 more on strike relief than it had received, including donations from its own locals. The charge then shifted that some of this money had gone to buy railroad tickets for strikers' children sent out of town. This was dropped when the Boston Local of the Socialist Party testified that its donation of $3000 was intended for whatever strike purpose it could best serve. The IWW was cleared in the courts, but the SLP, which, throughout this wave of textile strikes interfered, masquerading under the name IWW, issued a pamphlet again accusing the IWW of these exploded charges.

These railroad tickets had been bought to send strikers' children to sympathetic families away from hunger-and-militia-ridden Lawrence. This was a new strike tactic in America. The children liked it and were effective reminders of the strikers' needs in the communities to which they went. They traveled in guided groups, each child with an identification card signed by its parents. This went well until Feb. 24. That morning parents and friends assembled to see a group of children off on the seven o'clock train. When it pulled in, the militia

crossed bayonets across all doors. The children had
their tickets clutched in their hands and some who
tried to run to the train were clubbed down on the
platform while police beat the strikers in the station. "There was a hideous struggle" reported Solidarity. "The women fought and kicked and
scratched with the mad frenzy of mothers fighting
for their young. The police choked them and clubbed
them and knocked them down. Finally the officers
pitched the women and children into a great arsenal
wagon and drove them off, a screaming, fighting
wagon load, to the police station where the little
ones were booked as neglected children."[8] Since
this was interference with interstate commerce, the
U. S. Senate investigated and brought forth two
fat volumes on the strike.[9]

On March 13 a rank and file committee that
could talk shop better than the company lawyers
met with American Woolen that raised its previous
best offer of a 5% flat increase to a 21% boost or
2 cents an hour for those getting 9½ cents, ranging
down to 1 cent for those getting 20, along with other
improvements in reckoning the pay and bonus. Next
day a mass meeting on Lawrence Common accepted
these terms. Eight companies that refused were still
struck until they gave parallel gains. There were
sympathetic increases in mills elsewhere.

The impact of this strike on thinking about American labor was expressed by Harry Fosdick in Outlook of that June: "Wages have been raised, work
has been resumed, the militia has gone, and the
whirring looms suggest industrial peace; but behind
all this the most revolutionary organization in the
history of American industry is building up an army
of volunteers. The I.W.W. leaves behind as hope-
lessly passé, the methods of the American Federation of Labor."[10] Others felt the same way about
it.

Strike methods and oratory both contributed to
this impression. Speakers talked of a day when the
endless haggling with employers would be replaced

by an industrial democracy in which those who did the work made the industrial decisions. They explained that the solidarity in the strike and the solidarity of labor toward the strike were steps, not only to two cents more per hour, but to the organized competence of labor to run industry for use instead of profit. The exodus of children to sympathetic homes was part of the strategy of making the working class feel as one. The endless chain picketing, devised in this strike when regular picketing was stopped, so that strikers walked one after another around the entire mill section of town, made each worker in that line feel that however helpless he might be as an individual, as a link in that chain he tied up industry. The democracy that welded these workers of 16 tongues together, and that enabled them to determine strike policy, was a foretaste of what labor, rightly organized, could do.

The Lawrence strike was followed by other textile strikes.[11] In Lowell 18,000 textile workers struck immediately after it. In New Bedford in July 15,000 textile workers responded to the call of the IWW to support the independently organized weavers who had struck against the fining system. The various craft unions refused to act jointly with the IWW but the 15,000 stayed out until the weavers on their own account had returned. In Little Falls, N.Y., a major center for knit goods and underwear, the state law limiting female labor to 54 hours per week became effective Oct. 1, 1912 and produced an unorganized walkout at the Phoenix and Gilbert Mills on the 10th, much like that in Lawrence. The IWW organized the Polish, Austrian and Italian workers, but had less success with the $6.40 a week "Americans." To hamper the strike, meeting places were denied and outdoor speaking prohibited. The socialists from Schenectady, including Mayor Lunn, furnished most of the force for the free speech end of the fight and won, not only their constitutional rights, but considerable support from the English-speaking workers. On Oct. 30, when a thug struck a girl picket, a fight broke out with the result that organizers Legere (an actor) and Bochino got convicted of stabbing a detective "in the seat of the pants" and sojourned at Auburn until July, 1914. There were hundreds of individual arrests, and a mass arrest of strikers meeting in the Slovak Sokol Hall. On that occasion the police broke heads, musical instruments and furniture alike. Next day other strikers paraded, playing the Marsellaise and International on their broken instruments, and requested troops to curb the police. The request was denied. When, shortly after this, children were sent out of town, and truant officers attempted to stop them at the station, they had papers in proper legal form to assure their departure. On January 3 the strike was ended on terms arranged by state mediators, reinstatement for all, increases to range from 5 to 18%, no one to get less for the 54 hour week than for 60 hours.

A week later when the National Industrial Union of Textile Workers held its fourth convention, it was proud of its achievements. Then came Paterson.

Paterson was an old silk center, with some big firms and about 290 smaller ones. Its technology lagged behind that used in the newer silk towns, like Allentown, Scranton and other places where miners' wives and daughters worked on high speed looms. (Their wages averaged $7.01 in 1912; male earnings were lower, only $6.06) The industry was beginning to trustify. Haywood said: "The strike would undoubtedly have ended much sooner had it not been for the desire of the richer manufacturers to see the smaller ones starved out and driven into bankruptcy. . . . The competing Pennsylvania mills are largely owned by the same interests."[12] Under these circumstances victory required industry-wide solidarity; it could not be attained by lone action in the technologically backward center from which the industry was moving.

When the 4-loom system was introduced into the Doherty Mills in Paterson late in January 1913, the weavers, unorganized, came out spontaneously. In

Paterson the IWW had a substantial local, including such capable organizers as Ewald Koettgen and Adolph Lessig, silk workers themselves. The weavers asked their help, and they took the gamble of trying to make the strike industry-wide. On the last day of February the local struck the 1930 mills and dye-houses in Paterson,and, with the aid of socialist locals at or near the more modern silk centers, sent strikers and organizers to bring them into the fight too; but there had not been the necessary preparation, the fight was confined to Paterson. There 25,000 struck until September 24; 1473 were arrested; five were killed. Outside labor support brought in $59,957.79 for strike relief, and this time to prevent rumors, the funds and expenses were checked by a public accountant. A pageant staged by John Reed, using the strikers to portray their struggle, toured eastern cities; the poster design was later used on many editions of songbooks and other pamphlets. But all this could not win in the old silk center against modern technology in other towns, with the better looms owned by the same large interests. By the time the strike was given up, hard times were on their way again, hitting, as they often do, the textile industries first. The IWW spent the last cent it could raise on this fight, and it almost did for the IWW as the Pullman strike of 1894 had done to Deb's ARU.

In April and May, 1913, while the Paterson strike was on, the union engaged in a struggle in Ipswich, a town where the previous fall the IWW had won prestige by action enabling workers to collect $60,-000 in back wages held from those who had quit without giving two weeks' notice. Arrests, police clubbings, and the impossibility of getting any place to meet except a churchyard, made the strike a dead issue when an ordinance was passed forbidding meetings in churchyards.

The National Industrial Union of Textile Workers persisted until March 11, 1916.[13] Then the General Executive Board put its remaining members in directly affiliated locals until it should have a membership of 5000 or more. Since then there has been only a scattered membership in that industry and a few minor efforts at organization. Already at its 1913 convention, full of sucess, the older members whose persistent plugging had built it up in the lean years of 1908-1911, refused to accept nominations. The GEB reported to the 10th convention that immediately following the Lawrence strike "a campaign of slander and insinuation was launched against the officers and most of the old active workers." That 1913 convention resolved that only those who had worked in the textile industry should serve it as organizers, though the organization had been built largely by organizers from other industries. But most important factor was the unemployment and hard times that set in late in 1913. The policies of the 1913 convention, the friendship of the socialists and these hard times all combined to undermine the newly grown union. Despite the arguments over "sabotage" and the unseating of Haywood from the National Executive Committee of the Socialist Party in 1912,[14] actual relations were friendly, and the harm done by the socialists was evidently done unwittingly, even though its policy right along had been and still was to favor the AFL. With hard times the socialist activities appeared to offer a better outlet for whatever aspirations for a new social order these workers had retained from their strikes and past experience. Dropping the old guard of organizers as strangers to the industry pushed them in this direction for they could have mapped out a program to make the union serviceable to its members no matter how hard the times, just as it had survived the bad years 1908-1909. While many had been organized for brief periods during the strikes, and while every effort, short of contracts, was made to hold them after the strike, post-strike locals were small. In Lawrence it was claimed that 10,000 out of the 25,000 strikers joined the IWW, but by the fall of 1913 the Lawrence local had only 700 members.[15]

To some extent this decline of the National Industrial Union of Textile Workers came from the difficulty of hitting the right balance between an industrial union program so different from prevailing thought that it struck most workers as alien, and a program so confined to job unionism that it lacked the spirit and vision necessary to hold workers together, as they had been held in 1908, when jobs disappeared and strikes were out of the picture.

Throughout the years since some of the old battlers and some younger textile workers who shared their vision have maintained Textile Workers Industrial Union 610 of the IWW, mindful of the need for industry-wide bargaining to cope with geographical shifts and persistently low wages even as in the days of Paterson. They may yet provide the union the textile workers need, for their need very plainly has not yet been met.

1. For general story of the period, see series "IWW Tells Its Own Story" for greater details, and articles by Chas. Miller who actively participated in these strikes, in *Industrial Worker*, July 1945.
2. *Solidarity*, Nov. 18, 1911.
3. Report of Organizer J.P. Thompson to 7th convention of IWW.
4. Chas. Miller, series July 1945, *Industrial Worker.*
5. *Solidarity*, No. 114.
6. Al Priddy in *Outlook*, Oct. 1912.
7. H.E. Fosdick in *Outlook*, June 15, 1912.
8. *Solidarity*, No. 114.
9. They are 62nd Congress, 2nd session, Senate document 870.
10. *Outlook*, June 15, 1912.
11. Details of these strikes are in papers of period and summarized in "IWW Tells Its Own Story," *Solidarity*, Sept. and Oct. 1931.
12. *International Socialist Review*, May, 1913.
13. Proceedings, 10th Convention IWW, p. 73.
14. See below, chapter VI, on ideological conflicts of period.
15. Levine, *Political Science Quarterly*, Sept. 1913. Winston Churchill's novel, "The Dwelling Place of Light" depicts the Lawrence strike fairly well.

V. The Pre-War Crest

(Period 1912-13: Union activities outside
of textile industry)

While the IWW was building a name in the textile industry it fought some great battles among
Canadian construction workers, Louisiana loggers,
Washington saw mill workers, on the docks of Philadelphia and Duluth, in auto and other metal industries, in the Pittsburgh cigar industry, and for hop-
pickers in California. Its rapid extension — much
like that of the Knights in 1884-86 — was possible
only because it developed the organizing abilities
latent in its ranks. It had not yet developed the program of "every member an organizer," and the job
delegate system that grew in 1915 out of its activities in agriculture, but had as organization staff
all its General Executive Board members, four national organizers, and 16 organizers with "voluntary
credentials," weekly listing them in its papers and
warning that no others were accredited organizers
for the IWW.

The prestige of Lawrence resulted in victories in
other fields: a victorious one week strike of molders
and others at National Malleable Casting in Indian-
apolis in March, 1912; the organization of a successful strike of piano and organ builders in New York
in April and May. Again in May a two week strike
against American Radiator in Buffalo won boosts
and better hours there and brought other nearby
plants to do likewise so that over 5000 benefitted.
In June the IWW won increases at Warner Refining
in Edgewater, N.Y., and at Corn Products Refining
at Shadyside, N.J.[1] In Peoria in June occurred one
of the few events that give some substance to the
myth of the IWW blowing into town, fomenting a
strike and pulling out again. Visiting organizer
James P. Cannon there turned a socialist meeting
into a local of workers at Avery Implement. A cou-

ple of the boys were fired, and the rest pulled the
whistle without any preparation for strike or getting
many organized. It took aggressive picketing to
make the strike click, and pickets got arrested, including Cannon's fellow evangelist, Tom Moore,
who sent out a call from jail for "jail material and
lots of it." It threatened to turn into a free speech
fight to rival San Diego, but, to prevent this, new
organizers came to town and arranged a settlement
including the release of all in jail, and the evange-
lists departed.

Along a five hundred mile stretch where the Canadian Northern was penetrating the mountains of
British Columbia, six thousand "dynos and dirt-
hands" struck on March 28, 1912.[2] They soon tied
up everything from Hope to Kamloops, and before
it was over the IWW had another strike of similar
size on the construction of the Grand Trunk. Some
organization had been built among these men in the
summer of 1911 as they flocked into the area waiting for this work to open up. Those doing preliminary work for the sub-contractors, and others camp-
ing along the right of way waiting for work, sent
for organizer J. S. Biscay to unionize them so they
could start the big job with union demands. Their
competition had brought down wages on this preliminary work to $2.25 a day. By Sept. 6, 1911 over
900 had been organized into Local 327 and the men
on a 160 mile section decided to hold out for higher
pay. The contractors asked for the army to force the
men to work, but didn't get it. Local business interests hoped for a wage boost and business men even
donated funds for Local 327 to build its hall in
Kamloops. Organization had reached over 2000 or
a third of the men before the big strike began.

This was the first time the IWW had to establish
its "thousand mile picket line," extending not only
over 400 miles of construction, but much further to
employment offices in Minneapolis and San Francisco. The IWW kept many from shipping, and sent
its missionaries among those shipped to induce them

to quit en route, and the railroads were left holding many old suit-cases filled with bricks and newspapers by those taking the trip part way.

The contractors after finding that neither violence nor the remote recruiting of scabs could break the strike, hit on "station work," a form of subcontracting by small groups of "self-employed" workers, with "piece work" rates that appealed to many of the strikers. The strikers were now divided first over whether or not to accept station work at any rates, and secondly, if so, how those rates should be set. Solidarity weakened and the strike ended with minor improvements, and earnings at station-work were no doubt raised by the strike and the sense of unionism. (A similar use of the "gyppo" system of piece work had much to do later with the decline of the IWW in Washington forests; and in post-mortems many on the scene later argued that the effective tactic would have been to accept this payment-by-results system but at rates that gave the employer no advantage over day-work. In both instances, to introduce it, much higher earnings were permitted than men made by it once it was established.)

This and the strike on the Grand Trunk lasted until late fall. Both were well supported by the labor movement of western Canada. The British Columbia Federationist served it as a regular weekly strike bulletin.

It was at this time that the term "Wobbly" as nick-name for IWW came into use. Previously they had been called many things from International Wonder Workers to I Won't Works. The origin of the expression "Wobbly" is uncertain. Legend assigns it to the lingual difficulties of a Chinese restaurant keeper with whom arrangements had been made during this strike to feed members passing through his town. When he tried to ask "Are you I.W.W.?" it is said to have come out: "All loo eye wobble wobble?" The same situation, but in Vancouver, is given as the 1911 origin of the term by

Mortimer Downing in a letter quoted in Nation, Sept. 5, 1923 with the additional information: "Thereafter the laughing term among us was 'I Wobbly Wobbly,' and when Herman Suhr during the Wheatland strike[3] wired for all foot-loose 'Wobblies' to hurry there, of course the prosecution made a mountain of mystery out of it, and the term has stuck ever since." Mencken in his American Language doubts this explanation. Some credit the term to Otis of the Los Angeles Times, an avid opponent of the IWW. Some lingual difficulty seems most likely to have been behind it, for in its sense of vacillating it fits no accusation ever made against IWW, and about the only meaning of wobbly that could conceivably fit is that of "wobble saw," a circular saw mounted askew to cut a groove wider than its own thickness.

In February 1912 the second national industrial union of the IWW was formed, the Forest and Lumber Workers. That summer the young Brotherhood of Timber Workers, centered in Louisiana joined it as an autonomous division. In contrast to the northwest, the Louisiana lumber worker was a "homeguard," often a "sod-buster."[4] Previous efforts from the Knights on had failed to give them stable organization. In 1902 around Lutcher they had formed a union, won, and dissolved. Again they had organized in 1907 to resist a wage cut, holding out longest around Lake Charles, and the union had died again. In 1910 the Brotherhood was formed, "swarming" around some 90 IWW's and "red" socialists—that is those who preferred Debs to Berger and Lee—and from the beginning was attacked by the lumber barons as IWW and alien. Its fights were lockouts, not strikes, and it was a revolt of the local people, including farmers and preachers and merchants and doctors, against the outside capital that was walking off with the riches of the area. (During its fights the lumber interests said they would deal with a respectable AFL union, yet in 1919 when AFL Carpenters tried to organize around Bogalusa, a mob of deputized thugs killed three at the union hall and stopped it.) The Brotherhood organized black and white workers together. It sent fraternal delegates to the 1911 IWW convention; its convention in May, 1912 was addressed by Haywood, and by referendum it joined the IWW that summer and was duly installed at the 1912 IWW convention.

The lumber companies opposed the Brotherhood with off-and-on lockouts, discrimination and "tin-panning," or the raising of such a din by beating circular saws that speakers could not be heard at union meetings. On July 7, 1912 at the cross-roads in Grabow, A. L. Emerson, president of the Brotherhood, held his audience together through such a "tin-panning" until shots came from the office of the Galloway Lumber Company, killing three. In the ensuing fight several more were killed. No company thugs were arrested, but 58 union men were lodged in the "Black Hole of Calcasieu" until after a two month trial they were acquitted in December. The jury was much influenced by the frank admission of state witnesses that their story had been framed in the offices of Congressman Pujo. Their victory in court was greeted with general jubilation by all southern labor.

After the strike the American Lumber Company discharged all who had testified for the defense, and, expecting further discharges of union militants, Emerson asked the 1200 workers involved to line up on one side of the road, and those who wanted to risk a strike to cross the road. The 1200 Negro, Mexican, French, Italian and native white workers crossed in a body, and a seven month fight was on that the Brotherhood lost. It had one more skirmish at Sweet Home, in December 1913, also lost. The Brotherhood persisted until 1916, but had been virtually killed by the blacklisting of 5000 members. They went west and later helped organize the oil fields of Oklahoma.

On March 4, 1912 the Forest & Lumber Workers Union of IWW struck all the sawmills in Hoquiam, Washington, and within a few days the strike had extended to Raymond, Cosmopolis and Aberdeen, tying up mill operations throughout the Gray's Harbor area. The demand was a wage boost from $2.00 to $2.50 per day. When the Mayor of Aberdeen tried to turn city laborers into deputies to break the strike, most of them quit. The Aberdeen Manufacturing Company turned out a load of heavy clubs to crack strikers' heads; the strikers went into the plant and seized them.[5] A Citizens' Committee prevailed on the Aberdeen Trades Council not to endorse the strike. This Committee was headed by bourgeois direct actionists whose vigilantes raided the union hall, arrested strikers, clubbed many in town, and kidnapped hundreds more, whom they took into the surrounding swamps, clubbed and left there. At Hoquiam these vigilantes put 150 strikers into box-cars for deportation, but the Mayor and the railroad workers stopped them. There were mass deportations of Greek and Finnish workers in particular from Raymond. Hindus were brought in to scab, but refused. Finally the Citizen's Committee recommended a raise to $2.25, but preference for native born American workers. The companies agreed, and the strike committee called a meeting and recommended that the men go back with this gain, and build organization for a further fight.

Next year, in May, the Forest and Lumber Workers, IWW, put out a ballot in all logging camps in that area on whether or not to strike for the following demands: a minimum of $3 for 8 hours; "clean, sanitary bunkhouses without top bunks and having springs, mattresses and bedding furnished free of charge, all camps to be supplied with baths and dry rooms"; end of employment fees. Though the vote ran 85% to strike, the strike was called off July 3 for lack of pickets.[6] A similar short-lived strike in the Missoula region also failed. The lumber worker was doomed to remain an unwashed timberbeast until 1917.

In August, 1912, Local 101 of IWW, tobacco workers, won short strikes in its old battlefields of

Pittsburgh and McKees Rocks, making the Penn, Zasloff and Webster companies revoke a cut. It followed up with a strike against Standard Cigar in both towns, precipitated by a fire in one of its factories that killed four girls and injured 17 others. The union had overcome a prejudice stirred up by the company between the McKees Rocks girls who were mostly Jewish and the Pittsburgh girls who were mostly Irish, and thereby won an 8 hour day, wage boosts ranging from $3 to $4 per week, and a clean-up of the shops and greater protection against further fires.[7]

The following summer the employers in the "hill district" of Pittsburgh, where the three for a nickel variety of stogies were made, locked out the IWW when it struck a member of their association, Dry Slitz Stogie. Twelve hundred were locked out, and the IWW called the remaining 800 stogie workers out. It was an unfavorable time, the beginning of the summer slack season, but the IWW held these workers, mostly girls, together to victory. The lack of organization in this field points up the craft viewpoint. In the nineties the stogie makers had organized, but been turned down as outcasts by the Cigar Makers, and for a time were part of the Knights. When the machine-made "four for a nickel" variety came in, this union turned these down too. The IWW welcomed them all. In the Labor Day Parade the IWW local entered a float depicting child workers and tuberculosis in the Dry Slitz factory. On Sept. 4 the agreement binding employers into an association ended, and many made separate offers. The IWW demand had been 12 to 15 cents for stogies, per hundred, and soon all settled at 11 to 14—all but Slitz. It had moved out of town.

In Akron on Feb. 10, 1913, 150 Firestone tire builders walked out when their piece rates were cut 35%. This led to a six week strike in which the local socialists and IWW with the aid of Haywood and other outside speakers competed with John L. Lewis, then an AFL organizer, and William Green,

Solidarity staff in Newcastle jail, 1910. L–r, 1st row: G. Fix and V. Jacobs; 2nd row: B. Williams, E. Moore, A.M. Stirton, C.H. McCarty. See p. 44.

San Diego free speech fight, 1912. See page 51.

Pat Quinlan, Carlo Tresca, Elizabeth Gurley Flynn,
Adolph Lessig and Bill Haywood, Paterson, 1913. See page 61.

Families with hop picking bags, Durst ranch,   See page 78

Knit goods strike, Little Falls, N.Y., fall 1913. Ben Legere's hand on shoulder of Matilda Robbins (Rabinowitz). See pages 59–60 and 74.

Vincent St. John, general secretary 1908–1914.

then an Ohio State Senator, the one side to organize
the rubber workers industrially, the other to .stam-
pede them back to work rather than see the IWW
grow.[8]

It was an unorganized industry. Unionism had
been held back by craft claims of Boot & Shoe
Workers. When the Amalgamated Rubber Workers,
AFL, was launched in 1902, Akron rubber workers
welcomed it, while the companies launched an Employers' Association and fought it by discriminatory
discharge, espionage through Corporations Auxiliary Company, "voluntary" increases, and company
unionism. The Amalgamated had lost its push by
1904 in a major defeat in Trenton.

When these 150 tire-builders walked out, unorganized, they soon brought the rest of the Firestone
tire-building department after them. There was an
IWW local of 50 or 60 members, closely associated
with the Socialist local, and the hall they jointly
used was offered as strike headquarters. In a short
time they brought out the entire local rubber industry, about 20,000 workers. It was a revolt against
industrial poisoning, lack of sanitary facilities, and
especially the speed-up and Taylor system of which
Sieberling boasted. No one had expected this spontaneous revolt, yet it was orderly. The Akron
Beacon-Journal of February 14 said: "It is safe to
say that no strike was ever started so peacefully or
with less excitement," and again on the 17th "With
the factories depleted," it commented, "throughout
Akron there is only praise for the very orderly way
in which the strikers have behaved up to date."

The Mayor promptly asked for the National
Guard. The Governor instead sent in the State Board
of Arbitration, and Senator William Green, later
president of the AFL, set up a committee to investigate, and the AFL sent in John L. Lewis and other
organizers to take over. The AFL issued a statement
explaining that it had intended to organize in Akron
earlier, but had been delayed "on account of the
enormous work devolving upon its organizers in

textiles and iron and steel, as the result of interference . . . by the people who have assumed control
of the strike in the rubber industry."

It took the strike committee of 100 close to two
weeks to iron out a wage scale acceptable to all
occupations. The AFL drew up its own wage scale,
but withdrew it as workers protested against the
obvious inequities in it. Later, as in regular Mo-
hawk Valley formula style the loyal citizens were
equipped with badges and clubs to crush this "invasion of alien unionism," and with meetings and
picketing stopped, a back to work movement was
promoted to the tune of clubbings, then, says Roberts in his study of the Rubber Workers, "The AFL
put it self in the unfortunate position of aiding the
back-to-work movement, thereby helping defeat the
strike."

The dirty work of the AFL went deeper than that.
The issue was whether or not there was to be collective bargaining. Sieberling who had done much
with his stop-watch to promote the strike, hurried
back from his Pacific cruise to say he would deal
with no union, and to denounce the strikers as anarchists. Organizer Bessemer replied that in the
common usage of anarchist as an extreme individu-
alist, Sieberling's refusal to deal with a union made
him the leading anarchist in town. The entire managerial side in its dealing both with the State Board
of Arbitration and with Senator Green's Committee,
made it clear that there would be no collective bargaining. Yet the AFL forces, including Green's committee, made much of IWW aversion to contracts as
though this could prolong the strike in an industry
whose management refused contracts. On the contrary, the IWW proposals were workable ways to
settle the strike and achieve some progress in industrial relations. Since the companies refused to deal
with any union, the strike committee proposed instead:

"The right of employees to present grievances
collectively by committees of their own selection,

composed of employees of each factory, to negotiate
with each manufacturer, should be established for
the adjustment of all grievances in the future. The
right of workers to organize in labor organizations
of their own choice should not be infringed upon."

This was a workable basis for unionism and collective bargaining without official union recognition. (In most instances the criticism of IWW for not
making contracts in these years falls equally flat
for almost identical reasons.) The language of the
proposal, considering its adaptation to the specific
circumstances, later acquired a familiar ring, in the
proposal by which Gompers broke up Wilson's Industrial Conference of 1919, and later incorporated
in section 7-a of NIRA to go on down into Wagner
and Taft-Hartley Acts. It appears to have originated
in this proposal made by the executive committee
in an IWW strike on March 7, 1913. The committee
also proposed that the 8 hour day it demanded could
be introduced gradually. Probably the greatest damage the AFL did to the rubber workers was their
denunciation of the IWW as an impossible organization that could not carry on collective bargaining.
This and the similar line of Green's Committee did
much to ease the conscience of the Citizen's Police
Association, and its recruitment in churches and
YMCA. The employers refused to meet even with
committees of their own employees insisting that
strikers were not employees, and issued statements
that made the local AFL inclined to pull a general
strike. At that point the sheriff put the city under
martial law, the more loyal AFL local leaders
joined in the back-to-work movement, police club-
bing grew, and on March 31 the IWW called off the
strike by a vote of 140 to 58—a marked contrast
from the thousands who had gathered in Perkins
Park to hear Haywood say: "We are standing in the
shadow of a monument of John Brown to discuss
and fight a greater problem than he ever faced."
The strike is usually called a defeat. It did not establish the collective bargaining it aimed at, but it

did stop the 35% cut that precipitated it, and so properly cannot be called a defeat.

The following January a startling disclosure was made by James W. Reed, secretary-treasurer of the Akron local in an affidavit that he had hired out as a spy in 1908 to look out for labor agitators at Diamond Rubber, and that during the years 1912-13 almost all officials of the local had also been in the pay of this Employers Auxiliary Corporation, an industrial espionage outfit.[9] While few knew of this, several of those involved attended the Jan. 14 meeting, and a picture of all was taken first, and then the story disclosed. The incident shows the futility of such espionage in an organization of the IWW type, where the strikes are handled by committees of strikers and not by the secretaries or other officers. Thus there seems to have been no great harm done by the spies, and instead a rather good technical performance of the clerical duties to which they were elected.

In the auto industry of Detroit the IWW had a small local, No. 16, which for several years had sought members by speaking in parks about social evils or distributing occasional leaflets without much success. In the spring of 1913 it too began to concentrate on industrial unionism at factory gates, and it began to grow. An able speaker was Matilda Rabinowitz, one of the four national organizers, who had come to Detroit originally to raise funds for the Paterson strike. She was a little woman and after one noon-day meeting a police officer complained: "You take advantage of us because you are a woman." Within the one month of May Local 16 grew from a mere skeleton to a promising start of 200.

In June Studebaker changed from weekly to monthly pays. There was dissatisfaction over this and members of the local in the Delray or west end plant of the company sent in a committee to ask about it and to report to a meeting for all Studebaker workers that the Local had called for June 14.

All the committee got for an answer, was the discharge of one of its members. The Sunday meeting elected another committee to see management; it got told that the company would give its answer in a week. The men feared that week would be used to thin out union ranks, and struck on the morning of the 18th at Delray. They all held a meeting in an adjacent vacant lot and marched in a body the seven miles to Plant No. 1, arriving there at noon and bringing out its 2000 workers. Next day the men from both plants brought out plant No. 5 bringing the total on strike to about 6,000 or a tenth of the local auto workers at that time. They accepted the police restriction of 30 pickets to a plant, but somehow the urge to soap-box turned the strike into a free speech fight, and it seems the entire strike evaporated into this evangelistic activity.[10]

Industrial unionists in the local then went to work on the three companies providing most of the wheels for the auto industry. First they won a short strike at Metal Wheel, gaining a 10% boost, a 9 hour day and better sanitation. This enabled them to get similar gains by strike threat next day at Toledo Metal Wheel, and on July 29 by a four hour strike at Foyer Brothers.[11]

The IWW in Detroit must be distinguished from the still-born faction of De Leonites who left the IWW in 1908 and were known as the "Detroit faction." The factual Detroit IWW plugged along, but found it could not build a strong union in autos, though neither were AFL nor independent attempts successful either. This period should make plain that in all these fields—textiles, rubber, autos, out-of-town construction, and whatever the IWW hit—it was there simply because all those who disdainfully spoke of IWW instability, had proven even more unable to organize than were the Wobblies. The IWW did not leave Detroit, but has been there ever since, though many workers it has organized and won gains for have deserted it.

In 1911 the IWW had gone on record against "boring from within." The urge, and often the need, to belong to whatever union one's fellow workers were in, led, of course, to many IWW members belonging to other unions in those fields where they had organization. In three fields this resulted in efforts to alter union programs: in the Western Federation of Miners, among the Hotel and Restaurant Workers of New York, and in the maritime industry. On the New Years Eve that ushered in 1913 a strike accredited by press to IWW started among the members of the Hotel & Restaurant Workers, AFL, first at the Astor, and soon extended to other leading hotels. The New York Times of the period makes much of accounts that Elizabeth G. Flynn urged an end to tipping and an exposure of food adulteration or that Ettor urged strikers to poison food of patrons, which he plainly did not advise. A running fight between AFL and IWW in that local field ran through the year.[12]

In the spring of 1913 the Marine Transport Workers of the IWW was launched. In February the Marine Oilers, Firemen and Watertenders moved to affiliate with the IWW.[13] No such event occurred, but the desire for industrial organization led a number in this and other maritime crafts to build up an IWW organization that by 1916 was to have considerable to say about conditions aboard ship on the Atlantic coast.

In Philadelphia on the docks the IWW found a chance to build its first clear example of stability, a longshore organization that lasted from 1913 to 1925 and exercised job control through most of those twelve years.[14]. About May 10 the small Philadelphia local got wind that the unorganized longshoremen were in a mood to organize and favored the IWW. An organizer was assigned to the job, but he could not find those who had such ideas. George Speed of the IWW was addressing a meeting of sugar workers, and a group of longshoremen came in and asked would he organize them. He said he would and got it settled that in this industry where Negro and white workers had regularly been pitted against each other, a union would have to unite them, and got them to formulate the demands they felt the union should go after. Word of these demands spread along the 20 miles of dock like prairie fire, and resulted in a strike which the IWW had not called. But the response to its appeal for Negro and white workers to stick together so took the company by surprise and so shattered its customary means for keeping these Negroes, Poles and Lithuanians apart — through threats to assign docks to men of another hue—that the strike was won in a short time. In the early stages of the strike, the strikers calmly deliberated on the proposals of both AFL and IWW and chose the Wobblies. After the strike the AFL with booze parties and a press accusing the IWW of mismanaging the strike, tried to recover but the MTW-IWW held the fort and grew.

An effort was made to build this Marine Transport Workers on the Great Lakes, where the AFL had just given up a three-year strike, but the only Lakes success was on the docks at Duluth and Superior, where an IWW strike put in the safety devices still used on the ore docks. On the Superior docks two workers were killed through what their fellow workers felt to be company negligence. Organizers Leo Laukki and J. P. Cannon were there and built up strike sentiment, and were soon joined by Frank Little. Many of the workers were Finnish and at this time the Finnish socialists were leaning toward IWW views, and had founded the daily paper Socialisti, made into an IWW paper in 1916, and still published as an IWW Finnish daily, Industrialisti,* in Duluth. With this support they spread the strike to the ore docks of the upper end of the Lake. On August 8, GEB member Frank Little was kidnapped and taken to a farm 35 miles out in the country and held there until newspaper reporters caught the trail and rescued him. He got back in time to make a dramatic entry, haggard and unshaved, at

*Industrialisti ceased publication October 21, 1975.

a strike mass meeting in the Duluth Armory. The
demand for safety equipment was won, the strike
called off and other concessions obtained in the
settlement were spread by the Finnish socialists to
other docks.

In this period of active industrial organization
there were many smaller strikes not mentioned here.
One strike of workers employed by Utah Construction near Soldier's Summit, Utah, resulted in a mass
deportation from the camp, an incident that later
became part of the background of the Joe Hill
case.[15]

Another sortie that achieved fame out of its aftermath was the strike at Durst's hop ranch at Wheatland, between Marysville and Sacramento, Calif.[16]
Durst advertised for pickers to flood the market.
Some 3000 camped on his land, whole families,
waiting for a chance to work, though the earnings
averaged only $1.28 a day and tents were rented
to them for 75 cents a day, and all groceries were
to be bought at his "pluck 'em" store. The camp
had no facilities for garbage, nine crude toilets, and
five wells, garbage-contaminated and usually dry.
To the thirsty pickers he sold a mixture of citric
acid and water for five cents a glass. Dysentery and
other sickness was common. Among them a few,
perhaps a hundred, had IWW cards, for the IWW
had been making repeated efforts among west coast
agricultural workers. These called a meeting to consider strike action Sunday noon, Aug. 2, 1913, using
a dance pavilion to speak from. On it Dick Ford
took a sick baby from its mother's arms and said,
"It's for the life of the kids that we're doing this."
At that moment two cars filled with drunken deputies, brandishing their guns, broke into the peaceful
meeting and proceeded to arrest Ford. The crowd
hollered, and some drunken deputy started shooting. Before it was calmed down, two strikers and
two of the sheriff's group lay dead. Hop-pickers
believed that one of the wounded strikers, a Puerto
Rican, had grabbed the gun of a deputy before he
died and evened the score.

Hundreds of hop-pickers were arrested, "investigated" and put under pressure to turn state's evidence, but among all these 3000 starvelings not one such could be found. At the trial in 1914, Ford and Suhr were convicted of the murder of Deputy Sheriff Riordan. In 1928 Ford was released on parole and promptly re-arrested on orders of District Attorney Manwell for the murder of his father, the other officer killed in the scrimmage. The trial resulted in such an exposure of the previous miscarriage of justice that both Ford and Suhr were liberated—fifteen years too late.

Thus ends the story of the pre-war crest of the IWW. Focusing its attention on industrial activity, it had jumped from the approximate 4,000 members of its first six years to have an average membership, as reckoned by per capita of 18,387 for 1912, and 14,851 for 1913.[17] A figure for all who were members at any time during those two years would be at least double, and probably quadruple these figures. In 1912 it had been almost consistently winner in its fights; it won some in 1913, but was progressively less successful. When hard times hit in the fall of 1913, they fell on an organization that had spent its resources on Paterson and Akron, on the trials arising from Paterson and Wheatland and Louisiana—a union in bad shape to face tough times and with many enemies, both in and out of the labor movement.

1. *Solidarity* of period, especially issues 122, 128 and 148.

2. British Columbia accounts from IWW press and *International Socialist Review* of period.

3. See Wheatland strike, end of this chapter.

4. For account of Louisiana lumber, see Jensen "Labor and Lumber" (Farrar & Rinehart, 1945), pp. 87-92; also Spero & Harris "The Black Worker" (Columbia Univ. Press, 1931), chapter 15. This account taken largely from writings of Covington Hall, including article in *International Socialist Review*, Sept. 1912, reports in IWW press, 1912-1914, series on Louisiana in 1945 *Industrial Worker*, July 14, 21 and 28, and unpublished mss., "Labor Struggles in the Deep South."

5. *Solidarity*, No. 119. For general account of strike, Jensen, "Labor and Lumber," p. 121, etc., and Bureau of Labor Statistics Bulletin 349 (1924), though Jensen repeats confusion of 1913 woods strike with 1912 mill strike. Woehlke in *Outlook*, July 6, 1912, has a story of strikers scaling fences around Lytel Mill to pull out scabs that is not corroborated by accounts or memories of participants. Account of end of strike, *Solidarity*, No. 124.

6. *Solidarity,* No. 178.

7. Pittsburgh cigar: *Solidarity* Sept. 7, 1912, and No. 198; extensive account by Cooper in *Survey* for Nov. 29, 1913.

8. For details of Akron read "The Rubber Workers" (Harper's, 1944) by Harold S. Roberts, senior economist National War Labor Board. Other data taken from *Solidarity* and *ISR,* April 1913.

9. Affidavit given in full, *Solidarity,* Jan. 17, 1914.

10. *Solidarity* No. 127.   11. Ibid Nos. 184 and 192.

12. *Solidarity,* through Jan. 1913, and *N.Y. Times* 1913, see own index.

13. Grover Perry in *International Socialist Review,* May 1913.

14. Spero & Harris, "The Black Worker," chapter 15, give the more commonly held account of IWW start on Philadelphia docks, based on reminiscences. This follows record in *Solidarity* by McKelvey, Oct. 4, 1913; also *N.Y. Times,* May 13, 1913, for May strike.

15. Soldier's Summit account, *N.Y. Times,* June 13, 1913, p. 13.

16. For details of Wheatland read Report of Executive Secretary of State Housing and Immigration Committee, by Carlton Parker, published as appendix to his book, "The Casual Laborer." (The rather Freudian analysis of migratory workers in this book has struck some of them as much like the distorted descriptions of primitive peoples by well-meaning outsiders, including even anthropologists.) Both the story of Wheatland and a record of the failure of AFL attempts to organize agriculture in California is given in Williams "Factories in the Fields," Little Brown & Co., 1939.

17. Figures from table in Brissenden, p. 354.

VI.   "Those Bomb-Throwing I Won't Works"

The hard times that set in toward the fall of 1913 cut down chances for job organization and strike activities and turned the attention of the IWW toward agitation, particularly among the unemployed. The first effect of the war in 1914 was to cut jobs further. Joblessness, this war for trade and dynastic ambitions, the breakdown of international socialism, the evils of militarism and conscript armies, the obvious need for world-wide working-class solidarity—all these gave soapboxers much to talk about, and audiences to talk to.

When the IWW again became effective in industry, it was in new fields: lumber, metal mining, oil fields, agriculture, construction projects, and its area of influence, outside of the Philadelphia waterfront and east coast shipping, was chiefly west of the Mississippi. The pre-war depression and early war years make a definite break in the story of the IWW, the more so because of a change in its reputation. Before this, it had been derided as being ahead of its time and had been called the "International Wonder Workers." After this break in its story, it was ridiculed instead as the "I Won't

Works" and depicted as a bunch of bums with bombs in hip pockets, advocating violent sabotage.

This weird reputation has no relevance to the facts, but it became so widespread and such an influence on its subsequent history, that the history of the myth must be told alongside the history of the actual organization. Perhaps the simplest answer to the myth is the finding of an extensive study issued by Johns Hopkins University in 1939:

"Although there are contradictory opinions as to whether the IWW practices sabotage or not, it is interesting to note that no case of an IWW saboteur caught practicing sabotage or convicted of its practice is available." [1]

Brissenden, whose studies should have enabled him to know better, writes in the Encyclopedia of Social Sciences that the Socialist Party was so deeply incensed by the sabotage propaganda of the IWW that its national convention in 1912 put a provision into its constitution excluding those who advocated sabotage. This is a widely accepted opinion. The facts indicate instead that IWW discussion of the subject developed as a consequence, not as an antecedent, of this Socialist Party action, and that the roots of the entire hullaballoo lie not in any American situation at all, but were transoceanic migrations of earlier quarrels between socialists and other theorists in Europe.

Prior to the May 1912 convention of the Socialist Party, the only reference to sabotage or kindred ideas appearing in any IWW publication is to sabotage and direct action in Chicago strikes in 1910 mentioned in Chapter 3. The connotation of sabotage there is that of malingering or inefficient work. The currently accepted sense of malicious destruction is a later development, attaching itself to an absurd etymology. As Veblen in his "Engineers and the Price System" and other scholars have pointed out, the relation of sabots or wooden shoes to sabotage is this: the use of wooden shoes persisted among French peasants after industrial workers had shifted to leather shoes; the clumsiness of peasants, particularly when they entered industry as strikebreakers, led to their being called saboteurs, in much the sense that "hayseed" was once current here; and defeated strikers going back to work and expressing their discontent by work as bungling as the strikebreakers had done, referred to this imitation of the sabot-wearers as sabotage. The alternative derivation, to support the connotation of destruction, alleges a practice of kicking a wooden shoe into a loom, and thus involves the unlikely picture of the culprit with one shoe off, one on, standing by the damaged loom trying to deny his depredation.

The entire story of these disputes about violence, physical force, sabotage and direct action is a tale of strange fantasies told in words that keep changing their meaning. Not only has "sabotage" shifted in meaning from malingering to malicious destruction, but "violence" in the earlier discussions was an accusation against unionists that they violated the social concord of democracy by refusing arbitration; "physical forcism," dead as a social program since the decline of Johann Most's influence after 1886, was a DeLeonite epithet used to imply that any radical movement lacking an electioneering program must therefore anticipate the overthrow of government by force of arms; and "direct action," used originally to contrast action by workers for themselves with action for them by legislative or other representatives, has been contorted to cover all the implications of mayhem and destruction implied in these other terms.

The background of the IWW myth lies in France. (The background of the actual IWW is American industry.)[2] A class-struggle unionism had grown in France whose leaders, as Lewis Lorwin says, were "annoyed and hampered by the overshadowing prestige of the political socialist groups and by the disruptive competitive bidding of these groups for the loyalties of the workers."[3] Their Confederation Generale du Travail developed as antidote a philosophy hinging on the doctrine of union self-sufficiency: that whatever workers needed done for them, they could do for themselves through their unions by union action. This CGT philosophy was one of world labor solidarity, and thus anti-patriot, anti-militarist and distrustful of all government. It projected an increasing competence of organized workers to determine what should be produced, with union quality-control, and where it should go, and pictured the final showdown with the old order as a social general strike, with folded arms, that would so demoralize the old order that soon all or almost all sections of society would be happy to see the resumption of the work necessary for social survival by union workers producing for use under their own direction.

There was no scope in this program for the politician. All parties seeking the labor vote felt the urge to attack it, and the more so because then, even more than now, mid-19th century Utopianism had left as a hangover the notion that every program should be a complete procedure for performance in some social vacuum where nothing but the specified program itself went forward.

Liberals and reformist socialists, believing that the role of government is to settle all conflicts in the general interest, urged arbitration of industrial disputes and assured workers that they could get a better settlement that way than by striking, and without any trouble, if only they would elect friends of labor to office. French liberals argued that even the most peaceful strike, if it stopped work the community needed done, or stopped income that the shop-keepers needed, did violence to the social concord and was a crime of "lese democratie." In 1906, Sorel answered these arguments with a series of essays, "Reflections on Violence," emphasizing the demoralizing influence of compulsory arbitration or of statism in general, and urging that the will of the working class to create the good world could develop only from daily practice of a class struggle ethic. This was the content of the term "violence" in this dispute between French radicals, and it continued as the content in British discussions, such as Ramsay MacDonald's articles on syndicalism; but when this discussion moved to America where labor disputes had often become pitched battles, "violence" was taken to mean Most's "physical force."

The more Marxian wing of the socialists used a different attack. It conceded that in times of business activity, strikes could be effective but argued the final battle might come instead when masses already unemployed could not effectively strike. To counteract this argument, the syndicalist movement elaborated various forms of possible sabotage: that of the "open mouth" by which workers let out trade secrets or disclosed the wrong-doing of employers, particularly in the foodstuff industries; that of "misdirection" of shipments; that of giving employers the services of "hands" only, if workers were to be treated and hired and paid only as "hands"—and sundry other forms of the "conscientious withdrawal of efficiency." There was disagreement among syndicalists as to the effect of these practices on proletarian morale and the development of labor's ability to create a good world, but the syndicalist consensus was that by the discriminating choice and adaptation of these means, the morale of capitalism could be shattered and organized labor emerge as a constructive force. This became official CGT doctrine in 1897.

In the socialist movement of pre-war years, particularly throughout Europe, there were internal power disputes presented as conflicts of theory as to the nature of the state, the relation of politics to unionism, the determinants of historic development, the choice of programs of reform or programs for the simple abolition of capitalism, acceptance of posts in capitalist governments, attitudes toward nationalism and war, and whether to oppose war by a general strike or by parliamentary action. While there was no neat polarization on these issues, in a general way all socialists denounced syndicalists as sinners, and the gradualist-reformist socialists denounced the doctrinaire-"impossibilists" as sharing the sins of the syndicalists.[4]

In America, the fact that many of the "doctrinaires" were out of the Socialist Party and in the SLP delayed the breaking out of this dispute until 1912. Then the IWW replaced the CGT as the goat. Those who hoped to catch support by catering to the AFL pushed through the new Article II Section 6 by a vote of 191 to 90, which read: "Any member of the party who opposes political action or advocates crime, sabotage or other methods of violence as a weapon of the working class to aid in its emancipation shall be expelled. . . ." In consequence of this, Haywood was recalled from the National Executive Committee of the SPA in February 1913. On local levels, IWW and Socialists remained as friendly as ever, often sharing halls. In 1917 the Socialist Party rescinded Section 6.[5]

The argument over violence led to a resolution adopted at the 7th Convention of the IWW, September 1913:

"At all times it is the rulers who, being in power, are in a position to determine in great measure just how and when the struggle will be fought. . . . It is the employing class and their agencies who provoke violence and then cry out the loudest against it. . . . The program of the IWW offers the only possible solution of the wage question whereby violence can be avoided, or. at the very worst, reduced to a minimum. If the ruling class of today may decide, as their prototypes in the past have decided, that violence will be the arbiter of the question, then we shall cheerfully accept their decision and meet them to the best of our ability—and we do not fear the result."

The weird reputation that the IWW acquired in this period is the outcome of this right-left quarrel inside the socialist movement, combined with a depression situation that led to "sensational soapboxing." Although many writing in the IWW press were familiar with the European labor press, the

only portion of CGT philosophy prior to the 1912
convention in IWW publications were statements
by Vincent St. John supporting the doctrine of
union self-sufficiency. In other literature a reference
exists to a pamphlet issued by Trautman in Pittsburgh in 1912, entitled "Direct Action and Sabotage," but no mention of it occurs in the IWW press.
In February of 1913, Solidarity ran a series of articles on the CGT by Leon Jouhaux, with editorial
comment that it was necessary to get a clear picture
because of misrepresentation in socialist and capitalist press, and pointing out that the IWW was
not anti-parliamentary but non-parliamentary, asking the politicians only to leave the labor movement
alone. Later that year as Andre Tridon's "New
Unionism" came out, the IWW press promoted its
circulation, and took note of translations from the
French being issued of Pouget's "Sabotage" and
Pataud and Pouget's fictional description of the
general strike, "Syndicalism and the Cooperative
Commonwealth". In Spokane, on his own account,
an IWW speaker, Walker C. Smith, issued a booklet
on sabotage and it was advertised in the IWW
papers in 1913; this was followed by another booklet describing sabotage by Elizabeth G. Flynn issued
in Cleveland in 1915. For neither of these could the
IWW be properly held responsible. It was this irresponsibility of the Cleveland autonomous "IWW
Publishing Bureau" that led to its dissolution next
year and the consequent move of Solidarity to Chicago. For a while a few internal critics of the IWW
in Los Angeles, who attacked IWW policy as "cen-
tralist" issued a paper "The Wooden Shoe."

Soapboxers found that talk of sabotage gave their
audiences a thrill, and since the dispensers of the
above publications were happy to send them for
sale on commission to all who would handle them,
there was nothing to stop spielers, whether they
were IWW members or not, from procuring these
booklets, mounting a box, talking about the IWW,
taking up a collection and selling the literature.
The actual effect on IWW practices was evidently

nil, as shown by the Johns Hopkins study given at
the start of this chapter; but its effect on the popular conception of the IWW was definitely damaging.
There are curious consequences of this disparity of
practice and reputation: in one IWW strike after
another local papers commented on the amazing
orderliness and peacefulness of the strike despite
the "known fact" that the IWW was notoriously
violent everywhere else; the imprisonment of hundreds of exceptionally non-violent men for allegedly
aiming at the violent overthrow of organized society; or the confusion of the North Dakota farmer
who regularly hired IWW help and who made the
distinction: "The IWW's I know are swell fellows,
but them alleged IWW's I read about in the papers
are holy terrors."[6]

IWW ideas on violence have been shaped by practicality. Organizers regularly pointed out to strikers
that if they used violence or induced violence toward themselves, they handicapped their strike by
putting the police openly on the side of the scab-
herders; and that the violent strikes of labor history
are almost regularly the lost ones; that violence
was often found to be the work of employer agents.
At all times their concept of the "social revolution"
in an industrial society was that of industrial action,
not violence. In February of 1913 when a mysterious
explosion in a New York roominghouse occupied
by radicals (incidentally not Wobblies) led to much
talk of dynamite in the local press, Joe Ettor wrote
in the Call: "The IWW has neither advocated nor
participated in violence against the social order.
The general strike is the method we favor for over-
throwing the capitalist system, and that is the only
kind of force we are in favor of." E. G. Flynn took
exception to this stand; Ettor and others replied
with arguments that there was too much talk of
violence and it would be best to stop it. But there
was no puzzle why strikers felt like punching scabs
in the nose; and when McNamara of the Structural
Iron Workers, which had systematically blown up
scab-erected bridges, always with certainty that no

lives would be lost, was induced by the promise
that his fellow workers would be let off, to "confess" to blowing up the Los Angeles Times Building
(which evidently went up from a defective boiler),
the IWW frankly called him a victim of the class
war and, with all his friends deserting him, provided
him to his death in San Quentin with tobacco
money.

Before the IWW got back to substantial organizing, war came. The IWW stuck to the position that
had been typical of the labor movement in peace.
When Gompers wrote his "Labor in Europe" in
1910, he did not hesitate to concur with the CGT
slogan "the workingman has no country" or to
assert that "workers will forever refuse to kill one
another merely because authority has put them in
different uniforms."[7] Because the IWW did not
change its tune with the new winds of war, it became the wartime bogy of the propaganda press,
which picked up all the canards that had developed
about the IWW and broadcast the cartoon conception of the Wobbly as a bomb-toting "I Won't
Work."

1. History of Criminal Syndicalism Legislation in the United States,
by Eldridge Foster Dowell, Ph.D., John Hopkins University Studies in
Historical and Political Science, 1939, Series LVII, No. 1, p. 36.

2. Both Levine, in 1913 article cited next note, and Brissenden in
both his books on IWW and in article in Encyclopedia of Social Sciences,
point out the native American origins of IWW, and its industrialist program a response to the more developed American industry.

3. In article "Direct Action," Encyclopedia of Social Sciences.

4. Socialist background of this period given in W.E. Walling, "The
Socialists and the War," Holt, 1915, or L.L. Lorwin, "Labor and Internationalism," McMillan, 1929.

5. James O'Neal and C.A. Werner, "American Communism," Dutton,
pp. 29 and 37. Theoretical differences in SPA given in John Macy's "Socialism in America," Doubleday, 1916 (very readable with considerable
information bearing on IWW).

6. For a positive presentation of IWW philosophy, see Frank Tannenbaum: "The Labor Movement," Putnam, 1921, or the section on
Syndicalism in Bertrand Russell, "Proposed Roads to Freedom," or
pamphlet "IWW in Theory and Practice" by Justus Ebert.

7. Gompers: "Labor in Europe," esp. p. 274 et seq.

The data and place of publication of the following material is significant of the migration of the content of the questions discussed in this
chapter: Sorel, "Reflexions sur Violence," Paris, 1906; Roller, "Die
Direkte Aktion," Berlin, 1910; R.A. MacDonald, "Syndicalism," London, Constable, May 1912; Arthur D. Lewis, "Syndicalism and the General Strike," London, Unwin, 1912; Levine, "Syndicalism in France,"
Columbia University Press, 1912; A.W. Kirkaldy, "Economics and Syn-

dicalism," University Press, Cambridge, 1914; in America the following, in 1913: John G. Brooks, "American Syndicalism"; Spargo, "Syndicalism, Industrial Unionism and Socialism"; Hunter, "Violence and the Labor Movement"; Tridon, "The New Unionism," and the following scholarly accounts: Levine, Sept. in *Political Science Quarterly,* and Brissenden, "The Launching of the IWW," University of Berkeley Press, and in 1914, Hoxie, "Truth about IWW," in *Journal of Political Economy.*

Fictional treatment of IWW follows similar diversity later, ranging from Zane Grey's poisonous "Desert of Wheat," Harper, 1919, which helped send many Wobblies to jail, to such sympathetic treatment as Upton Sinclair's "Oil," Boni, 1927. Winston Churchill's novel, "The Dwelling Place of Light" uses the Lawrence strike of 1912 as general situation with a rather neutral treatment. Eugene O'Neill's "Hairy Ape" has a scene in IWW maritime workers' hall that realistically dramatizes the conflict of myth and reality; Stavis' "The Man Who Never Died" is a somewhat Stalinoid drama of Joe Hill, with very informative preface. Probably favorite IWW fiction has been Jack London's "Iron Heel," 1907, and "Dream of Debs."

VII. Hard Times — 1914-1915

When the pre-war depression hit in 1913, IWW members were as jobless as any. Inclined toward collective action, they felt their chances for food and a place to sleep were better if they went after these necessaries organized. First notes of their activity among the unemployed are in the various organizations that grew spontaneously in different cities. In some instances the IWW substantially directed these. In other instances it formed unemployed auxiliaries with dues usually at a nickel a month. Soon these began the collection of food and the provision of lodging for their members, not only to meet creature needs, but to escape the demoralizing influences of the souplines and missions, and to provide a sociability and sense of solidarity that was needed as much as soup. By September 1914 when the 9th Convention met, it was agreed that it was folly to join parades to City Halls where there was nothing to eat anyway, but that the unemployed should be organized to give them union principles, to enable them to go after what they needed, and to prevent their being used to batter down wages.

There were various outcomes: free speech fights; fire-hoses turned on "unemployed armies"; a busboy became a college professor; "Solidarity Forever," marching song later of millions of American strikers, came to its author, Ralph Chaplin, out of an unemployed demonstration in Chicago;[1] Henry Ford announced $5.00 a day minimum; the hall of Butte Mine Workers Union No. 1 got blown up; in Sioux City a group of jobless men descended upon a banquet at which the Chamber of Commerce was considering their plight, and relieved their plight by eating the banquet. Probably the chief consequence for the IWW was that their activities laid the foundation for building a substantial organization of agricultural workers, and thus later for substantial victories in western lumber and other industries.

Early in March 1914 a big snow storm hit New York City. The IWW agitated that the unemployed should not shovel the snow for less than 30 cents an hour. Shelter from the cold was important for the penniless. A bus-boy, Frank Tannenbaum, led a number of jobless men to the Church of St. Alphonsus on West Broadway, to sit there for the night; but a fight developed and Tannenbaum was sentenced to a year on Blackwell's Island. Agitation for his release merged with protests against the Rockefeller Ludlow Masscare and the brutal treatment of the striking Michigan copper miners as major issues at the unemployed demonstrations, including the Union Square riots of April 6. (Tannenbaum went ahead with his education, and his early book "The Labor Movement," especially in its opening chapters, is an outstanding constructive statement of basic IWW attitudes.)

In Detroit on February 12, 1914, the IWW staged an unemployed demonstration in front of the Employers' Association to demand a municipal lodging house; about 3000 jobless gathered before the police started cracking skulls.[2] In December Organizer John F. Leheney formed the Unemployed League as an IWW auxiliary which set up kitchen in a former church building donated by the Unitarians. There it combined public forums with mulligan stew and found that even with a shortage of Wobbly speakers, the IWW points could be made by systematic Socratic questioning of invited orators. This IWW effort managed also to maintain close cooperation with the AFL.[3] With street meetings and leaflets the Unemployed League steadily argued that to get rid of depression it was necessary to cut the hours and boost the pay; Ford's policy of $5.00 minimum has been attributed to this pressure.

On West Coast the trend was to participate in other organizations of the unemployed. There were frequent arrests at the daily mass meetings held in 1914 at 5th and Howard, then a vacant lot, in San Francisco. Kelly's Army was starting its parade eastward and at Sacramento got chased off the sandlots with fire-hoses.[4] When the millionaire hobo Eads Howe obtained the San Francisco Civic Auditorium for an Unemployed Convention (February 18th to 23rd, 1915) the IWW participants took substantial control from the big names, on the grounds that the term unemployed meant workers seeking work, and not the habitually idle, rich or poor.[5] Taking it over yielded nothing much but resolutions on behalf of various imprisoned workers, as the McNamaras, Niles, Ford and Suhr, and Pancner.[6]

In Butte hard times brought the automatic blacklist system to a head. It had been started in December 1912 by connivance between the companies and the copper clique, as those in Butte Miners' Union who sought to propitiate the companies were called.[7] Under the new scheme all miners had first to go to the Butte Mutual Labor Bureau, maintained by the companies, and get a rustling card without which they could not apply for work at the mines. The militant and especially the pro-IWW element which up to 1912 had exerted a healthy influence in the Butte WFM local could readily be deprived of employment by this scheme—an objective common to some of the local labor union leaders and management. However so many of the more competent miners were in the red-tagged group that it had not been practicable to try to get rid of them until slack times had set in. The separation of the

WFM from the IWW in 1908 had set it out on the futile path of trying to imitate the union-company collaboration of various AFL unions in a field where management was not inclined to collaborate with even the most supine of unions. In 1913 the Moyer faction had brought it back into the AFL where it was to be the International Mine Mill & Smelter Workers. The rustling card, the affiliation with the craft-separationists, the futility of discarding militancy as shown at Hearst's Homestake and elsewhere, and distrust over handling funds for the Michigan copper strike, all produced dissension and a substantial decline in members in Butte Miners Union. When the latter insisted that all miners show their cards to go to work, dissidents launched a new organization, the Butte Mine Workers' Union, often called "Muckie McDonald's union." The IWW forces supported the new venture, and the Socialists, who administered Butte in 1914, were also friendly. The dispute between the two organizations was used by company provacateurs to rid Butte of miner unionism—and it stayed that way until the spontaneous rebirth of unionism after the Speculator disaster of 1917. In the dispute, against the instructions of the new union, a mob was led against the old union hall; shooting broke out evidently from inside the hall; dynamite was obtained from the mines and the old hall was blown up with 26 separate blasts, Miners Day, June 13, 1914. Many accused the IWW of this, but even the editor of the Western Federation Miners' Magazine wrote that he had reliable information that the dynamiters were gunmen of the Waddell-Mahon agency.[8]

In Sioux City the IWW opened up a hall in October 1914 as it was a strategic point for new plans to organize the wheat hands. IWW activity on behalf of the unemployed led to a series of skirmishes and free speech fights, in which IWW had the backing of a substantial local Socialist movement. The Sioux City free speech fight was "good stage." Every night crowds of about a thousand witnessed a Wobbly mount his box and talk until arrested; 82

were in the stockade by mid-April. The police started a rock-pile and led the prisoners there. They sat
down in passive disobedience. A fight developed
with police over this refusal to work and over the
burning of lousy blankets issued to the prisoners;
three cops got laid out with a pop-bottle. Public
sentiment grew for the Wobs, and as more free
speech fighters arrived, the City sought terms, proposing that the men would be freed if they would
promise to leave town. The men insisted that whether
they went or stayed was up to the individual pref-
erence of each. They were released and, as a final
gesture of contempt for the rock-pile, they gathered
the ingredients for a mammoth mulligan stew, built
fires there, cooked the stew in Standard Oil cans,
and ate their "victory banquet" on top the rockpile.[9]

More significant was the beginning of organization among the wheat hands. Kansas City Local 61
set out in earnest in the spring of 1914, aiming at
$4.00 a day, but pushed the going wage only to $3.00
from a previous $2.50. Organization of agricultural
workers had been attempted by AFL and other unions without success except for an independent local
of sheep-shearers.[10] The 1914 experience showed
how the problem shaped up, and what structural
changes would be needed in the IWW to handle it.
Reduced to bare elements, building unionism in a factory or on a construction project amounts to getting
men together, agreeing on terms of employment,
and enforcing the terms by collective refusal to
work on lower terms. Here the job was the vast
wheat belt of America, running up into Canada.
The job seekers gathered in box cars, rode empty
gondolas, huddled in hobo jungles, idled around the
one Main Street of a thousand towns and villages.
But hardly any lived in the wheat belt; they came
into it from outside. It was too big a job for Kansas
City Local 61. It would require the coordinated
effort of IWW members all around the wheat belt,
organizing the job-seekers as they came in, and pro-
ceeding inward with the new recruits to maintain
wages and enforce union terms.

The 1914 convention arranged for a spring convention of the locals directly concerned with such a campaign for Kansas City, April 16, 1915. This led to several new developments which soon became the general plan of operations throughout the IWW. Up to this point IWW members had been members of locals, with these locals occasionally, as among the Textile Workers, banded together into a National Industrial Union. Membership cards were issued by the secretaries of the locals, but no secretary of Local 61 could write cards all over Kansas and the Dakotas, nor was there reason for forming local unions scattered through this area. Thus one organization was set up—the Agricultural Workers Organization 400 (later changed to Agricultural Workers Industrial Union 110) with a national secretary issuing blank cards and dues stamps to job delegates, and an organization committee to be responsible for operations everywhere in that industry. This system of industrial union secretaries issuing organization supplies to local secretaries and even more to job delegates, soon became the regular IWW pattern in all industries.

The new organization was tempted into free speech fights, but soon learned to avoid these as distractions from its main job, organizing, raising the pay and cutting the hours. It did find it was necessary to clear the jungles and freight trains of hi-jacks and card-sharps. At first the policy was to get the job-seekers to withhold their labor waiting for farmers to meet the union demands. Soon they found this meant that the work got done by "wicks" below union scale. Policy then changed to going on the jobs at the going wage, then pulling a quickie strike at an opportune moment for their demands.[11] This often resulted in benefits to their successors rather than themselves, but, if acted upon generally, as later it was in the lumbering industry, it became of mutual benefit to all workers.

To achieve better conditions, it was necessary to deter those who would not co-operate with the union from reaching the harvest fields. Since they rode box-cars, this meant keeping them off unless they joined or talked like union material. Soon many train crews aided them by asking all free riders for their red cards, or else, get off. This speeded up initiations, so that for quite a few years, up to 1925, the dues collected by the Agricultural Workers ran to about half of the total dues collected while initiation fees were an even more disproportionate share of the total. A further consequence was that the process of sifting out the non-unionists or "wicks" was the more complete, the further one penetrated the wheat belt. This difference gives some measure of the union's effectiveness. In the interior of the wheat belt a 10 hour day prevailed, and on the fringes the day was sun-up to sun-down, and wages in the center of the wheat belt were usually double those on the fringe. This sort of organization remained effective to about 1926, when the wide use of the combine, previously restricted to Kansas, cut down the labor market, and the cheap second hand car brought in the wicks on rubber tires in a manner difficult to organize. The net effect of the IWW on agriculture is perhaps most clearly shown in the statistics in Louis J. Ducoff's "Wages in Agriculture in the United States" issued by the Bureau of Agricultural Economics in 1944. These figures show that if farm wages in 1943 bore the same ratio to industrial wages that they had during World War I, they would need to have been 80 to 85% higher. That difference is attributable to the fact that the Wobs were there in World War I, but not in World War II and largely because union demands had made it pay to mechanize agriculture.

Looking backward in 1945 one of the IWW organizers active during the First World War period, Joe Ettor, wrote in a series of articles "The Light of the Past"[12] that this relatively easy way of obtaining about 15,000 initiation fees per year had sidetracked the IWW from other fields of industry that might have yielded more permanent results. Others point to the fact that many of those re-

cruited in the harvest field became active for the
IWW elsewhere, and that the large amount of literature circulated in these harvest drives resulted in
an understanding of IWW unionism that both made
for a readiness to respond to organizing efforts elsewhere and for some insistence that other unions
come closer to IWW ideals.

The most popular piece of IWW literature was
the little red song book. In box car, jungles and on
the job, its songs were sung, until even the farmers
and their boys were singing them too. Many of the
more favorite songs were written by Joe Hill. When
it became known that he faced death on flimsy and
unconvincing evidence, public concern developed
into international proportions comparable only to
that shown in the Sacco-Vanzetti case. A grocer (an
ex-policeman) had been shot along with his son by
masked men who, according to the remaining son,
had entered his store at closing time crying out
"We've got you now." Since no theft was attempted,
the obvious motive appeared to be revenge, However Joe Hill was arrested and convicted on the
grounds that he had been wounded about the same
time. Conceiving that the grocer may have
shot, the lower and finally the Supreme Court of
Utah proceeded on the strange logic that to have
a bullet wound for which no explanation was offered by the defendant was as damaging evidence in
this murder trial as the possession of goods from his
store had it been a charge of burglary. However it
is very doubtful whether the grocer shot at his as-
sailants. Had he hit Hill, since Hill's wound went
through his body and clothing, the bullet would
have been in the store; but it wasn't. Further the
bullet hole was high in Hill's chest but low in his
coat, showing that he had been shot with his hands
up. Also the bullets that killed the grocer and his
son had not been fired from Hill's revolver.

To the IWW—and to many outsiders who investigated the case— there was no doubt that Hill was
prosecuted because he was considered a dangerous

agitator, a writer of rebel songs that growing thousands sang, and out of vindictiveness for previous skirmishes in the mines of Utah, free speech fights in Salt Lake City, and particularly for winning a victory at Tucker against the Utah Construction Co. On November 19, 1915, Hill was executed, despite the protests of the AFL and the labor bodies of other countries, the objections of the Swedish government and the intervention of President Wilson. His funeral in Chicago was attended by an unexpected 30,000 mourners who blocked traffic for their long parade to the cemetery in an amazing demonstration of concern for a framed-up working stiff.

1. R. Chaplin, "Wobbly," University of Chicago Press, 1948, p. 168.

2. *Detroit News*, Feb. 12, 1914, quoted in *Solidarity*, No. 215.

3. *Solidarity*, No. 272.

4. Account of Kelley's Army at Sacramento with good photos, in *International Socialist Review*, May 1914.

5. *Solidarity*, No. 269.

6. Niles was in San Quentin on trumped-up charge of horse-stealing and subjected to brutalities described in Jack London's novel, "The Star-Rover." John Pancner: Public Service Workers Local 111 had won the 8-hour day in all miner boarding houses in Tonapah, Nevada, except two, which it boycotted. Drunken thugs raided its hall July 11, 1914, tore down the boycott signs, and seized a member, threatening to lynch him. Pancner shot one thug in the leg and they fled; he was convicted on charge of assault with intent to kill.

7. Brissenden: "Butte Miners and the Rustling Card," in *American Economic Review*, Dec. 1920, and Perlman and Taft, History of Labor in U.S., p. 257 (good summary).

8. *Miner's Magazine*, July 2, 1914, quoted in Jensen's "Heritage of Conflict," Cornell University Press, 1950, p. 336. Jensen gives detailed account, marred however by a bias that leads him to imply on page 347 that the IWW had an impossible three-month advance knowledge of this occurrence, on the basis of a letter from Leheney to Dan Liston, sent in care of Bradley, subsequently secretary of the new union, containing the statement, "Fearing that the hall may have been lost, am addressing this letter in care of him." The reference in letter is plainly to IWW hall, for Wobblies at that time might as well have used the Anaconda as a mailing address as the Butte Miners' Union. The dispute ended with martial law, despite objections of the Mayor, and the imprisonment of McDonald and Bradley on charges of deporting objectionables, i.e., requiring that they leave town. See also P.F. Brissenden's pamphlet "Labor Conditions in Butte," and *Solidarity*, Nos. 233, 254 and 255.

9. Sioux City affairs described quite fully by Wallace Short in *Survey*, Oct. 15, 1915; see also *Solidarity*, Nos. 263-264 and 273-277.

10. AFL lack of success in attempts to organize agricultural workers, detailed in Williams, "Factories in the Fields," Little Brown and Co., 1939, and in Jamieson, "Labor Unionism in American Agriculture," *Monthly Labor Review*, Jan. 1946.

11. The role of the IWW in devising and developing union techniques is roughly indicated in chapter 16 of Taft's "Economics and Problems of Labor," Stackpole, 1942.

12. Series in summer of 1945, especially issue of July 21.

13. Most complete account of Joe Hill available is the non-fiction half of Barrie Stavis "The Man Who Never Died," Haven Press, New York 1954. (The other half of the book is a fictional drama about Hill.) A summary of the evidence is given in special Hill edition of *Industrial Worker,* Nov. 13, 1948, answering attack on Hill by Wallace Stegner. A boiled-down version of same article in *New Republic,* Nov. 15, 1948. In Swedish there is Ture Nerman's "Joe Hill," Federatovs Forlag, Stockholm, 1951, giving his original name as Joel Haaglund, born Gavle, Sweden, July 12, 1887. Detailed account of funeral is given in Chaplin's "Wobbly."

VIII. Events of 1916

In 1916 the IWW became involved in an inter-union dispute in the Baltimore Garment industry. It had started a local for clothing workers there on May 1, 1911 which remained small until the spring of 1913 when the independent Lithuanian Tailors' Union joined it, followed a little later by a body of Italian clothing workers. By September 1913 it had control of some of the largest shops in the city, among them Schless Brothers four big shops. A fourteen week strike against Schless ended dismally when the United Garment Workers furnished scabs. For nearly two years the IWW remained ineffective in the Baltimore garment industry but began to grow rapidly again in 1915. The United Garment Workers (AFL) relied less upon the organization of workers and putting up a battle against employers than it did on the demand for union label clothing by other workers who did not question under what conditions or for what wages the clothing had been made. Consequent dissatisfication led to a split and the formation of the Amalgamated Clothing Workers after the 1914 convention of the UGW.[1] During the early part of this split the IWW was the largest union in the industry in Baltimore. IWW policy forbade time agreements with employers and it sought no closed shop. The pattern of unionism throughout the local industry was less like the current "sole collective bargaining agency" device and more like the pattern that until recently prevailed in Europe, with workers in the same unit acting through whichever union tendency they individually preferred. The IWW was the majority in some shops, the minority in others; in either case, though it competed with both ACW and UGW for members, it took action to defend members of either union. For this "it got about the same thing as the neutral Belgians" observed organizer E. F. Doree.[2]

Grief & Company had five plants one of which in the Coca Cola Building was three quarters IWW, the rest UGW with a few members of the Amalgamated. In 1916 the UGW and ACW began demanding closed shop and wanted the IWW to pull this plant in support of their respective demands. The IWW issued a circular stating:

"The IWW always has and always will work in conjunction and strike with any group of workers anywhere, whether organized or unorganized when they have a grievance against any boss, but will not permit itself to be used as a club by any organization to fight another union."

The Amalgamated sent pickets with clubs and knives to bring out the Coca Cola Building; other members rallied to the free-for-all to even up the odds with the result that ACW left them alone there.

Soon after this the pocket makers at Strouse—20 of them IWW and ACW—decided to strike for the abolition of the sub-contract system and a straight price of 15 cents a pocket. The ACW tried to settle for less, proposing to replace any who struck against its settlement. The cutters in the plant were UGW and decided to strike in support of the original pocket makers whether IWW or not. A long strike of 700 AFL and IWW followed with 300 ACW recruits inside working. The clothing industry in Baltimore went to the unions that bid against each other for collective bargaining agreements and the IWW faded out of the picture.

Organizer Doree pointed out to the 10th Convention that the IWW was handicapped by its provision that no time agreements could be made and that as a result the IWW organizes, fights and lets other unions derive the benefits. However the reluctance to let agreements prevent sympathetic action continued this constitutional ban to 1938 when the constitution was amended to permit industrial unions to adopt their own regulations for agreements provided that nothing in the agreement obligated the workers covered by it to undertake any work that would aid in breaking any strike.

In contrast on the Philadelphia waterfront similar IWW policies achieved substantial union stability. The Marine Transport Workers there had a branch of 3000 members in the spring of 1916 and on May 20 with a parade of all 3000 members—and a band—to the three non-union docks, won union recognition (without any written agreement) and the same condition as prevailed on the docks previously organized. In June, with all docks now acting jointly, it struck and raised the scale to 40 cents for day work, 60 cents for night work and 80 cents for Sundays, holidays, Saturday afternoons and meal hours. The union branched out to other industries. Shoe Workers Local 162 won a strike in 23 shops. A local of coopers was organized, and a Spanish language local with a paper Cultura Obrera. An AFL local of lumber handlers left the ILA even though it meant leaving their treasury behind to join the IWW. In 1917 it began the organization of the sugar refineries.[3]

In Detroit workers at the Solvay Process plant struck without organization for a nickel pay boost, showers and lockers. A couple came to organizer Weber who arranged a meeting attended by 700 strikers. There was some difficulty over forming a committee, so it was decided to get the manager, Mr. Greene, to come to the meeting and negotiate with all. Mr. Greene said that only the back east directors could grant their demands and urged the men to return to work while he saw what he could do for them. Weber pointed out that the long dis--tance lines were open to New York and said the men would continue their meeting while Mr. Greene talked to the Directors. Soon he reported that they had been considering a one cent raise but agreed to the demands. Weber insisted this meant that penny plus the five cents just granted, showers and lockers. On these terms the men returned, but no permanent organization resulted. The local Auto Workers of IWW did better with a strike of 3000 against Kelsey Wheel, adding a tenth of them to its local.⁴

The most novel of IWW organizing campaigns was that of Jane Street among the housemaids of Denver. By persistent contact with them she compiled a card index by employer giving the "salaries paid in each of these positions, the number of people in each of the homes, the kind of work, the hours, and the characteristics of the mistresses," later adding a turnover record. The list soon grew to cover 2500 homes hiring servants with the pay going up largely because each time a girl managed an increase her successor would know of it and insist upon starting in at that figure. Both the Post and News in Denver ran cartoon-illustrated articles about the new union, implying it sabotaged the soup with too much pepper and won raises by putting too much starch in shirts. The union provided job information, employment service and social gatherings for the girls on their days off. It planned on having its own clubhouse in the residential area where girls could also stay between jobs, but it fell flat when its index list was stolen from its office. Unsuccessful efforts to imitate it were made in Seattle, Chicago and Duluth.⁵

In May 1916 the IWW began organization efforts on the Mesaba Iron Range on the urging of the Finnish Socialists who were strongly entrenched in that area. In Duluth they had a daily paper, the Socialisti, a residential labor college and a fine hall. Through the Iron Ranges they were responsible for the election of scattered Socialist administrations. They favored the IWW; some had participated in the IWW strike at Gray's Harbor in 1912 and others in the Duluth and Superior dock strike of 1913;

they had earlier been staunch supporters of the
Western Federation, but had been alienated by its
futile efforts at company collaboration and in particular its rustling card deal in Butte which first
victimized several hundred Finnish Socialists over
a Socialist proposal to tax mine tonnage for the
benefit of the city.[6] Though enthusiastic socialists
their ties with the Socialist Party also had been
loosened ever since Article 6 had been born over
disappointment with the effect of the McNamara
confession on the Los Angeles mayoralty campaign,
and now they saw a chance to help build a union
that would give them socialism on the job. In April
the staff of Socialisti advised Walter Neff, secretary
of the IWW Agricultural Workers in Minneapolis.
that there was unrest on the range, and that if the
IWW could provide organizers speaking English,
Italian and the various Slavic tongues, it could assure the support of the Finns and Swedes. There
were already Finnish speaking delegates, including
Geo. Humon on the Range.

Before organization had proceeded far, a strike
broke out at Aurora on June 2. It spread rapidly for
the strikers paraded to nearby mining towns and
when miners there struck, they did likewise. By
June 14 the entire Mesaba range was out, 16,000
strong and 4,000 IWW cards had been issued. Demands had been formulated into one program:
"$3.50 per day for wet places; $3.00 per day for dry
places; $1.75 for surface work; 8 hours to constitute
a day in and around the mines; miners to enter and
come out on company time; pay twice a month; Saturday night shift to be abolished and miners receive
full pay; abolition of all contract work; all miners
to be paid as soon as they quit work for a company."
They had been working 10 to 12 hours per day and
getting from $1.38 to $2.50.

The IWW tried to run a peaceful strike, but the
companies recruited over a thousand thugs from
various cities, often with the aid of police chiefs
who had "something on them," to break up meetings and to prevent even small groups of miners

meeting on the streets. On June 9 as the miners were parading from Aurora to Biwabik, eight organizers were nabbed from their ranks by the company police. An Oliver Mining Company gunman shot a miner, John Allar, as he and some other miners stood talking to each other on a street in Virginia. There a Citizens Committee ordered all IWW's out of town. The Duluth Herald held that resistance to this illegal vigilante group which represented about two percent of the citizens of Virginia was a defiance of law and order. Company lawlessness overruled local administrations that allowed civil liberties. On July 6 a posse of deputies, led by one who had recently been a bouncer in a roadhouse, entered the home of Phillip Masonovich to arrest him and a miner who boarded with him, Joe Hercigonovich. Mrs. Masonovich objected, and was knocked down on the floor. Somehow two of the deputies got shot. According to a boy in the house they were shot by the previously mentioned roadhouse bouncer. The two Montenegrin miners already mentioned, and another, Joe Nicich, and others were arrested as directly participating and also a group of organizers who were not in the vicinity, Carlo Tresca, Sam Scarlett, Joseph Ahlgren, Joe Schmidt, Frank Little and James Gilday, on the theory that their speeches had led to the deaths of the deputies. No trial was held; though the coroner's verdict had been "death at the hands of persons unknown," Judge O. N. Hilton, who had been called in as defense attorney, arranged for the three Montenegrin miners mentioned to plead guilty to manslaughter and for the others to go free. It soon developed that this arrangement had been proposed by Elizebeth Gurley Flynn who was handling publicity, and that she had sacrificed these miners to secure the release of her friends among the organizers. Her connections with the IWW were promptly terminated.

In mid-August a meeting at Crosby brought out the Cayuna Range. Organizers were busy in the Michigan iron mining country. At Ironwood the vigilantes drove eight organizers out of town. On August 16, Frank Little was arrested at Iron River, Michigan, taken out of jail, beaten, and threatened with lynching—with a rope around his neck—in a futile effort to make him lead his persecutors to the organizers speaking Italian and other languages. They knocked him in the head and he woke up dazed in a ditch near Watersmeet.

The labor movement felt obliged to support the strike. The Duluth Labor Herald, AFL, commented: "In 1907 there was a similar strike on the Iron Range. At that time there was a responsible labor organization supporting the strike. . . . Were not the same arguments being used in 1907 as are being used in 1916? Did not the press condemn the WFM as it condemns the IWW today?" On July 17 the Minnesota Federation of Labor convened in the strike town of Hibbing and promised support to the strike. The official organ of the Western Federation attacked the strike but its locals sent donations. Following the strike the State Federation attempted to organize the miners, but they wanted the IWW.

With mine production crippled, stock piles were shipped and then lower grade material. In Two Harbors the dock workers struck and stopped shipment; in Duluth a dock strike was broken by police; on the Allouez dock a 15% increase was promised if the men would stay at work. In Superior the coal dock workers struck for a 60% boost; Mayor Conklin told them he would help if they would join the AFL; instead they joined IWW.

There were tips that the companies were less reluctant to grant improvements to the miners than to grant them formally to the IWW; so in September with the Mesaba, Cayuna and Vermilion ranges out, the central strike committee discussed the proposal of going back to work with a strong organization, a market hungry for ore, and winning their points by action on the job. The proposal was referred to all locals; all voted in favor, and on September 19 the central committee called the strike off. A week later it reported: "The men are returning to work and thus far there has been no evidence of any discrimination against them and none is expected as the mining companies confess themselves exceedingly hard up for help." On April 1 next year Metal Mine Workers held its first conference in the Socialist Opera House in Virginia. Reports submitted showed that the gains anticipated when the strike was called off were being won; there was a 10% increase and a promise of the eight hour day May 1. To make sure of it the miners decided on a 24-hour strike that day—but meanwhile America was taken into the war.[7]

At the same time the IWW was recruiting miners on a smaller scale in the copper country of Arizona and in the Joplin lead district. In the coal fields of Pennsylvania it had a dozen locals who held a conference at Old Forge, Feb. 6, 1916. They established a district organization committee, uniform dues and initiation fees and formulated uniform demands: abolition of the contract system; an 8 hour day with Saturday a half-day; $4.00 for miners, carpenters, engineers and motor runners; $3.50 for laborers; $2.50 for mule leaders and $2.00 for breakerboys. A strike in the Lackawanna region to enforce these demands was broken by the State Constabulary, and of course hampered by the fact that the miners were under a 4-year UMWA contract against which they were chafing.[8] On June 14 a meeting of 268 members at Old Forge was raided by mounted troopers in a combination cowboy-and-Indian-and-Keystone-Cop manner. All were lugged off to jail and released by October for lack of any evidence against them, but the Scranton Republican on October 4 complained "The sheriff's opera bouffe at Old Forge has cost this county several thousand dollars."[9] This terrorism prevented further IWW organization in the field, but IWW influence still had one effect: while bituminous miners were kept tied during the war years to their contracts, the anthracite field permitted upward adjustments.

The Agricultural Workers had a successful year.

Their policy had taken the form of announcing in the IWW press what wages it demanded for different operations and areas, and where these terms were met the farmers had no labor trouble. The more intelligent farmers realized that no gain came to them from beating down labor, so long as they were not put at a differential disadvantage with other farmers, and the experience of 1916 led the farm organization, the Non-Partisan League, to propose all-over collective bargaining for the next year, an outcome prevented only by the anti-IWW war hysteria. This fact is far afield from the bogey-tales of sabotage. Harvest over, the AWO sent its members into organization efforts in the woods of Minnesota and the West Coast and the Western fruit area. In Yakima, Washington, the IWW was organizing among the apple pickers and opened up a hall. A few hours later the police closed it. The members started an open air meeting to discuss their grievance, and 60 of them were thrown into the city jail. This was lousy; they held a meeting, condemned it and proceeded to demolish it from the inside out. Police and fire department turned the fire hose on them, then marched them soaked to iced refrigerator cars and told a train crew to take them out of town. The train crew refused and told the vigilantes to get going. The men were released from the refrigerator cars and taken to the county jail, for the city jail was a relic. Protests from union officials resulted in permission to open an IWW hall and the release of the men.

A similar effort to drive the IWW out of Everett, Washington became a tragedy. The lumber barons ran the town through the Commercial Club and their lackey Sheriff McRae. They wanted no union IWW or AFL. On August 19 the striking Shingle Weavers were beaten by company thugs who waylaid them as they went over a trestle 30 feet above the water. When an IWW hall was opened, McRae closed it. On September 11th his thugs, sworn in at the Commercial Club, took IWW organizer James Rowan to the woods and beat him severely. During

October various groups of IWW members, totalling altogether about 400, were driven out of town by these organized hoodlums.

On October 30, forty-one members arriving from the wheat fields were taken to Beverly Park, beaten, forced to run a gauntlet over a cattle guard at a railroad crossing while the Commercial Club thugs beat them. A church committee investigated and found men's hair and skin still sticking to the cattle guard and the ground soaked with blood. On the advice of these ministers, the IWW issued a circular to the people of Everett announcing an open meeting for Sunday, November 5 at 2:30 and urging them to "come and help defend your and our constitutional rights." Wobs took passage on the steamer Verona, and the overflow came on the Calista. As the Verona drew in to the dock, the free speech fighters were on the side facing it. One lad, Hugo Gerlot, had climbed the mast and all were singing. At a signal from McRae his thugs on the dock and others hidden in a warehouse opened fire. Gerlot fell dead to the deck. At least five more whose bodies were recovered were shot. The pilot house was riddled with bullets, and without a pilot the engineer backed the vessel away through the bloody water, the Commercial Club thugs shooting at it until it was out of range of their highpower rifles.

As the vessels returned to Seattle, the men were arrested, and 74 held on the charge of having killed two deputies who were among those hidden in the warehouse where the men could not have even seen them. All demanded separate trials. During the trial of the first, Thomas Tracy, the lawlessness of the sheriff's thugs became a matter of record, and their plans to murder the free speech fighters; also that the two deputies had been killed by ricochet of bullets inside the warehouse; that the bullet holes in the boards of the warehouse all showed that the firing had been from inside it toward the Verona. Tracy was acquitted May 5, 1917. The others were released. But the bloodthirsty Commercial Club and its murderous hirelings were not even indicted.[11]

Organization in the woods went ahead despite this terrorism.

The Duluth District is a winter logging area. On December 24th a meeting of 1500 sawmill workers in Virginia voted to demand a pay boost and the 8-hour day, and struck on Dec. 28th. They were soon followed by the lumberjacks who demanded a minimum of $40 per month, free hospital treatment, and to go to and from work in daylight. In Idaho, a spring drive country, the men went to work at the going rate of $3.50 for 12 hours, struck at the opportune moment, and won $5.00 for 8 hours. The Seattle district was busy laying foundation for the history-making strike of 1917.[12]

Although the country had re-elected Wilson on the slogan "He kept us out of war," pressures were growing to bring America into the war. Through the British Empire, where the IWW had some degree of organization in England, South Africa and Australia, the IWW was already being victimized. The general viewpoint of its members was that the primary purpose of unionism is to prevent workers from being used against each other, and that a sense of their common interests should prevent them from shooting each other just as it should prevent them from scabbing on each other. The frank expression of this attitude in Australia led to the trial of its more active spokesmen for treason. They had been arrested in a raid on their headquarters by the militia on September 30, 1916. On December 3 seven were sentenced to 15 years, and others to 10 and 5 years. A press account states that one of them, Beatty, aged 30 when sentenced to 15 years "startled the assembly by saying that he had been sentenced thirty years ago to penal servitude for life, and that any sentence the court could pass would not trouble him." In contrast to America, these men were released promptly the war was over.[13]

The 10th Convention—the last before 1919—met in November 1916 with an organization well recovered from the slump of 1914, and, as shown in the reaction to the Mesaba strike and the Everett tragedy, winning recognition from most labor unionists as a significant part of the labor movement. The two chief outcomes of the convention were the reorganization of its forces, and its stand on war. Out of the former grew substantial industrial unions: Agricultural Workers 400, Lumber Workers 500, Construction Workers 573, Metal Mine Workers 480, Metal and Machinery Workers 300 and a General Recruiting Union to administer both mixed and industrial locals that lacked an industrial union on a national scale, and to encourage the formation of industrial locals until enough of them existed to warrant the formation of an industrial union structure for them. (These were renumbered in a decimal system in 1919.) This was a swing from the decentralist tendencies manifest in 1913 and not to crop up again until 1923, and reflected the need to coordinate recent gains. To make its publicity more responsible, the IWW Publishing Bureau was moved to Chicago and the GEB held responsible for publications, with Solidarity as the official organ. On the west coast the Industrial Worker had been resumed; the Finnish Socialisti of Duluth, a daily paper, had changed its name and become an IWW daily, which continues to this day; for non-English readers there were the following: Il Proletario, A Bermunkas, Pruslovy Delnik, Solidarnosc, Conscience Industrial, L'Emancipation and El Obrero Industrial.

The IWW stand on war took form in the following resolution:

"We, the Industrial Workers of the World, in convention assembled, hereby re-affirm our adherence to the principles of industrial unionism, and re-dedicate ourselves to the unflinching, unfaltering prosecution of the struggle for the abolition of wage slavery and the realization of our ideals in Industrial Democracy.

"With the European war for conquest and exploitation raging and destroying our lives, class

consciousness and unity of the workers, and the
ever-growing agitation for military preparedness
clouding the main issues and delaying the realization of our ultimate aim with patriotic and therefore
capitalistic aspirations, we openly declared ourselves
the determined opponents of all nationalistic sec-
tionalism, or patriotism, and the militarism preached
and supported by our one enemy, the capitalist
class.

"We condemn all wars, and for the prevention of
such, we proclaim the anti-militaristic propaganda
in time of peace, thus promoting class solidarity
among the workers of the entire world, and, in time
of war, the general strike, in all industries.

"We extend assurances of both moral and material support to all workers who suffer at the hands
of the capitalist class for their adherence to these
principles, and call on all workers to unite themselves with us, that the reign of the exploiters may
cease, and this earth be made fair through the
establishment of Industrial democracy." [14]

1. Perlman & Taft: History of Labor in the United States, McMillan Co., 1935, being the 4th volume of the History of Labor by Commons and Associates, p. 312 et seq.

2. Doree's report on Baltimore in Proceedings of 10th Convention. Budish and Soule in their "New Unionism", give a very garbled account.

3. Philadelphia account taken from Solidarity, Nos. 330, 333, 340 and 348. The 10th Convention proceedings indicate friction between the MTW and the centralizing tendencies of 1916.

4. Solvay account, Solidarity, No. 329; Kelsey Wheel, No. 331.

5. Denver housemaids account, Solidarity No. 328; cartoons repro- duced in Solidarity, No. 342.

6. A clear account of the victimization of Finnish Socialists by the copper trust unopposed by WFM is given in Perlman and Taft History cited above, page 258.

7. The account of the Mesaba strike is taken from Solidarity, and Survey of the period, Proceedings of 10th Convention, Industrial Com- mission and conversations with participants.

8. The two four-year contracts accounted Perlman & Taft, pp. 342 and 470.

9. The Old Forge arrest vividly described in Scranton Times of June 15, 1916, as quoted in Solidarity, No. 350.

10. Everett most fully described in book "The Everett Massacre"; also Survey, Jan. and May 1917, in two articles by Anna Louise Strong, and 30th memorial issue of Industrial Worker, Nov. 2, 1946, with de- tailed memoirs of Jack Leonard, one of the participants. For general background see Jensen "Lumber and Labor," Farrar & Rinehart, 1945.

12. Lumber strikes: Solidarity No. 364, and article by C.E. Payne in International Socialist Review, June 1917.

13. Full account of Australian arrests in pamphlet "Guilty or Not Guilty," by H.E. Boote, published by the Committee Appointed by the Labor Council of New South Wales to Secure a Royal Commission to Investigate the IWW Cases.
14. Minutes 10th Convention, 1916, page 138.

IX. The Fight with the War Profiteers

From the summer of 1916 through the summer of 1920 IWW efforts to improve job conditions met with an unparalled campaign of terrorism. During this period the IWW won some of its most enduring victories and built up its strength to what is probably its peak membership of about 40,000 in 1923.[1]

The campaign of terrorism was directed by employers anxious to resist unionism of any sort. At first these employers relied on their own plug-uglies and local vigilante movements; throughout this period this was the chief force the IWW had to fight. They were soon abetted by the local politicians and judiciary, all covered by the smokescreen of a subservient press. In March 1917 the Idaho and Minnesota legislatures passed the first Criminal Syndicalism laws, and the first victim of these was James Dunning, a Minnesota lumberjack convicted Sept. 29, 1917. From the spring of 1917 federal troops began herding off pickets, and in June several hundred sailors from the Bremerton Yards were given special leave and wrecked the IWW hall in Seattle; it was quite unofficial, yet before the event the Roseburg, Ore. News announced that these men had been given a few hours leave to drive the IWW out of the city. The Washington end of the government acted with at least outward propriety until September 5, 1917, and in August had assured the editors of Survey that Washington had receive no information on which to take action against the IWW despite horrendous stories in the press depicting the IWW as a gang of arsonists in the pay of the Kaiser.

That this campaign, masked with the patriotism that Johnson called the last refuge of scoundrels, was the work of corporations fevered with high profits, is plain from the geography of the struggle and the acts and assertions of the corporations themselves. Where the IWW had already made employers take unionism for granted, as in Philadalphia, no campaign against it developed; the impetus to destroy the IWW came from the non-union fields it was invading: lumber, copper, iron mining and oil. Federal prosecutions were based on opposition to the war and interference with conscription; where the IWW had small propaganda locals there was evident sentiment against registration but where it was engaged in substantial union activities it avoided being sidetracked from the struggle with the employer by such issues; yet the men arrested were those engaged in practical union effort, and of them, all but one of draft age, had registered. The copper corporations fought the IWW with thugs, deportations and lynching, all on the pretext that the IWW interfered with war production; yet these companies were selling the government copper at 30 to 34 cents a pound which it cost 7 to 10 cents to produce, and to maintain the scarcity had to store away over three billion pounds of the essential metal;[2] moreover to fight the unions Phelps-Dodge kept the ablest miners out of the mines, thus restricting production.[3] In the oil industry when the Tulsa tar-and-feather outrage, the federal raiding, the closing of halls by force, and the Wichita indictment had not stopped organization and a strike started in January 1918, the oil companies told the federal investigators that they would close down their wells rather than permit government interference with their labor relations.[4] Or, as a large lumber operator told Robert Bruere: "We have fought the IWW as we would have fought any attempt of the AFL unions to control the workers in our camps, and of course we have taken advantage of the general prejudice against them as an unpatriotic organization to beat their strike."[5]

In these war years profits soared to where they equalled capitalization, but the average real wage, which had climbed from its 1914 base of 100 to 125 in 1916, fell to 116 in 1917 and did not get up to its pre-war level until after the war. Yet in those industries where the embattled Wobblies fought, substantial gains were won.

The foundations laid in 1916 enabled the IWW through 1917 to organize rapidly on several fronts. Efforts that had been made in the southwest oil fields now blossomed into an Oil Workers Industrial Union chartered January 1. When the Metal Mine Workers were chartered on January 29th they already predominated over the AFL Mine-Mill in the Globe and Miami districts of Arizona, and the Miami scale became the standard for bargaining in other areas. On the east coast the IWW was rapidly organizing seamen and a major chore for its MTW secretary in Boston was to make up menus for all vessels on the Atlantic run; these were stamped with the IWW seal, posted in every mess hall, and the stewards were instructed to abide by them.[6] The U.S. Shipping Adjustment Board recognized the IWW as the bargaining agency for the Philadelphia longshoremen and on February 7th, 1918 asked that it provide a member for its three-man adjustment commission empowered to settle wage disputes. The General Executive Board wired that this was autocratic and the Shipping Board made an exception for IWW democracy and accepted the MTW representative on the understanding that he was at all times under the instruction of the union.[7] As a result no strikes were necessary on the Philadelphia waterfront until 1920. At the same time on the Great Lakes where AFL unionism had been wiped out in the long strike of 1909-13 a fair start at organization was made, but with entrapment into war, arrests and hysteria stopped it.

A new national Industrial Union for General Construction Workers was launched at a conference in Omaha April 29th 1917. It conducted a strike on an irrigation project at Exeter, Calif. in April. On May 14 a short strike won complete job control on all grading jobs around Seattle, including the arrangement that all workers be hired through the IWW

hall. At Rockford, Illinois, an active construction
local won a strike about the same time; here there
was also a budding Furniture Workers' local, but
both got strangled in the anti-draft activities that
made Rockford briefly famous. Throughout the
Inland Empire as construction work opened up in
the spring, job delegates got busy recruiting. It was
the age of the mule team and fresno for most of
this work and the Wobbly mule-skinning clan was
known to hold tightly enough together so that without formal agreements, their announcement of wage
rates enabled the contractors to reckon their labor
costs with certainty. Through most of 1917 the organization efforts of this Industrial Union 573 went
ahead relatively unmolested, until Guthrie, Grant
and similar large operators turned loose the same
campaign of terrorism as had been loosed on their
fellow workers in lumber, copper mining and the
oil fields; yet their organization survived to be a
major part of the IWW in post-war years as Industrial Union 310.

During the early months of 1917 there was wide
apprehension that America would be taken into the
war and that conscription would follow. A division
of opinion grew as to how to apply the 1916 resolution on war. A minority that included many of
the Finnish and Irish members in Butte and on the
Iron Range, and GEB member Frank Little, and
Clyde Hough, secretary of the Rockford Furniture
Workers, and a number of propaganda locals, felt
the IWW should concentrate on open opposition to
the war and defiance of the draft. The majority felt
this would sidetrack the class struggle into futile
channels and be playing the very game that the
war-profiteers would want the IWW to play. They
contended that the monstrous stupidity by which
the governments of different lands could put their
workers into uniforms and make them go forth and
shoot each other was something that could be stopped only if the workers of the world were organized
together; then they could put a stop to this being
used against themselves; and that consequently the
thing to be done under the actual circumstances

was to proceed with organizing workers to fight
their steady enemy, the employing class, for better
wages, shorter hours, safer and more sanitary working conditions, keeping in mind the ultimate ideal
of world labor solidarity. There was no opportunity
for referendum, but the more active locals took this
attitude, instructing speakers to confine their remarks to industrial union issues, circulating only
those pamphlets that made a constructive case for
the IWW, and avoiding alliance with the Peoples
Council and similar anti-war movements.[8]

Lumber Workers Industrial Union set out at its
initial convention in Spokane, March 5, 1917 with
the set of demands they aimed to achieve in lumber
camp and sawmill. The lumber worker of that day
was still the victim of the employment shark. He
was a "timberbeast" set off from the rest of his
fellow workers; he had to furnish his own blankets,
and these with his working gear were enough to
carry without ordinary dress clothes; as a result
when he came to town he was permitted entry only
to the dives that lived off him and so tolerated the
caulk shoes his work required and that would soon
tear up a floor; camps lacked shower baths or facilities for washing clothes, and the timberbeast was
often a smelly, scratching specimen of humanity in
town; at camp he spent his little leisure after a 10
hour day in a bunkhouse of double deck bunks, re-
dolent with the acrid odor of sweaty work clothes
drying. The Wobbly demands ran:

    1. 8 hours with no work on Sundays or holidays;

    2. Minimum wage of $60 per month and board;

    3. Wholesome food in porcelain dishes, no over-
crowding; sufficient help to keep kitchen clean and
sanitary;

    4. Sanitary sleeping quarters, not more than 12
men in each bunkhouse; single spring beds and mat-
tresses with good clean bedding to be furnished free
by company; bunkhouse to be well lit and furnished
with reading tables; dry room, laundry room and
shower baths;

5. Free hospital service;
6. $5.00 per day minimum for river drivers;
7. Two pay days per month by bank check without discount;
8. All men to be hired on job or from union hall; free transportation from place of hiring to job;
9. No discrimination.

Quick victories were won on the river drives in the short log country during last part of April. The 12 hour day was cut to 8 and the pay raised to $5.00 from $3.50. Militia raided the hall at Whitefish, Mont.; men were arrested for refusing to work, but the river drive strikes were complete victories. IWW plans for the woods had been for a July strike in the short log country, then later a strike on the coast, but events moved faster. Scattered victories along the hump between the two areas were won in May and "in camp after camp the union was moving from the hall to the bunkhouse." Spontaneous action started the wave of short log strikes on June 20th, general by July 16, on which date, in response to strike calls by both AFL and IWW the long log country came out solid too.

The use of federal troops in the lumber and other strikes lacked legal sanction. The National Guard had been called into federal service as soon as America was taken into the war, and so only federal troops were available. No record seems available that any governor or state legislature certified that insurrection or disorder beyond the capacity of the state to suppress required such intervention— though such certification is required by law. To the contrary "prosecuting attorneys in Montana and Washington and special agents of the Bureau of Investigation testified to the peacefulness of the lumber strike and the lack of violence and intimidation by the I.W.W." Though the law of 1878 provided that federal troops may not be used as a posse comitatus to federal law officers, War Department Authorizations to local army officers passed down the line of authority to platoon level, in effect provided for such service to sheriffs and district attorneys. Arrests could be made to protect public utilities essential to the war or for "acts in pursuance of prearranged plans contemplating violence." These pretexts were used to arrest strikers committing no offence. Those arrested were not subject to habeas corpus, as the local Councils of Defense agreed that the sheriffs should answer any such petition that "the prisoners are held by military power."[9]

Concurrent with this general northwest lumber strike was the copper strike in Montana and Arizona. The repressive measures urged by the copper barons and behind the scenes moves in Washington shaped the novel and successful process of carrying the strike of the lumber workers back to the job. A correct depiction requires a switch of attention here to these copper miners, then a return to the lumber strike.

By June 1917 the IWW in Arizona had edged ahead of the old Western Federation, then known as AFL Mine Mill & Smelter Workers, but neither organization was in position to engage in effective bargaining. The Mine-Mill members often carried two cards and favored joint action by the two unions; most local officials didn't, yet were opposed enough to Moyer policy to want statewide autonomy. At Globe and Miami the two forces working together had pushed wages up to the highest in the industry. Early in June the IWW won a 12½% pay boost at the Humboldt smelter at Prescott and in the mines at Mayer with a short strike. Mine-Mill had given notice to the Clarke interests that it wanted a wage boost at Jerome and a contract with check-off. The IWW called a mass meeting there, explained that it would support any strike for improved conditions, but opposed the check-off and contract, proposing instead that where two unions were involved a policy of no discrimination and a grievance committee elected by all workers would protect all miners. The men were solid for this policy, and the company promptly met these de-

mands, including the Miami scale. At Swansea the
same company granted the same demands after the
IWW had staged a strike for one half shift.[10]
   At this point things began to move in Butte where
there had been no miner unionism since the turmoil
of 1914. On June 5 many Irish and a number of
Finns were arrested for demonstrating against the
draft. On the 8th came the Speculator Mine disaster. With flames blocking the shafts men rushed
to the bulkheads that separate the level of one mine
from adjoining levels of the next mine. To save a
few dollars for iron manholes in them required by
safety law, they had been concreted solid, and 190
miners were burned to death. Indignation resulted
in a strike on June 11 and a new union, the Metal
Mine Workers, formed to ensure mine safety, end
the rustling card and espionage system, and bring
wages up with the high cost of living. The new
union was unaffiliated; the miners would have none
of Moyer's Mine-Mill, nor of the handful still liqui-
dating the assets of old Butte Miners' Union No. 1,
and the IWW avoided any action that would jeop-
ardize their solidarity. The AFL however would not
let them use the Carpenters' Hall, so they met in
the hall of the Finnish Socialists. On the 18th the
AFL electrical workers, as the result of a long standing dispute, walked out and soon were followed by
other AFL crafts. The miners and electrical workers cooperated and to July 20th issued a joint strike
bulletin. Arizona miners quickly saw that with
Butte struck, a strike throughout Arizona was the
best help they could give to restore unionism to the
Butte mines and to settle their own grievances, particularly their safety demand of two men on all
piston and Leyner machines, two men in all raises
and stopes, and no blasting in raises, stopes or drifts
during shifts. By June 26th IWW organizer Grover
Perry could wire: "Bisbee, Jerome, Miami and
Swansea strike in support of Butte; other camps
await call." On the 27th the Silver Bow Trades and
Labor Council resolved 44-28 that the new mine
union was "in the best interests of organized labor"

though the AFL crafts still disowned it. There was some talk of getting an AFL charter, but Mine-Mill's jurisdiction prevented that and the miners were told they would have to join Moyer's union as individuals—which they didn't.

With Arizona mines tied up tight, the federal government sought a settlement by its Conciliation Service, to which it appointed former Governor Hunt, who had been re-elected but had been temporarily counted out by the copper companies for his friendliness to unions. The IWW insisted that settlement should be nationwide so as not to leave the Butte miners holding the bag, and proposed that the government could save a lot of money by granting union demands and taking over the mines. Since the government was paying Phelps-Dodge three times the production cost of copper it was horrified and denounced the IWW as working for the German government. Then working on a plan laid out by a German army captain for him, Walter Douglas, head of the Phelps-Dodge Copper Queen Division, set out to rid Arizona of Wobblies. On July 10 at Jerome, the company officials with a posse of business men and a handful of Mine-Mill members, rounded up those they considered IWW agitators and jailed them. A Mine-Mill organizer secured the release of 37 of the 104 on his assurance that they weren't IWW's and the rest were shipped to Needles, sent back and released. At Bisbee before dawn on July 12 a similar posse rounded up the strikers as they prepared for break-of-day picketing, and searched homes until they had a total of 1164, not counting the three they killed, marched them to Warren, held them in a ball park until they could be put into cattle cars and shipped to the desert. They were packed tight standing up, parched with thirst, and many had been clubbed in the round-up. After 36 hours of this torture they were put into a detention camp at Columbus, N. M. All was carried out under the direction of Mr. Douglas of Phelps-Dodge.

Scattered strikes continued in Arizona, but with many of the more experienced Wobs at Columbus or in jail at Prescott and Tombstone (for protesting these outrages), settlements were made for wage increases and other improvements, leaving the Copper Queen run with imported scabs, and the Butte miners fighting the copper trust alone. There on August 1, again in the dark early hours, a gang came to the boardinghouse next to the Finn Hall where Frank Little lay in bed, his leg recently broken, and dragged him to the Milwaukee railroad trestle where he or his already dead body was hanged. Instead of intimidating the miners, it put them the more solidly behind the IWW whose spokesman Frank Little was. His funeral was the largest Butte had ever seen, even the AFL unions joining the procession with their banners. On August 11, Federal troops began to patrol the streets. Phelps-Dodge stirred up additional wrath when, upon taking over a coal mine at Gallup, N.M. it declared open shop, and subsequently deported the UMWA coal miners. William Green of UMWA threatened a national strike of coal miners unless these men were protected in their right to return. The fight between labor and the war profiteers everywhere (the AFL had of course far more strikes than the IWW) was threatening to demolish the fabric of lies against the IWW woven by the press and to lead to recognition of the IWW as spearheading this fight with the profiteers in the areas where it was most competent to do so. On August 25 the new union in Butte, by this time thought of usually as pro-IWW, by a picket line closed the Anaconda smelter and the Anaconda shut down what mines it had been able to operate and its smelter at Great Falls. On September 5th federal authorities abruptly changed face and raided IWW offices and halls across the country all at 2 p.m. central standard time and seized all records—over five tons of them.

This was the situation that led the lumber workers to switch tactics. By September 1 the short log country had been out from eight to ten weeks in different sections and the west coast six weeks. On the coast the IWW had been hesitant about calling the strike because most of the workers had gone back nearly broke after the July 4 holiday. In the short log country in particular repression had been rough. At Troy, Mont., Frank Thornton had been put in a wooden jail and the jailed burned down. All halls had been closed, Spokane being the last to remain open; as it was being closed and the authorities at one end were taking possession, at the other jacks were still lining up to have their cards written out. In Klamath Falls strikers had been kangarood, local lawyers refused to defend them, while lawyers from out of town were told to travel. In Portland when strikers were arrested, the MTW answered by tying up river transportation. Arrests for vagrancy and other charges grew on the coast, and in its issue of August 15, the Industrial Worker pointed out that if this continued the strikers would be compelled to shift to a new kind of strike—one on the job where the police would not be so handy to club them. On August 31 the District Organization Committee for the Seattle District carried the following motion: "That we ask all branches and picket camps to call a meeting for September 7th to determine the sentiment in regard to transfering the strike to the job for the purpose of enforcing the eight hour day. We wish to impress on the minds of the membership the importance of understanding this motion clearly. The meaning of the motion is that if we did transfer the strike to the job we would only work eight hours and quit. Kindly inform the District Office of the results of your meeting of Sept. 7."

The nationwide raids of Sept. 5 ended any doubts about the proposed tactic. To the employers it seemed that the men were accepting defeat; the lumber workers who had discussed their tactics, and agreed upon them almost unanimously, went to the camps as they opened up. Some took their own whistles with them, blew them at the end of eight hours and

went in to camp. If they were fired, the next crew
did the same. In some they soldiered on the job;
in others they played "dumb"—but whatever their
form of the new tactic, they were eating and sleep-
ing on company territory, away from the police, and
the employers did not know what to do. Senator
Borah explained: "The IWW is about as elusive a
proposition as you ever ran up against. . . . It is in-
tangible. . . . You cannot reach it . . . it is simply
an understanding between men."—and it could not
be jailed.[11]

The case of the lumber workers was clear. The
President sent Carlton Parker as a peace envoy and
he said they should have their demands. Secretary
of War Baker and the Governor of Washington
urged the 8 hour day. But the west coast operators
said no. As the strike on the job tactic was enforcing the 8-hour day in camp after camp, the operators of the Inland Empire passed a resolution calling
on the government to establish the 8-hour day for
industrial peace. The Spruce Division headed by
Colonel Disque of 4-L fame announced it officially
May 1, 1918—but the lumberjacks knew that they
themselves had got it. They had celebrated May 1
1917 with a big parade to strew Joe Hill's ashes.
They observed May 1, 1918 with a bigger celebration in camp after camp, burning the old bedding
rolls so that the companies had to furnish bedding
or have no workers. Where double deck bunks persisted, the top sections got thrown out. By a continuous battle, intermittent but never lost sight of,
the process of "conditioning the job" went on to the
transformation of the shunned timberbeast of 1916
into the respected lumber worker of 1919, eating
the best and dressed the best of any worker in the
country, and also sobered up. The IWW had changed
not only the conditions of the timberbeast, but also
his wants and habits. A wage boost can at times be
taken away—but not the habits and standards of an
entire occupational area; the gains of 1918 have

withstood depressions, wars and complete disorganization to this day.

In the copper strike no such permanent victory was achieved. Following the raids of Sept. 5, 1917, it seems that the higher brackets of labor leadership effectively clamped down on sentiment in their ranks favorable or even tolerant toward the IWW, though to that date its prestige in the labor movement had been gaining. In the Butte,Anaconda situation, on Sept. 11 the AFL staged a meeting to urge the return to work; the Butte miners were left out, and their strike and their new union faded out by December 28th. Once the new union had given up, the IWW job delegate system felt free without imperilling solidarity to build for itself, and achieved sufficient strength by September 1918 to pull short strikes protesting the convictions in the IWW and Socialist cases, and by March 1919 there were over 5000 in the Butte IWW local. In Arizona the Mediation Commission set up machinery for union representation, but with the proviso that those belonging to organizations refusing to make contracts or disloyal to the government be excluded. Thus the commission by excluding the IWW slapped the war-profiteers on the wrist for their lawless interference with production, and gave them exactly what they wanted.

The espionage charges, to support which the nation wide raids were made, had nothing to do with espionage, and were an improvisation hit upon after other plots to wreck the good work of the IWW had proved ineffective. The first scheme was to rely upon the new deportation provisions enacted in 1917, which allowed deportation for beliefs acquired by the foreigner during his stay here. Deportation procedure was felt to have the stealthy advantage of permitting no "snail-paced court trial," little or no publicity, and putting the burden of argument on the deportee. It was felt that extensive deportation arrests would intimidate enough to prevent the IWW from using the war to establish decent working

conditions. This snagged on three facts: the Wobs
didn't get scared; most of them were native born;
and the employers didn't want them removed from
the labor market, but only wanted to stop them from
having any voice in that market. Use of federal
troops got snagged on the same facts. Western governors proposed that all IWW agitators, without any
bother about court procedures, be apprehended and
secretly interned somewhere so as to "mystify and
frighten" the remaining members. This plan was
considered and then given up for the program said
to have been formulated by former governor John
Lind of Minnesota for the state Commission of Public Safety—arrest all officers, editors, etc., under
the wartime provisions of the Espionage Act.[12]
IWW-membership lists secured from the raids were
given to Samuel Gompers to arrange for general
blacklisting.

On the basis of the five tons of "evidence" seized
in the September raids, indictments in Chicago, Sacramento and Wichita were i s s u e d against those
whom the advisers to the federal government considered the back bone of the IWW.[13] These were
charged in many pages that the IWW was interfering with the war by strikes, sabotage and discour-
agement of conscription. The strikes were legitimate
disputes not with the government but with the profiteers who were milking the government. The evidence of hostility to conscription dated from pre-
war days when it too was not unlawful. The alleged
sabotage consisted of unsupported tales as far back
as 1911 by company henchmen. The defense objected that if charges were to be based on these
tales, the accused should be tried in the district
where the offense was alleged so that witnesses
could be secured and cross-examined, and all this
within a reasonable time of the commission of the
alleged offenses. But this and the old literature
were admitted by the court as evidence of the
"frame of mind" of the IWW, and the court conced-
ing that these alleged acts were not within federal
jurisdiction, let them go before the jury without

One base for 1917 spring drive: Sand Point, Idaho, Nov. 26, 1916.

Deportation of union miners, Bisbee, July 12, 1917. See page 119.

Throop St. farewell for men headed for Leavenworth, April 24, 1921. See pages 125 and 137.

Colorado police shot up union hall, 1928. See page 153.

Chicago IWW Unemployed Union gathers clothes for
striking Kentucky miners, 1931. See pages 157–158.

any requirement thus that they be proved. Most
of this trash got thrown out by the higher courts,
but the conviction was sustained. On August 17,
1918, the Chicago jury in less than an hour reached
a decision on the tons of evidence—which the court
conceded had been illegally seized—and the evidence it had been hearing since April 1, and the
fate of over a hundred men. Judge Landis gave
fifteen men 20 years, thirty-five 10 years, thirty-
three 5 years, twelve a year and a day and the rest
nominal sentences.

In Sacramento the men did not go to trial until
after the war was over—when Australia was already releasing its IWW prisoners. In the long
delay five of the 51 had died under bad jail conditions. The defendants decided to treat the proceedings frankly as a kangaroo court and remained silent. The results were the same as if they had lawyers to interpose overruled objections. The Wichita
proceedings were even further delayed.

On these federal indictments, on Criminal Syndicalism charges and on various other pretexts arising largely out of strike activities, probably close
to two thousand IWW's were arrested during this
time. Further IWW stationary delegates, branch
secretaries and job delegates were chased from
home or job by plug-uglies and vigilantes, often
with beatings and tar-and-feather parties. The arrests required an almost complete change in official
personnel of the union, and a concentration on legal
defense that led to the formation in October 1917
of a General Defense Committee to coordinate defense work nationally. It was handicapped by a
general reluctance of lawyers to serve, not only
because of the prejudice built by press against IWW
but because of such instances as the deportation of
lawyers from Klamath Falls, Ore., or from Bisbee,
or Staunton, Illinois where defense counsel Metzen
was tarred and feathered along with the IWW he
went there to defend.[14] On October 30, Solidarity was denied the mails; a Defense News Bulletin
was issued instead. Its mailing was interfered with

so that distribution had to be by small bundles mailed from various places in other publications as wrapping.

In retrospect sober judgment has looked upon this period as one in which the IWW was engaged in activities that were not only legal, but positively praiseworthy, and that the lawlessness was that of the war-profiteers and of their political and judicial henchmen. The positive results were improved job conditions and a growing IWW with its attention focused on "conditioning the job."

1. Average annual membership calculated by dividing dues stamps sold in calendar year by 12; probably peak membership for any month may have been in August 1917 and comes close to 100,000

2. For war profits, see Senate Document 259, 65th Congress, and chapter 17 of Seldes, "Iron, Blood and Profits."

3. Jensen, "Heritage of Conflict," pp. 480 and 422. Jensen has a detailed account of the copper strike, biased by Mine-Mill contentions that IWW was imported by the mine companies!

4. *Defense News Bulletin* No. 17.

5. As quoted in Gambs' "Decline," p. 44.

6. Correspondence with Jas. Phillips, MTW sec'y. Boston, at time.

7. Exchange of wires in *Defense News Bulletin* No. 16.

8. Foregoing paragraph digests many letters, minutes, etc., used as evidence in the Chicago trial, gathered from briefs filed with U.S. Circuit Court of Appeals, 7th District, October term 1919, docket 2721.

9. This paragraph is based on information in a manuscript by William Preston of History Department, Denison University, on "The Ideology and Techniques of Repression." This author had access to Washington files for his study.

10. Account of copper strike is compiled from IWW papers of the time, Jensen's "Heritage" and correspondence with A.S. Embree and report of President's Commission.

11. Account of lumber strike from IWW papers of the time and reminiscences in later IWW publications, discussion with participants. Fairly good accounts by others are given in Jensen, "Labor and Lumber" and Perlman & Taft with considerable documentation. An ironic epilog to Disque's Spruce Division and its efforts to get the lumber workers to work harder occurred through the 1950s as Hoover's economizers tried to get the Spruce Division abolished on the grounds it had been collecting its pay and doing nothing since November 1918. Borah quotation in Congressional Record, Mar. 3, 1918.

12. Sources same as Footnote 9 above.

13. There is extensive literature on these cases by American Civil Liberties Unions and others. All three summarized in *N.Y. Nation,* 1919, XVIII, p. 383. The cases are Haywood v. U.S. Fed. 795 (1920), Anderson v. U.S. 273 Fed. (1921) and 269 Fed. 65 (1920). W.D. Lane described Kansas City jail conditions in *Survey,* 1919, XLII, 807. Cases are summarized also by Gambs and Perlman & Taft. While Dowell's book previously cited concentrates on the Criminal Syndicalism cases, it is the best study so far of the psychological and economic processes involved in this effort to get the IWW. It is still hoped that some thorough Ph.D. thesis will be written on the role of the federal government and how it was induced to take that role.

14. *Defense News Bulletin* 16—the mob was led by the District Attorney.

X. Revolution Around the Corner

The First World War ended in a wave of revolutions that brought great hopes for those who wanted the world to be different, great fears for those who wanted it to remain the same, and great problems for those who wanted it not only different but better. These are the hopes, fears, and problems that characterize the age in which we still live.

News of the March and November revolutions in Russia was welcome to the IWW. Revolts in Austria and Germany brought the war to a halt; in January workers in the Ruhr seized the industries in which they worked; in March Karolyi peacefully handed Hungary over to a Communist regime; Britain and France had strikes for workers' control and for "Hands Off Russia"; with all this the term "revolution" lost its customary overtone of distance. Capitalists believed revolution imminent, feared it, legislated against it and bought books on how to keep workers happy. Workers too favored change, but most held hopes in the vague promises of wartime politicians for a "world fit for heroes to live in." A minority in the labor movement believed world social revolution a possibility that needed only some nurturing, with a bit of conspiracy and the properly formulated theses. This minority consisted typically of those who conversed (or debated) mostly with other members of the same minority and who thus lived "in a miasmata of their own effulgences." Those whose manner of living kept them in steady contact with the general run of workers were not so prone to let hopes distort their perceptions. This was the situation with most of the IWW, but a few managed to acquire the view of the self-appointed "militant minority" and to do such harm as the forces of repression had not been able to do, with results not fully apparent until 1923-24.[1]

No major consequence of the revolutionary upheaval in Europe appeared in America until 1919.

Not until late summer was the divisive effect of the Russian revolution upon the general anti-capitalist movement evident. A new bogeyman was replacing the IWW as a newspaper stereotype, and the left wing was playing with Soviet terms, running strikes under Workers' Soldiers' and Sailors' Councils in Seattle, Butte and Toledo—or trying to.

The Seattle General Strike of February 6th to 11th, 1919 was an AFL strike, but many held it showed IWW influence, the more so as under wartime conditions many IWW's had become "two-card men" active in Seattle AFL circles. The purpose of the strike was to back up the 25,000 metal trades workers in the shipyards against a Macy award that cut wages. It was a marvel of orderliness, with the Central Labor Council officially responsible, but in the background this Workmen's Soldiers and Sailors' Council. (The business group later boasted it had its man there too, drafting a constitution fit to send any man to jail who signed it.) It was abruptly ended by threat of invading international officers to revoke the charters of the participating unions. In the open shop reaction that followed, both the Socialist Party and the Equity Press where the Industrial Worker was printed, were raided; also 31 members of the IWW were arrested charged with trying to overthrow the government by participating in the strike. That the rank and file of the unions favored the strike was shown by its orderliness, its completeness and the fact that all local officials were re-elected.[2]

Butte followed with a general strike two days later, February 8th. It was precipitated by announcement of a dollar a day cut on the 7th. To cope with craft disunity that had wrecked the 1917 strike, it was necessary to create some inter-union body. In the Soviet fad this was called a Workers' and Soldiers' Council; its veteran members wore part of their military uniform. The IWW Metal Mine Workers furnished a large part of the strikers and also delegates to this Council. To give the crafts an excuse to stay home, for lack of transportation,

they picketed the streetcar barns. When the strike
was on for a few days the Silver Bow Trades &
Labor Council ordered all members to join the
strike, but international officers were soon on hand
to threaten revocation of charters. This broke the
strike. The paycut was put across temporarily, but
soon put back to the $5.85 rate again by resistance
action on the job.[3]

(In 1919 Metal Mine Workers Industrial Union
800 had an average annual membership of 8000
roughly divided into 2500 in the Great Lakes iron
district and 5500 in the copper district; there was
considerable turnover for with about the same membership through the year, there were about 6000
initiations. It struck again in August in Butte in
support of the AFL crafts, and at Oatman, Arizona
for a 6-hour day and a dollar an hour. They had the
mines tight, but the Moyer union signed an agreement for a 50 cent increase with the proviso that
no member of the IWW be hired.[4])

Another "soviet" formed in Toledo gave the IWW
its first disillusionment with this phenomenon. Early
in May workers at the Ford plate glass factory walked out and joined the IWW. Overland workers followed, and soon the Autolite, bringing the total on
strike to 13,000. To unify it all the left wing formed
a Soldiers and Sailors' Council. The IWW learned
that the funds raised for this body for strike relief
went instead to pay for printing its revolutionary
propaganda. The IWW didn't object so much to the
lurid phrases, but it did object to the tapping of the
strike funds, and the strike appears to have fallen
apart.[5]

The 11th Convention of the IWW met May 5th to
16th, 1919. It was the first convention since 1916.
The financial statement for the intervening 31
months showed per capita income of $77,968.18,
which, at 7½ cents per dues stamp, indicates an
average membership during those 31 hectic months
of about 33,500. The current membership was figured at 35,000. Defense activities had required ma-

jor expenditures: $101,808.54 for lawyers' fees; $29,-
603.43 for relief of prisoners and their families; and
$8,985.13 for witness fees. The IWW press had two
English weeklies and an English language monthly
magazine; seven weeklies and two monthlies in other
languages, and the Finnish daily. About this time
there was considerable recruitment in Chicago and
cities east, "language branches" formed for propaganda and social activties and pride in "redness"
rather than for conditioning the job. In an effort to
insure an industrial focus this 11th Convention elim-
inated the Recruiting Unions. Soon however it was
found necessary to make other provisions for the
membership of those who wanted One Big Union
but for whom local industrial unions did not exist.
Subsequent constitutional changes set up a General
Recruiting Union with the intent of generating industrial locals and eventually new national industrial unions.

Through the summer of 1919 the IWW carried on
in harvest field and lumber camp despite the additional harassment of the anti-red frenzy of 1919. The
Agricultural Workers had an average annual membership for the year of about 4,000 but recruited
about twice that number, 3,039 of them in August
alone. Its techniques made it the most unstable part
of the IWW, engaged in the selling of union cards
rather than in the organization of men. Its spring
and fall conventions were newsworthy. Mayor Short
of Sioux City announced he would open the spring
convention with an address of welcome; citizens met
to protest and he read them the constitution. The
Mayor and other citizens, including a government
agent and his stenographer attended; after the
Mayor's speech all outsiders left except the agent
and his steno, and for two days the 103 members
conducted their affairs in peace. Then the sheriff
closed the hall. The convention moved to the corner
of 4th and Jennings and completed their convention
in front of a large and interested audience who
joined in closing it with the singing of "Solidarity
Forever," the government agent and his steno not

participating. The boys found Sioux City such an interesting place they set their fall convention for it too. Haywood was out on bond and was scheduled to attend it and speak on the street. Permission was denied, so he addressed a largely hostile crowd of about 5000 from the windows of the hall, and soon had them with him. The indignant editor of the Tribune ran his car back and forth through the crowd until the Chief of Police arrested him. (This was about the only instance in the year of the law favoring the IWW; arrests were as numerous as in 1918, with the Criminal Syndicalism laws providing the new technique.)[6]

The lumber workers were the sturdiest industrial union in the IWW with an average annual membership of close to 20,000 through 1919. During the year they initiated 8,800 new members, but about half of this represented growth, not replacement of others dropping out. In the northwest it had from a third to a half of the lumberjacks organized and about a sixth of the mill workers. It had no competition except the dying 4 L's which retained some membership in the mill towns. A spring strike on the river drives got the same bedding gains for this work as had been won already in the camps. In October a generalized wave of strikes in the short logs against adding the cost of blankets to the board bill ended with return to work and winning again by job action. The strike had two novel demands: release of all class war prisoners and withdrawal of troops from Russia. In the Great Lakes area, small walkouts and job action won some minor improvements in camp conditions and maintained a fair degree of organization. When a mob attacked the district office of the lumber workers in Superior, Wisconsin, those inside let the mob see that they were armed, and there was no further trouble. In Centralia, Washington, the lynching fever of the business class was not stopped by similar action, but following these two examples of resistance, raiding of halls was checked.

When the Armistice Day parade, November 11,
1919, stopped in front of the IWW hall in Centralia,
there was no doubt what the intent was. Once before on April 20, 1918 a parade had stopped at the
IWW hall and demolished it, the banker taking the
secretary's desk. In June of 1919 a Citizens' Protective League was talking of driving the IWW out
of town, and the blind IWW newsboy had been kidnaped, taken out of town and told not to come back
at the risk of his life. A ways and means committee
of the Citizens' Protective League was elected to
attend to the details of driving the IWW out of
Centralia, and it was common talk that the Armistice Day parade would be used for this purpose.
IWW lumberjacks consulted a local attorney, Elmer
Smith, who told them they had a legal right to protect their hall by arms. On November 7 it was
announced that the parade would march to Third
and Turner and return—that is, march to the corner
past the IWW hall, turn and march past it again.
That left no doubts. When the parade came, the
postmaster and ex-Mayor McCleary were each carrying a coil of rope, conspicuously prepared for a
lynching bee. Paraders after the turn of the line of
march broke out and when they broke through the
door of the IWW hall, IWW members shot and killed
three of the attackers. Then the mob surged in,
beat and arrested the defendants, except one, Wesley
Everest, a returned soldier, who went out the back
of the hall, holding the mob at a distance with his
automatic as he retreated toward the Chehalis River.
There he offered to surrender to any officer of the
law, but not to the mob. Dale Hubbard, son of the
banker who had taken the IWW desk in the 1918
raid, stepped out to take him; Everest shot and
killed. Then his revolver jammed and the mob had
him. They beat him, rammed a rifle butt down his
throat, and threw his bleeding body in the center
of the jail where his fellow workers, locked in cells,
could see him but do nothing for him. That night
the mayor and city electrician shut off all lights in
the city and the businessmen opened the jail, took

Everest out to lynch him, cutting off his genitals before they did so.[7]

A reign of terror followed in the region. It was open season on Wobblies. When the defenders of the hall were brought to trial on a charge of conspiracy to murder, troops surrounded the courthouse at Montesano. The evidence clearly established that the conspiracy was that of the businessmen to drive out the IWW with a threat of lynching and with the probability of an actual lynching such as they did indisputably perpetrate, and that the first shot was fired after the invasion of the hall. A Seattle labor jury, sent by the AFL to witness the trial, judged the men completely innocent. The jurors found them guilty of the impossible charge of second degree murder on a conspiracy indictment. Later affidavits from the jurors declare that this verdict was wrung from them by intimidation, and fear what the business class could do to them in the community where they had their homes. Elmer Smith, the lawyer who had advised them, was acquitted and spent most of his time until his death in 1930 in efforts to obtain their release, but his efforts and the findings of church and other bodies left the governors unmoved; probably because to recognize the men's innocence was to recognize the guilt of the American Legion and the business men. Lumber Workers Industrial Union survived the terrorism and remained a sturdy organization until 1925 when it was rendered ineffective by dissension and the "gyppo" system.

At this period the program of revolutionary industrial unionism was growing internationally by extensions of the IWW and the birth of similar movements with which the IWW had friendly relations. In Canada, where the rather small IWW had been repressed during the war by orders-in-council, a similar movement, the One Big Union swept the western area largely because the conservative leaders refused to join the western bodies in protests against these order-in-council which suspended civil rights for radicals.[8] They proposed a reorganiza-

tion of the Canadian labor movement on an industrial basis, were turned down, and formed the OBU
originally representing substantially all labor from
Port Arthur west. The Winnipeg General Strike,
though arising out of disputes antecedent to the
OBU, brought it great publicity as it was headed by
the active spirits in the new movement. These men
were convicted of trying to overthrow the government on the grounds that permitting milk deliveries
was assuming governmental powers. The loss of
their chief spokesmen occurred at a time when AFL
officials were threatening that bodies with the old
treasuries would take over existing contracts and
would bar OBU men from their jobs, and the OBU
was reduced to a few occupational groups, in mining,
streetcar transportation, lumber and the railroad
shops. In the lumber industries of the Great Lakes
and coast areas, an interchange of IWW and OBU
cards was arranged, and these lumber workers
eventually joined the IWW in 1924 after the OBU
had further declined with pro-communists shifting
it from an industrial to a geographical or mass basis.
The Canadian OBU persisted for years in Winnipeg,
and even had branches in the United States trying
in San Francisco to build an industrial union in the
building trades and also in eastern textiles; its paper
the OBU Bulletin for years was a sort of Reader's
Digest of the left wing and liberal press sustained by
a betting pool rather popular because of its honest
conduct, but eventually declared illegal.

In Latin America the Marine Transport Workers
had established a branch in Buenos Aires with its
own paper in November of 1919, and in December
IWW adminstrations were started in Mexico and
Chile. Through the summer of 1920 the Chilean
union conducted a three month strike to prevent
the export of cereals from the country at a time
when this export was producing famine, and famine
prices and profits. The profiteers retaliated on July
22 with a raid at Santiago, starting a reign of terror
against the IWW and other unions that lasted for
years, the favorite punishment being to send the

men to stony islands off the coast where not a blade
of grass grew, and tell them to build their Utopia
there. On June 2, 1921 the IWW hall at Tampico,
Mexico, was raided, and the IWW called a general
strike in the area which won them the right to have
their hall.[9]

In Great Britain wartime attacks on union standards had resulted in a militant Shop Steward movement; in January 1920 this body resolved to link
itself to the IWW, and at the 12th IWW Convention,
May, 1920, arrangements were made for the interchange of cards. But the major international question was Moscow. The IWW had been invited to
join the Third International and to send a delegation
to its Second Congress in the Kremlin, July 19 to
August 7, 1920. The IWW did not attend, but its
General Executive Board, very friendly to the general idea, had set up a committee to arrange for
contact with the various revolutionary movements
around the world. The Second Congress adopted the
21 points as conditions of affiliation, and set up a
provisional body to found an international of red
trade unions, to convene January 1921. To this the
IWW was again invited and sent delegates. A preliminary caucus of syndicalist bodies was held in
Berlin in December 1920 and it aimed at a union
international based on the class struggle and free
from political party domination. When the Red
Trade Union international met eventually in Moscow in 1921, both the IWW delegate and the delegate from the Canadian OBU reported that it was
a body to manipulate unions at Kremlin dictates and
not a union body at all. By referendum the IWW
turned down all of the various proposals, though
with a remarkably small vote that gave only slight
negative majorities. The three questions were a bit
confusing and the entire ballot later declared void.
It appears to indicate a refusal to be dominated by
Communists and at the same time a reluctance not
to participate in a gesture of left-wing unity.

IWW relations with the communists slowly but

steadily shifted from an original comradely disagreement to open hostility. When the American Communist and Communist Labor parties were born out of the splintering of the Socialist Party Convention in Chicago 1919, the IWW, though friendly to the Socialists too, allowed them temporary use of one of their local halls. In the eyes of reaction IWW and anarchist and communist were all alike, and in the mass arrests especially around New Years 1920 in the deportation delirium, hundreds of IWWs were included in the round-ups in Chicago, Detroit, Cleveland and elsewhere.[10] The Wobs ridiculed the early spouting about "mass action" especially in the sense of armed insurrection, pointing out that if military superiority was to be achieved, those looking for dimes to keep their organizations alive might take a peek at the combined federal, state, municipal and private corporation arms budgets before adopting that policy in place of the sure bet of workers' industrial solidarity. Lenin's doctrine of scrapping the left wing unions to facilitate capture of the trade unions was not acceptable to the IWW, nor the Communist demand that it appoint the editors for IWW publications. Their maneuvers inside the IWW eventually ended Wobbly tolerance for them. Philadelphia became the end of any brotherly love.

There the Marine Transport Workers struck on May 26 for a 20 cents an hour increase. They had good support from other unions, Marine Firemen refusing to provide steam for scabs, but the strike continued through all of June 1920 to July 10. The stevedores wanted to settle on foreign trade only; the shipping board wanted the men to go back on the promise of whatever terms the ILA negotiated in New York, but the IWW insisted on settling for all, and on July 10 marched back to all docks, including some that had previously escaped organization, with all workers wearing the button to assure complete job control. It was a union the communists could not maneuver, but early in August they spread talk that the IWW in Philadelphia was loading arms for Wrangel to use against the Soviet Government. In August the General Executive Board ordered the Philadelphia local suspended. The local insisted no arms were loaded for Wrangel and asked for some proof, some record of the shipment, but none was forthcoming, though the rumor persisted. This charge dismissed, the local was kept suspended on the grounds that it charged a $25.00 assessment actually as initiation fee in disguise. (The constitution of the time required universal rates for all industrial unions, with initiation fee of $1.00, but this active local needed a strike treasury.) It was not until a new General Executive Board was elected, less sensitive to communist approval, that the Philadelphia local was reinstated. Actually on all coasts the IWW was stopping shipments to the interventionists, even where it did not have job control.[11]

Other events moved the IWW in the same direction. The repression of the Kronstad revolt in Russia, the role of the communists during the seizure of industries by Italian workers in September 1920, and their division of the Italian labor movement the following winter and spring into two sections fighting on the streets against each other—all such events made the IWW realize that no matter how "left" the Communists might be, they were still politicians, primarily concerned with getting and holding the power to rule. [12] In April 1921 those out on bail on the Espionage indictments had to start serving their sentences. The Court of Appeals had thrown out the first and second counts of the indictment (interfering with the execution of the Espionage Act and Selective Service Acts, and injuring those employers who were supplying the government) but sustaining the charges of conspiring to deter men from registering and to bring about insubordination in the army. This did not reduce sentences. Of the 46 out on bond, Haywood and eight others did not show up; they had been spirited away to Russia. The communists said they would make good the bond losses, but never did, though publicly announcing that Haywood went to Russia on orders of the Communist Party. [13] It soon became plain that the communists in the IWW were operating under instructions to wreck it.

The discussion did help clarify IWW thinking. It became recognized that putches and insurrections cannot achieve industrial democracy in a complexly industrialized country. IWW periodicals began to put their emphasis on technical articles and descriptions of industrial processes and avoidable wastes. The chief damage done by the Communists to the IWW was the cultivation of the notion of a militant minority, priding itself on its revolutionary consciousness and holding in contempt the mere "union consciousness" of the majority of members. This was to show itself in the lumber strike of September 1923 and later, and do irreparable harm.

1. For events of time, see Borkenau "World Communism."
2. Seattle General Strike: see Crook "The General Strike," for accounts of this and other major general strikes, and W.I. Fisher in *New Solidarity* No. 16. Perlman & Taft v. IV, p. 440 et seq. *Nation* 108-487.
3. Butte strike: see *New Solidarity*, issues 15 and 16, and for a record of the scheming on the employer side, a stenographic record published in *Industrial Pioneer*, August 1926. Another bitter strike was fought by the IWW in Butte in April 1920, turned into a job-action strike by the massacre of pickets on Anaconda Road April 21. (See *OBU Monthly*, June 1920.)
4. Oatman strike: *New Solidarity*, No. 45.
5. Toledo strike: *New Solidarity*, No. 29.
6. Spring AWO Convention: *New Solidarity*, No. 5.
7. Most complete account is Chaplin's "Centralia Conspiracy." See also Jensen, "Labor and Lumber" for affidavits of jurors given in mid-thirties.
8. For circumstances giving rise to OBU, see Logan, "History of Trade Union Organization in Canada," University of Chicago Press.
9. *Solidarity*, No. 137.
10. Fully described by Louis F. Post (Assistant Secretary of Labor) in "The Deportation Delirium of 1920," Kerr & Co.
11. Facts on Philadelphia most clearly given in pamphlet issued by MTW No. 8. It was not reinstated until October 1921.
12. Communist maneuvering most thoroughly documented in Borkenau's "World Communism."
13. Chaplin's "Wobbly" gives details of efforts to induce communists to pay for the loss on bond-jumping.

XI. Peak, Split and Recovery (1922-1929)

In the early twenties, the Marine Transport Workers progressed steadily. It had a firm basis on Philadelphia waterfront, reinstated in October 1921, and among seamen, engine crews and stewards department on Atlantic Coast and Gulf, particularly among the Spanish-speaking personnel.[1] Its expansion into Latin America and its alliance in Britain and elsewhere added to its prestige and to the service it could render its members. The AFL crafts grew increasingly disserviceable. In New York the ILA in the fall of 1920 had struck to keep up with the high cost of living, and its officials, lauded by the press, had broken their own strike.[2] In 1921 the seamen fought cuts in base rate and overtime that took about half their pay, but the dictatorial action of the President of the Marine Engineers pulled out his craft and broke the strike.[3] After that strike an effort was made on West Coast to form a federation of the various crafts, but Furuseth, head of the Seamen's Union fought it from fear that landside workers would have too much to say, and even accused the editor of his Journal of being pro-Wobbly for supporting such an idea. Furuseth developed an anti-IWW mania, charged in Congress that the shipowners were coddling the IWW to disrupt the AFL.[4] He induced the AFL Convention in Portland, 1923, to authorize an investigation of the IWW on these charges. The IWW wired the convention it would help it investigate, but the challenge was not accepted.[5]

Back of all this was the actual growth of the MTW. The IWW actively participated in all maritime strikes as good union men and won increasing esteem from their fellow workers. Where it could not aim at job control, it recruited the staunchest unionists in all classifications, so that MTW membership became a mark of prestige. Its Maritime

Worker published news of the industry and propaganda for its immediate needs.

In Portland, Ore. the ILA and MTW struck jointly on April 23, 1922 when employers announced that hiring would be through their new "Fink Hall," instead of by the union list system which had worked fairly. The Shipping Board induced the ILA to work its vessels, though this meant going through their own picket line. MTW held a meeting for all strikers and the decision was that all would go through unless ILA quit doing so. The ILA settled for the right to have their man stationed in the Fink Hall. The IWW began a program of job action that brought it considerable growth. In October there was talk of a joint MTW and ILA strike, voted down at ILA meeting by narrow margin of 215 to 200. The employer association tried to bribe the ILA with an agreement providing that no IWW would be hired; the ILA did not sign it, and the strike was on. Some scabs were obtained, but the vessels they loaded made more trouble for their owners when Australian workers refused to unload them. The right to be a Wobbly was thus safeguarded in Portland.[6]

During that same month unsuccessful efforts were made to drive the MTW from Philadelphia and Hoboken. In the former the issues were a blacklist imposed by leading shipping companies and the 44 hour week. The MTW tied up the port from October 27 to November 19, winning its point and remaining solid on the Philadelphia waterfront until 1925. (Its disappearance then seems to have come from the dissatisfaction of its chief personnel over interference by the general organization, though there was little of this after its reinstatement in 1921, and disappointment with the 1924 split in the IWW; this situation, coupled with a threat that vessels would be unloaded at nearby ports where ILA was in control, induced the secretary, Baker, and others to take their following into the ILA.) In Hoboken, October 1922, repeated attacks by thugs, who MTW said were hired by ILA, also failed to drive them out. In February 1923, the Mobile, Ala., police ordered IWW to take their sign down; the 14 members in the hall held a meeting, decided not to, and went to jail. Others opened up and soon joined them, until they won out. But this sort of fight was eclipsed by the May Day strike.

The General Executive Board had recommended that where members felt they could strike effectively on May 1, 1923, they should do so, primarily to demand the release of all class war prisoners, but also for appropriate economic demands. Many were still in jail on wartime indictments; the number convicted under Criminal Syndicalism laws particularly in California was growing; the Centralia victims were in jail, and a number, such as Mooney and McNamara out of labor trials not connected with IWW. Protest strikes occurred in northwest lumber, on many construction jobs and elsewhere, but nowhere with such effectiveness as in the maritime industry. San Pedro, port of Los Angeles, was tied up tight, as was Aberdeen, and on east coast, New York, Baltimore, Philadelphia, Mobile and Galveston. In most of these ports it was a short protest strike but won pay boosts of 15%. In San Pedro it developed into a lengthy free speech fight on Liberty Hill. It broke out again July 12 when 27 members, many of them seamen, were convicted of Criminal Syndicalism after a long trial in which they defended themselves to enjoy the freedom of saying what they wanted to. This was a five day protest strike in which all shipping in the port was tied up.

The free speech fight in San Pedro was the last such large scale effort by IWW. Various liberals joined the fight, and Upton Sinclair got arrested for reading the Declaration of Independence. Stockades were built and filled with speakers; it was hopeless to arrest the hundreds who joined in mass singing of IWW songs. Young fellows on roof tops made speeches while cops chased them as in movie comedies.[7] In June of the following year, the morale

of the upper crust was shown by a raid on the San
Pedro IWW hall during a social evening; men and
women were beaten; young children were scalded in
a coffee cauldron; the place was demolished, and five
members were taken out into the desert and tarred
and feathered.[8] Light on all this was given by
Captain Plummer of the police in the following
statement:

"Somebody has been making holy asses of us
policemen. Last summer at the time of the harbor
strike I went to see old man Hammond. He told me
to take a bunch of my men, arm them with clubs,
go up on Liberty Hill and break the heads of the
Wobblies. I replied that if we did that, they would
burn down his lumber piles. 'They will do it any-
how,' he answered. But they didn't. Not an overt
act have they committed. The police who raided the
IWW hall in San Pedro recently did commit an overt
act however. In fact we policemen have been made
the tools of the big business interests who want to
run things. I'm ashamed of myself for consenting to
do their dirty work. The big fellows in this town
can do anything they like and get away with it, but
the workers can't even think what they want to
think without being thrown in jail." [9]

The Marine Transport Workers reached their peak
of influence in 1923. In such a field organization can
grow to a sizeable minority on the conviction that
there should be the better unionism that it offers;
after a certain point it must forge ahead to replace
the unionism it has criticized, or its new adherents
lose hope and drop out. The MTW could not cross
the gap; it was left once more a small minority
championing the cause of direct action and industrial solidarity, but completely unable by 1926 to
give any support to the British General Strike, or
to prevent the shipments of American coal that
broke the miner's strike. (Coal from Europe was
effectively stopped by unionists.) Its solid core continued and was able in 1934 to put up a good fight
once more.

In railroad transportation the IWW has had similar ups and downs, recruiting significant minorities of "two card men" from time to time in the hopes of building the industrial solidarity that all railroad workers realize they have needed. One such wave was in the years following World War I. Their activity prompted Attorney General Daugherty during the 1922 railroad shopmen's strike[10] to charge that the IWW was preparing to take over transportation and the government. Secretary Carlson of the Railroad Workers' Industrial Union issued a statement that IWW members in all crafts were backing the shopmen, and that the IWW was quite willing to run railroads or any other industry, but didn't want to bother with the government because they could not see that it was in any way useful.[11] Up to the 1924 split there was considerable growth of this Industrial Union particularly among the shopmen in western divisions, though also among train crews.

Despite the persistent strike demand for release of class war prisoners, the IWW of this period aimed deliberately at practicality. A favorite cartoon of the time depicted the sundry radicalisms as pointing at the stars, while the IWW was pointing to the industries, shouting "Organize." A pamphlet of the Construction Workers Industrial Union 310 centered on "Immediate Demands and Ultimate Aims," its argument that only by the unionism that could win immediate demands could workers develop the capacity to achieve the ultimate aim of Industrial Democracy. The oustanding orator of the IWW, James P. Thompson, persistently argued against the theory that a working class beaten down enough would some day turn to revolt with these contentions: the worse off the workers were, the more docile, and the more likely to settle for a bowl of soup; the workingclass was changing from the lot of the man with the hoe, to the man with education, technical training, organization and self-respect; and a workingclass lacking the organized competence to maintain decent job conditions certainly lacked the power to take over industry or the competence to run it. The IWW press emphasized similar teachings; its magazines were given largely to articles on industrial techniques; it started an Industrial Encyclopedia of booklets each giving the history of a major industry, and emphasizing its capital integration and the need for modernized unionism in it.

The Construction Workers of .this period were especially engaged in a campaign to improve job conditions, for safety and better living. The large construction projects of the time were built mostly by single men, housed in camp until they made their "stake," then back to a sojourn on the skidroad, and another job. The IWW had largely established free fee or hire on the job, and in many places the job-seeker could stay overnight and clean up before rustling the next camp. Perhaps more effective than the numerous strikes was the less publicized practice of systematizing the quitting. Three weeks was about average stay; if some quit from one to five days earlier than they had planned, and other a few days later, this meant a sizeable number would quit at the same time; without strike, their complaints about job conditions were effective, and usually a job delegate recruited new members out of these men practicing painless unionism. But to raise wages took the consent of absentee management and usually required a strike.

In April 1922 camps of Guthrie and Grant Smith along the Great Northern were struck for pay boost, better conditions and uniform 8 hour day. The men returned May 28 with subcontractors still working their men 10 hours. Mess halls were induced to refuse meals at the hours this schedule required, and soon the general contractor posted notices of a nickel pay boost and 8-hour day for all subcontractors. Strike victories on the Cazadero power project in Oregon and on the Skaggit Tunnel job in Washington soon followed, winning a 50 cent minimum, free blankets and waterproof clothing.

In November two large projects were struck in California, the Hetch Hetchy which was to furnish water for San Francisco, and the Edison power and irrigation project at Big Creek, up in the mountains from Fresno. The Hetch Hetchy strike grew out of organization in some of the camps; the men walked out almost 100%, but scattered so that non-strikers were needed for picketing, and picketing was important because of the large number of, operations under various subcontractors and various names, and it was the time of year when many of America s most ragged and rugged individualists were heading for "sunny Cal" with "wrinkles in their bellies and flat broke." Because of difficulties maintaining a picket line, the strike was called off December 2nd, with no direct gains; the union had to operate on the job with new faces after the strike, and even mail got opened in company offices.

On the Edison job a major grievance was the cold "nose-bag" at mid-shift in the tunnels when the men wanted a hot lunch. On November 13 a job delegate was fired, and the men in his camp walked out with him. Meeting other IWW's, some of them from Agricultural Workers 110, in Fresno, resulted in a call to strike all camps on the project. All the lower camps came out by the 18th and 3500 strikers staged the largest meeting Fresno had seen in the Opera House. News got to the upper camps, snowbound, through the press, and the men had to improvise skis and snowshoes to get out. The demands were $6 per day in tunnels and $7 for shaft men; 50 cents increase for all other labor; 8 hours portal to portal; two men on all machines; hot meals and other improvements. The strike petered out like the one on Hetch-Hetchy. Calling it actually deprived the former strike of manpower necessary to make it effective. The late arrivals from the upper camps were indignant about how it had been called. It was called off Dec. 22, a total loss. Some of the 310 members claimed it would not have been called if it hadn't been for the irresponsibility of the 110 "strawcats" in the valley; that such strikes should be called only by a conference of delegates from the various camps.

Many of the strikers from both jobs, no longer likely to be hired on these major projects, went to work for the Warren Construction Co. on a job out of Fresno. On January 3, 1923, they struck for reinstatement of a discharged IWW cook, enforcement of sanitary laws, $4.00 for 8 hours and no discrimination. The company settled, posting a notice of agreement to these terms. A second strike followed January 21 on complaint that company did not live up to its agreement, and additional demands were made, including the right to hold an Open Forum every Wednesday night in camp. There was some dissatisfaction by those who preferred fewer strikes to interfere with the process of making a stake, and this second strike was never definitely settled. The various protest strikes on construction jobs May 1, 1923 increased this apprehension of many construction hands. The problem was actually to enforce IWW teachings of rank and file control against the maneuvers of a professed militant minority.

The major demonstration of this injudiciousness of the "jawsmiths" occurred in the northwest woods. Lumber Workers' Industrial Union had been strong enough to prevent any appreciable reduction of standards in the Harding "return to normalcy" depression, and the extensive construction work of the era made a firm market for lumber. The IWW had the field to itself: the AFL Timberworkers' last battle had been fought at Klamath Falls in 1922, and is surrendered its charter in March 1923.[12] These standards had been kept by innumerable small job actions. The employers now found a divisive force: the gyppo system, or piece work. They brought it in with a sugar coating, letting men earn three and four times as much as they would make at hourly rates, but wiser heads knew this was to get it going: the need to settle prices for each operation would bring individual bargaining, and eventually less pay for more work. It worked out that way in the later twenties after the union had lost its strength. Opinions among IWW members how to cope with this differed. The general sentiment was that no Wobbly would work gyppo. Many, who took little part except to pay dues and strike with the rest, felt it foolish to pass up big money. A few who knew their economics suggested that given these circumstances of a money-hungry majority, and the current high rates offered for piece-work, the judicious thing was for the union to allow it on the proviso that rates be set for each operation by collective bargaining and kept so high that unit costs would exceed those resulting from hourly rate. Outcome was that those who worked gyppo dropped out of the union. Even more critical was the difference of opinion on the rather haphazard strike policy that had been developing in other industries. May 1, 1923 brought an orderly 4-day protest strike; a longer strike might have broken ranks. There was talk of a September strike but delegates from the camps in conference warned against it, that it might play into the employers' hands. However the "militant minority" who seemed to have talked to each other more than to the men on the job, felt it must be called, to demand release of class war prisoners and had a strike call distributed by airplane, the leaflets fluttering down into one surprised camp after another. The men came out solidly and later made an orderly return to work; but confidence in the union as their instrument was greatly weakened.

This strike was memorable for a side-line activity: the "dehorn squad." This was the prohibition era; but there were bootleggers, and in the Seattle area in particular the "smilo joints," usually operated by Japanese. Knowing that alcohol and strikes don't mix well, that "you can't fight booze and the boss at the same time," the dehorn squads told the smilo joints to close up for the duration of the strike. Those that didn't were closed by Carrie Nation direct action or the threat of it. The daily papers felt they must approve the resultant sobriety of the strike, and could hardly object to union enforcement of the

prohibition law, but felt obliged to denounce such
lawlessness just the same, and many of the dehorn
squads were thrown in the clink by police who
had been tolerating and perhaps profiting from the
smilo joints. The IWW was concerned only that
booze should not disrupt the strike; it did not cham-
pion prohibition, but ridiculed intemperance and did
induce most of its members, recruited from a hard-
drinking lot, to maintain customary sobriety.[13]

Metal Mine Workers won a strike in Bingham
Canyon in September 1922 and at the same time in
Butte, getting a 50 cents increase. This was the last
IWW strike there, though a skeleton membership
was maintained in Butte into the fifties, and considerable organizing effort was made in Butte during the twenties. Company intimidation and the
rustling card system make a partial explanation; but
since these cards could be obtained easily enough
for soapboxers to ridicule the system by tossing them
out to the crowd beneath the nose of company gunmen who were the most assured audience, it seems
that failure to maintain a union came chiefly because
somehow those who favored it figured it hopeless.

An effort was made to organize the oil fields of
the southwest early in 1922. Organizers Erwin and
Hickey were given 90-day vag sentences. Attorney
Mulkes went to Shreveport to defend them, was kidnaped from his hotel and so badly beaten he had to
go to hospital. American Civil Liberties Union finding it could not secure an attorney asked American
Bar Association to provide one, but none accepted
the challenge. Oil Workers Industrial Union sent in
more delegates. A number were arrested at Eldo-
rado, Arkansas and Attorney Julian went to their
defense. He was jailed with his clients. In court he
won freedom for them and himself. Outside the
courthouse they were met by a Ku Klux Klan mob;
Julian drew his revolver and he and his clients left
unmolested.[14]

Metal and Machinery Workers Industrial Union
440 without strikes or attempting to bargain, kept

up a steady growth in the early twenties in Chicago, Detroit and other eastern areas, working chiefly on a propaganda and social activity basis. In the harvest fields I.U. 110 kept selling "red ducats": 15,217 in 1923; 9,219 in 1924, and 8,507 in 1925, though the average annual membership for these same years was 6,483, 4,503, and 4,175.

Apart from MTW activities in eastern ports, IWW efforts were largely concentrated in the areas of greatest repression, particularly California where CS prosecutions came in a steadily flow. To speed up the effort to jail the whole IWW, Judge Busick issued an injunction again all members so that they could be prosecuted without offering evidence to show that the IWW was in any way unlawful. To prosecute under Criminal Syndicalism statute it was necessary to show membership—regularly stipulated by the defendants—and to make some showing that the IWW practiced or preached sabotage, overthrow of government or other unlawful divertisements. This requirement was filled by two professional witnesses whose credibility could not have been high with any jury; their evidence was a formality to warrant convictions obtained by appeal to prejudice. Judge Busick became notorious also for his practice of arresting the defense witnesses who established their membership in order to qualify their competence to testify. The continued prosecutions, frequently appealed, resulted in stricter requirements for the prosecution and in a growing community perception that the IWW was a commendable rather than a vicious organization. By 1924 in California alone 317 members had been indicted under Criminal Syndicalism and 140 convicted. Sentences were 1-14 years, with prison board handing out a customary 4 year sentence, which with good time off made three calendar years. Over a hundred of the 140 were in San Quentin at one time and they continued their habit of collective action. If one was thrown in the dungeon for some breach of discipline, all struck and were thrown there too. Since the San Quentin bunch consisted

largely of the job conditioning members, they soon
set up machinery for reaching such decisions by majority vote instead of being precipitated into them
by a minority. Many used their time for education,
reviewing and going beyond their school work and
taking correspodence courses, several for the mathe-
matics of navigation; they also all bought books on
social and labor issues and had a library of their
own of close to a thousand volumes, which they kept
circulating even though this, like decisions on organization issues, had to be done under guards' eyes
during line-ups for meals, etc. Even though the big
split of 1924 occurred during this time, and some
prisoners were on one side or the other, goodwill
and friendliness resulted from these organized procedures, and as they came out they sought to heal
the breach. In contrast the men in Leavenworth
were largely top officers, speakers, writers whom
the job delegates often considered somewhat like
prima donnas; the enmities that developed among
them are generally considered the major source of
the disastrous split of 1924. The fact that the IWW
grew from the war years to the 1924 split, and that
this disaster occurred when these leaders were released, does not fit in with the conclusion of Perlman
and Taft and other historians that the decline of the
IWW was due to the loss of its leadership by imprisonment. The collective action of the IWW's in
San Quentin, by attracting attention to routine bad
conditions resulted in a great improvement in the
diet.[15]

The IWW split wide open in 1924. On the surface
the issue was over the degree of centralization, but
its causes lay deeper; personal rancors developed in
Leavenworth, especially over the issue of accepting
conditional pardons, found vent in it; dissatisfaction
with the haphazard strike policy and the associated
fear of lumber and construction workers that the
"strawcats" were trying to lead them around by the
nose, also underlay it. The immediate circumstance
leading to it was the reorganization of the general
administration in 1923, so that it consisted of gen-

eral secretary, general organizer and the chairman of the general organization committee of each industrial union. A rule that GEB sessions could be called by a two-thirds vote led to a situation where some said a two-thirds vote had called one and others said no and both had arguable cases. Two IWW's as a result competed for survival, one getting its name Four Trey because it moved from 1001 Madison Street to 3333 W. Belmont, Chicago (this being the body that exists to the present day), and the other body because of its "Emergency Program," dubbed the EP's. The EP was the smaller, but most members dropped out the middle.[16] Whatever its explanation, most IWW oldtimers consider this 1924 split the definitely worst thing that ever happened to it. Considering how the IWW had gone ahead to this event in years when the AFL was declining, it seems possible that if it had been avoided, and even more had the underlying factors been avoided, the IWW might have retained stability in the lumber industry and achieved it at least in general construction, metal mining and marine transport. As it was the woods went unorganized and gyppo; the only construction strike in the 20's after the split was one at Natron cut-off. It showed its vitality only in new fields, particularly coal mining.[16]

The first large IWW coal strike was in Alberta, Canada, where the miners, fighting UMWA checkoff since it did not actually represent them, had gone into the Canadian One Big Union. In 1924 the lumber workers and coal miners of the OBU switched affiliation to the IWW. They struck in November 1925 for abolition of this taxation without representation; companies offered a 10% increase if they would continue to accept the checkoff; this was refused as a bribe.

In Colorado the coal miners were unorganized. A. S. Embree who had formerly been an active organizer among metal miners, settled in southern Colorado after his release from a criminal syndicalism sentence in Idaho, and slowly built the skeleton

of a coal miners' union among the veterans of the
fight of 1914 and their sons. Progress was incon-
spicuous up to the Sacco-Vanzetti protest demonstrations of August 1927. The IWW had joined in the
world-wide protest, and pulled one day protest
strikes where it could, but the outstanding response
was among the miners of southern Colorado. Of the
12,000 miners in Colorado, of whom about half were
employed by Colorado Fuel & Iron, the 6000 in the
south struck almost to a man on August 21, and
stayed out three days to assure no discrimination.
Organization grew faster, and on September 8 a
conference was held at Aguilar to formulate economic demands. Colorado law required 30-day notice before a strike and this notice was given at that
time. The State Industrial Commission said the
notice must be given by the miners, not by the IWW.
The IWW suggested that the Commission check on
whether it represented the men by holding meetings
at each mine and taking a vote. The commission declined the proposal, and though the strike was postponed to October 18 in efforts to meet the requirements of legality, the Commission held the strike
outlaw, and the strikers fair prey for the mounted
police who could harass any gathering of them as
unlawful. Demands were a daily wage of $7.50,
checkweighmen, payment for "dead work" and recognition of pit committees and the miners' organization. Technically this was not the IWW, but the
organization of all miners who would agree to stand
by these demands whether IWW or not.

There are three coal fields in Colorado; this was
the first time all three had been struck together. To
assure completeness a caravan of singing miners left
Lafayette in the north and trekked to Walsenburg
by November 4th, leaving the habit of singing "Solidarity Forever" behind them. The open enemy was
the state police. Strike meetings were harassed by
them and by low-flying planes zooming close to the
heads of the miners and their families who also
attended. This hazard was least if the meeting were
held near a mine tipple, and various mine owners

were not as ferocious as their uniformed watchdogs. One such customary spot for meetings was the Columbine Mine of the Rocky Mountain Fuel Co. There on November 21 the state police turned machine guns on the miners, killing six and wounding many. On January 12 the hall at Walsenburg was raided and Chavez and Martinez killed. But these were only the murders in a campaign of terrorism.

Companies eventually offered a dollar a day increase in the south and 50 cents in the north, bringing the scale to the second highest, and on February 19 the miners voted to return to work. Following the strike came elections of pit committees and checkweighmen and procedure for grievances. White cards of the striking miners had been issued during the dispute with IWW cards only to a minority. It was a significant victory and all considered it an IWW strike, for UMWA did not participate, but little unionism came out of it, though efforts continued into the early thirties and a number of locals were maintained which assured election of checkweighmen and pit committees. This situation seems to have grown out of the strike arrangements with little actual union recruiting. It was later found that some officers of the union were planning during the strike to form a new miners body out of the Colorado miners, the Kansas followers of Howatt and dissatisfied miners elsewhere as those who followed the communist line in Pennsylvania and those who were to step over the traces in Illinois a few years later. Suits against Governor Adams and Louis Scherf, head of the police and who personally gave the order to shoot at Columbine, were lodged and dragged along to 1932 to claim damages for the widow of George Eastenes and other victims; but the court turned thumbs down.

A major organizing drive followed in 1929 in the Illinois coal fields where miners were under UMWA check-off, but chafing under it and divided as Fishwick men, Lewis-men and what not. The communists, who had switched from their no left wing

union program, attempted to horn in also. The IWW
secured a considerable two-card membership around
Benld and Collinsville. When the communist National Miners union announced a statewide strike
for Dec. 9, 1929, it had no following among the
Illinois miners, but precipitated a strike at Taylor-
ville by putting out a picket line which brought in
the militia. The miners there struck only to demand
removal of the troops. The National Miners then
picked out a mine where the IWW had about a third
of the miners as two-card men, and picketed there,
saying it was part of a statewide strike. The miners
struck for the day to ascertain what the facts were,
and voted with only one dissenting vote to return to
work next day. This led to communist accusations
of scabbing by the IWW. Batteries of speakers were
brought by IWW into the Illinois coal fields and a
sizeable membership built up. In the many cornered
fight in 1932 the IWW withdrew its organizers to
avoid a situation where no matter what they did
they would be cats-paws for one or another of the
warring factions. They left the miners with ideals
how a union should be run and advised them to try
to make whatever union they found themselves in
live as close as possible to those ideals.

Temporary success came among the gypsum miners employed by U. S. Gypsum Company in the
vicinity of Oakfield, N. Y. They struck in February
against a cut from 51 to 45 cents a ton and settled
on April 26 for an increase to 75 cents a ton. A
local of I.U. 210 was established, but despite the
victory and repeated efforts to maintain organization, the local died. The crutch of a contract might
have made for stability, but the IWW expected
grown-up men, as their columnist T-Bone Slim said,
to be big enought to pay their own dues without a
check-off. The repeated allegation that the IWW did
not try to maintain organization after a strike is
certainly not true of any of its strikes during the
twenties, if it is true of its strikes at anytime.

1. For this reason, activities are more fully chronicled in *Solidaridad* and *Cultura Obrera* than in English language publications.

2. Perlman & Taft, Vol. IV, p. 452.

3. Ibid. p. 495.

4. Gambs, op. cit., p. 138; Congressional Record, Vol. 62, pp. 2124 and 4500, and West in *Survey,* Oct. 14, 1923.

5. Wire given in *Solidarity,* Nov. 8, 1923.

6. *Solidarity,* Nos. 218-219, and pamphlet containing affidavits issued by Portland Branch MTW.

7. From accounts of the time, *Solidarity,* No. 238 et seq. Descriptions are given by Upton Sinclair in his novel "Oil," and his play "Singing Jailbirds."

8. *Industrial Worker,* June 25, 1924; detailed account and photos in pamphlet "The Blood-Stained Trail," issued by *Industrial Worker,* but not officially approved by IWW because of various inaccuracies; it does however contain much valuable material supplementary to this history.

9. Quoted in letter from Clinton J. Taft of ACLU who heard the statement in Gambs, op. cit., pp. 49-50.

10. See *New York Times,* Aug. 16, 22 and 23, 1922.

11. Given in *Solidarity,* 1930; for strike situation see Perlman & Taft, 519.

12. Jensen: "Labor and Lumber."

13. This "de-horn" activity written in various papers at time; *Seattle Star,* Sept. 7, 1923, *Union Record,* Sept. 6, and denounced by Mencken at time as puritanism.

14. *Solidarity,* Nos. 168-177.

15. Most complete account of Criminal Syndicalism is in Dowell's scholarly "History of Criminal Syndicalism Legislation," Johns Hopkins University, 1939. Much of the Wobbly library in San Quentin was sent to Work Peoples College, Duluth, and used there as it was a residential labor school controlled by IWW, chiefly supported by its Finnish members; some was still in use in 1955, dog-eared, in San Quentin.

16. The EP started publication *Industrial Unionist* in Portland in April 1925, ceased publication June 1926; later issued the *New Unionist* in Los Angeles, which appeared off and on to 1931 as last gesture of a union that had died.

Other sources for items not given: IWW press of the time and personal knowledge of events; Colorado strike described in "25 Years of Industrial Unionism" and fairly adequately in Gambs.

XII. The Stimulus of Depression (1930-'40)

The stock market crashed in October 1929 as accurately predicted by the Industrial Worker. Constriction of business activity, lay-offs, wage-cuts and the Big Depression followed, just as the IWW right along had been saying was the certain consequence of the increasing exploitation of labor. The IWW had no doubt what labor should do: resist all wage cuts to make them expensive; organize the jobless so that they would no longer menace those who still had jobs, while these fought to cut the workday and raise real hourly rates; back all demands with the determination that if employers did not employ, the working class could dispense with their disservices and establish planned abundance.

The IWW made a tremendous propaganda effort. Its effects cannot be measured, but the outstanding fact of the thirties remains this: For the first time a labor movement instead of shrinking in a depression, grew as never before. This turn from abjectness preceded Roosevelt and the Blue Eagle. AFL propaganda of the early thirties was craft union echoing of the assurance that business was sound. The various radical propagandas focused on political issues. The healthy change in labor attitudes can thus largely be attributed to the millions of pieces of IWW literature, straight to the point, issued at factories or where the unemployed gathered, and to the IWW soapboxers who held meetings daily at factory gates and at streetcorners in the evening, establishing regular schedules in even out-of-the-way places that they had to reach by box-cars or hitch-hiking.

This propaganda effort was constructive, educational, and put on by flat-broke members of a flat-broke union. The IWW had never recovered from the 1924 split. It lost its building and printing plant into which it sunk all its resources. To economize in 1929 it replaced its various Industrial Union offices with a Clearing House run by its general secretary. Even so the general secretary taking office in November 1932 found $29.00 cash all told with which to pay back wages, run the office, pay accumulated printing bills, and the industrial union funds that had been loaned to the General Office. Within a year it was all in the black again, but with less than a thousand dollars to run on. The campaign among miners in Illinois had like that in Colorado, meant expenses instead of income, and in May 1930 it was thrust willy-nilly into the Harlan, Kentucky fight.

Harlan had been UMWA territory to 1924; after that a faithful few held the charter. Some IWW literature falling by chance among these miners as they faced 10% cuts led them to write the IWW for information, and to organize themselves into I.U. 220. Their local charter was in the mail when headlines told of the battle of Harlan and of the arrest of over a score of miners charged with murder. The IWW General Defense Committee undertook impartially the defense of members and nonmembers. Its field representatives were beaten up, and so were visiting journalists. Communists nosed in but got no following. Illinois miners and Colorado miners responded to appeals for help. The picture developed in the courts was very different from that originally given in the papers; many were acquitted, all saved from the death penalty, and the last were released in 1941.[1]

In February 1931 the IWW stirred up its own members and sympathizers to greater activity with a leaflet "Bread Lines or Picket Lines," very widely distributed. This urged that the unemployed organize either in IWW or out of it, so that they could assure those still working that they would not scab, and then by demonstrations outside plants that cut pay or worked longer than normal days, promote action to abate the depression. In execution the program became much modified: the unemployed helped picket in strikes called independently of this

program; it was approximated among job-seekers
at out-of-town construction jobs, for example Cle
Ellum, and the Portland Unemployed Union did
assure success to a small loggers' strike. These Unemployed Unions were formed to provide housing
and food for footloose jobless members while they
carried on IWW agitation. The UU at 2005 W. Har-
rison, Chicago held meetings outdoors nightly
throughout the city, sold over a thousand IWW papers a week and many pamphlets, solicited their
own food in the large markets, defrayed rent etc.
from proceeds of social affairs. A similar venture
in New York made publicity even out of its move
from E. 10th St. to larger quarters at 133 W. 14th,
and accommodated personnel for an organization
drive in eastern industrial centers that did much
educational work though it secured few members.
In Seattle the less spectacular 6 Hour Committee
did its most effective work through influence in
other unions to demand shorter workdays. The
Portland UU beside housing soapboxers and leaflet
peddlers, managed to provide the food for the unorganized lumber workers at Biex Logging when
they struck and won them a 25% pay boost. The
chief result of this agitation everywhere was that
the morale of the unemployed became such that
workers dared to strike.

Construction Workers Industrial Union 310 was
active through these "threadbare thirties." It set
out to organize among the jobseekers at Boulder
Dam in April 1931. Those who were union minded
were welcome at the Wobbly jungles just outside
the reservation while they waited to rustle jobs.
On the reservation 11 were arrested for promoting
the union on July 15. On August 7 a wage cut of
a dollar a day was announced. IWW speakers rallied the men as they came off shift and got 1400 to
assemble at the cookhouse. On the 9th the Bix Six
Companies tried to deport the strike committee in
locked trucks, but the Federal Marshall set them
free. Jobseekers and local merchants favored the
strike, and even its 6 hour day demand. On the 12th

Young of the Reclamation Bureau ordered all strikers off the reservation. The IWW called the strike off so they could remain, but insisted their demands still stood.

Boulder Dam was a speed-up job, rushed ahead of schedule, where state safety laws were daily violated and where men collapsed from gas. By October 1932 when I.U. 310 held its convention in Las Vegas, 127 workers on the job had been killed. By that time a prolonged free press fight had convinced the Bureau that it might as well abide by the Bill of Rights, after repeated arrests and deportations of men selling the Industrial Worker. The final effort of the IWW on the job was made August 16, 1933 in desperation as all suspected of IWW sympathy were being fired. Those not yet fired passed handbills in the mess hall; those already fired tried to rally the men to demand safety, 6-hour day and no discrimination, but the majority went to work and there was no strike. This is the only instance known of the IWW attempting a strike and none developing. It occurred on a government project among bulldozed workers fearful of the loss of a job, in the daze of the New Deal, and working for a dollar a day less than the low of the Hoover era.

Near Cle Ellum, Washington 250 men were working for the Lahar Construction Co. on an irrigation dam for 30 cents an hour. As many again waited around town or in the jungles for a job—these were the days when any freight train might have 300 free riders. IWW members sounded out men on the job, in the jungles and the merchants in the towns nearby; there was agreement that if the men struck for a dime more an hour, the unemployed would not take their jobs, and the merchants would provide beans and bacon. The company saw the situation and granted the dime boost, in a short strike May 11, 1932. The job was 100% organized. A second strike in October raised the rate to 45 cents with walk to work on the company time instead of on one's own.

Other major e f f o r t s by this I. U. 310 were
made to organize the Mississippi Bridge job near
New Orleans (summer of 1933); on the Los Angeles
Aqueduct, where organizers had to demand jury
trials to stop arrests for vagrancy; on the Fort Peck
job in Montana, where it won a $15 boost for com-
missary workers, on the New York Water Tunnel
and among WPA workers. Only on the WPA jobs
did it win managerial recognition, but on all these
it recruited men and agitated for better conditions
and achieved them.

The days of the old harvest drives were over, but
Agricultural Workers I. U. 110 fought battles for
families of "fruit glommers" in Yakima in 1933 and
in Watsonville, Calif. in 1939. The Yakima skirmish
started with a strike of 200 hop pickers in May.
Some had been earning as little as 75 cents for 10
hours. Picket lines were crashed by ranchers' cars;
one picket was run over and many arrested. On
June 3 the strike ended with a 50% increase in
piece rates. The IWW stayed active in Yakima,
solidifying "homeguards" and migratories for action
in successive crops. Strikes were on again in August;
on the 25th over a hundred were put in a stockade.
Mike Capelik, disabled veteran who represented the
General Defense Committee, visited the jail, was
held for the convenience of a vigilante mob who
drove him 40 miles away, beat him and covered
him with glue. The trial of arrested pickets was postponed to December. The Yakima Central Labor
Council elected its own labor jury to keep an eye
on proceedings; all were released on the 17th of
December. The IWW local organization in Yakima
persisted for several years without further strikes,
but holding socials and lectures through winter
months.

The major IWW efforts of this period were made
in New York, Philadelphia, Detroit and particularly
Cleveland. In New York the Marine Transport
Workers at a time when seamen's unionism was at
ebb tide, started off the decade with a spectacular

meeting of the 1700 crew members aboard the Le-
viathan, then the world's largest vessel, April 9,
1930. No major waterfront action occurred, despite
steady organizing, until the strike of 1934, though
there was a victorious fight for the right to speak
at Coenties Slip and repeated squabbles with the
Muscovite Marine Workers League. A branch of
the MTW had been started at Stettin, Germany, in
1929, and it became part of the anti-Hitler underground, with the MTW getting its supplies of the
thinnest paper, ink, etc. ashore to it; eventually
contact was lost. A local of Building Workers I.U.
330 was started in New York in 1930; agitation
among cafeteria workers was stepped up when an
attractive hall noted for its class struggle murals
was opened on Fifth Avenue; the good start in this
field was undone by conniving between AFL and
Communist racketeers.[2] Also a local of Municipal
Transport Workers for bus and subway employees,
was launched and later a campaign among apart-
ment house janitors, called superintendents in New
York's provincial dialect.

In Philadelphia as the ILA agreement neared
expiration in September 1930, Wobbly speakers
addressed longshoremen from Richmond to Point
Breeze on the grievances endured since they had
left IWW in 1925, but the ILA won. During the
Cuban general strike of 1933, IWW picketed to stop
the unloading of scab-loaded sugar. That year a
drive started among stonemasons, largely Italian,
building suburban homes. Rates were far below
AFL building trade scale, and competition so keen
among the petty employers that rates could be
raised only a trifle at a time by repeated short
strikes progressing into 1936, by which time I.U.
330 had organized the quarry workers too. In this
campaign the IWW found it was impeded by its
anti-Mussolini propaganda, featured especially in
its Il Proletario; many of these workers believed
Mussolini was trying to get them a syndicalist commonwealth, and pointed to his labor head, Edmondo
Rossoni, a former MTW-IWW organizer who first

turned to Italian nationalism from his American
experience with the additional exploitation Italian
workers here suffered under the padrone system.[3]
Among other groups the IWW won a 25% boost
at Denston Felt & Hair Co. with the provision that
all should hire through IWW hall, but subsequent
indifference developed. During 1933-4 at the RCA
Camden plant, noonday speeches, leaflets, house-to-
house visiting rallied a sizeable membership, but not
enough to win the plant. Successes were scored on
a smaller scale: Women who knitted at home for
Mrs. Franklin's Shops, Inc., raised their rates by a
third. In the swank suburbs there were pockets of
Negroes who do the laundry, mow the lawns and
tend the golf greens. These organized and glowed
with pride when organizer James Price refused to
meet the links committee in their clubhouse unless
the strike committee came along too. To save hall
rent, they held their IWW meetings in a church
they had recently built and of whose congregation
they were the majority. Their first meeting in the
church was opened with a few words of prayer by
a venerable deacon who thanked the Lord that
though He had not blest these men and women with
the good things of life, He had given them the good
sense to organize and go after them. A drive among
the private enterprise garbage crews was stopped
by hoodlumism.

The Marine Transport Workers put up some hard
fights and lost some good men. In the early thirties
it held forth the demand of the 4 watch system, and
the restoration of the old Shipping Board manning
and wage scale; in the later thirties, as competitive
unions split maritime labor asunder, its main concern was mutual respect for all picket lines and
solidarity in all strikes. In the Gulf in the early
thirties only Lykes Brothers paid the old scale of
$62.50 for AB's (ablebodied seamen) but cut that
to $50 for time in port. Other lines pared rates
even slimmer, down to Luckenbach's low of $33 a
month. As of early 1933, the ILA had longshoremen on Atlantic and Gulf coasts and the port of

Tacoma; San Francisco longshoremen had been in an employer-dominated "blue card" association since 1921, but organized an ILA local that year; on the east coast the old Seamen's Union was as good as dead; Great Lakes and Inland waterways were unorganized; on West Coast the Sailors' Union of Pacific retained some life.[4] On May First 1934 the ILA struck the Gulf ports. Originally to support them so that crews would not furnish steam or assist scabs, the MTW issued leaflets urging crews to back the longshoremen and suggesting they go after demands for themselves. Outcome was packed meetings in IWW halls to demand the old Shipping Board scale. Lykes promptly agreed to end its port pay cut. With the longshoremen back and victorious, the MTW called off its strike May 31 with the intent of calling quickies on the various lines paying less than Lykes. This was a hectic waterfront month: the big west coast strike had started May 9 with the Frisco longshoremen, followed by other unions and the development for a few years of Maritime Federation of the Pacific; the IWW hall in San Francisco was raided during the big strike, and later the City agreed to pay $100.00 damages. During this time in Baltimore the IWW tied up the West Eldarado, the first time in nine years that an American ship on foreign run had been held up.

Results for IWW on east and west coasts were quite different. On the Atlantic the surprise action of the MTW led the mossgrown ISU to secure contracts from 28 lines on the assurance that it would keep "irresponsible agitators" from shipping. The communists, who had changed their Marine Workers League into a Maritime Workers Industrial Union, attempted a protest strike against these contracts; when it flopped, they switched back to boring from within. On West Coast at first the MTW found cooperation with the SUP fairly easy out of a joint fondness for "quickies" and an aversion to the political maneuvers of the clique around Bridges. This West Coast militancy and sense of solidarity irritated the resurrected ISU, and as it was nominally the parent organization for the SUP, it revoked this west coast charter at its February 1936 convention. It was perhaps even more irritated because West Coast rates were higher. On March 2, 1936 the ISU crew of the SS California struck in San Pedro to demand West Coast rates; Madame Perkins phoned that the issue would be settled when it got back east; on arrival in New York the crew was fired with the blessings of the ISU. Protest strikes under Curran that followed were the conception of the National Maritime Union. On Sept. 12, 1936 the IWW tied up the SS San Jose in Philadelphia as it was carrying explosives to Franco; the New York ISU sent a crew to board it unwittingly in midstream.

When the SUP contract expired Sept. 30, 1936, union minded seamen on Atlantic and Gulf wanted to grab the opportunity to achieve equality with the west coast and whatever it gained anew, and thus strengthen it. Instead the ISU hired scabs in the Great Lakes area in an attempt to break the West Coast strike, as its own members refused to scab. The ISU was hampering solidarity action wherever it could. One of its fink-herders shot an IWW member John Kane as Kane stopped him from taking off with the Marine Firemen's records, in Houston. MTW and SUP pickets tied up all Pacific vessels as they reached eastern ports; in so doing another IWW seaman Blackie Hyman was shot in Philadelphia. MTW members fought through the east coast strike called off on tankers Dec. 31, and sought to keep cargo and passenger vessels still hot after that, but the fight deteriorated into political conniving in Washington, and the birth of NMU. This development in turn soon brought about a waterfront "cold war" in which Lundeberg of SUP and Curran of NMU each brought their membership to heel with the threat that the other union would steal their jobs: thus Curran got acceptance of unfavorable contracts, and Lundberg, as a trade for ILA support in jurisdictional squabbles, got members to OK return to the "union" in

1938 that had hired scabs to use against them in 1936—it changed its name from Int'l Seamen's Union to Seafarers Int'l Union.

Next imposition on the corraled but disunited seamen was the Copeland Continuous Discharge or Fink Book. The MTW tried to rally the growing list of maritime unions to refuse to accept this. Two MTW members even obtained a court order requiring Philadelphia shipping master not to demand the fink book as a condition for shipment. (One of them Harry Owens, a soapboxer who helped in various campaigns when not at sea, soon after was killed in Spanish Civil War, where he too found politicians exploiting the needs of labor to put themselves in the saddle.) There followed the US Maritime Commission "Fink Hall" to put an end to shipping through union halls; SUP and MTW pickets prevented its use while Curran and the communists tried to make a grab by telling NMU members to ship through it; NMU rank and file was so disgusted that the Muscovites had to pack NMU meetings with furriers to keep control. At the end of the decade the MTW was the same minority arguing for basic unionism as at the beginning, but stronger and sturdier, only now surrounded by workers under contract.

Metal and Machinery Workers Industrial Union 440 almost organized the auto industry of Detroit, flopped, then achieved for the IWW a hitherto unparalleled stability in Cleveland. In Detroit in 1932 the IWW had a small but solid basis of seasoned members with extensive contacts who had moved into a good hall at 3747 Woodward capable of accommodating a thousand, where socials, lectures, dances, plays etc. kept up a good attendance. Through 1932 it engaged in extensive general propaganda, soap-boxing, leaflet passing, recruiting additional members. In January 1933 the local labor temper changed: a series of strikes which the IWW did not call but in which it participated, changed the local picture. First the 600 tool and die makers at Briggs Vernor plant on January 11; Motor Products on January 20; 6000 production workers at Briggs Manufacturing on January 23, and next day the Vernor plant out in support of these newcomers; Murray Body January 27. These were all strikes against wage cuts. On February 7th men at Hudson Body struck for a pay boost. At the largest of these, the Briggs strike, organizer Frank Cedervall made daily pep talks but without mentioning his IWW connections. Soon various groups sought to get control of the strike, and the IWW opened a branch office near the struck plants and started recruiting members from strikers and from the industry generally. Its prime argument was industrial solidarity, as opposed to William Green's "Tentative Plan" for federal unions which the various crafts would soon dismember.

Through the summer of 1933 the IWW in Detroit passed out an estimated two million pieces of paper specially mimeographed for the situations where they were distributed, beside large quantities of printed general appeals; this kept an organization crew busy at every change of shift; at lunch periods they staged meetings at the plants; in spare time they cranked the mimeograph or made house-to-house visits. In addition there were daily radio programs over WEXL which though aimed at auto workers, brought the start of a railroad workers campaign.

First IWW action of the season was among metal finishers at Briggs Highland Park plant. Wobblies were a minority among them, but they struck on second shift for a 10% pay boost, sitting down to get it. After shift they came to IWW hall and organized for action at 6 a.m., and won the 10% for several departments. With growth of a skeleton membership in every major plant, the IWW moved to a larger hall on Sproat Street, a lavish front for the growing union; in the kitchen back of it, the organizers survived on bread and beans and slept on benches. The drive centered on the Murray

Body plant with the unfortunate result that the
dribble of recruits swelled into significant numbers
only on the eve of lay-offs due to changeover in
body designs. Men who joined the union and were
laid off within a week felt it was discrimination,
especially as departments were thinned out rather
than closed down; since it was these men, and not
the non-unionists, who came to the union hall, the
same interpretation gained ground there. A meeting
of men from all departments decided to send in a
committee the next day to ask for rotation of work
during changeover. Management insisted there was
no discrimination and that rotation was unwork-
able; the committee asked for acceptance in principle, each department to work it out so that the men
available under the plan were those technically
competent for the work on hand. Management felt
it was going far in receiving a committee without
knowing to what extent it represented the men, and
would make no commitment beyond the declaration
that it intended no discrimination. The committee
went to their nearby branch hall and by a ballot,
with only one negative vote, decided to pull the
plant. It needed only a signal from the street for
members inside to blow whistles, shut off power,
and bring the whole force to a vacant lot for
speeches. The strike started September 27 with enthusiasm, but since there was no urgent need for
more men than supervision with a few favorites
could provide, the strike was doomed to fritter
away and was called off November 12. In restro-
spect it was later felt that had the committee used
the sudden strike at 11 a.m. as a rally to show the
men were behind the rotation plan, and sent them
back at noon the union could have given some protection to the men, gained prestige in other plants,
and even used the laid off men as part time organizers to develop the already started membership in
most other plants in the city.

The loss of the Murray strike was the loss of the
campaign in Detroit. Early in it the big hall and
the radio program were dropped. A block system

to provide pickets and contact with those who didn't show up was an economy measure that foreshadowed the wartime "share-the-ride" system. Through the strike, but on a reduced scale, organizing efforts continued at other plants; and after it house-to-house visiting centered on the Murray recruits; yet all but a few of the newly won members dropped out and new recruits became rare. The IWW in Detroit was left with most of its members the unswerving Finns and Hungarians who had constituted its backbone in 1930. But the new members were activists who planted a seed in the American labor movement: the sit-down. Some of the Murray metal finishers moved to Hudson Body and there in Dept. 3760 they pulled such sitdowns as they had used at Briggs Highland Park but this time with little cards that the IWW mimeographed reading "Sit Down and Watch Your Pay Go Up." The men did as the cards said and their pay did go up, in five successive increases during February and March 1934. (Frank Ellis, IWW, had sparked stay-in at Hormel, Nov. 1933; first Akron sitdown was in June 1934; sitdown wave came in 1937.) Job action with similar techniques (primarily designed to show the IWW was inside the plant rather than outside it) won improvements at Budd Wheel and cleaned up the spray booth even at the lost Murray Body plant.

These slight successes put the union in no shape to seize the opportunities presented by 1934 when through the auto industry there was hope for a general strike and growing suspicion of the AFL and its domineering policy of appointing disliked personnel and its threat of craft division. In the spring 230,000 workers were finding that "hope deferred maketh the heart sick," and accepted the General Motors representation plan. Self-critical Wobs contemplated what they might have been able to do had they not lost all their eggs in one Murray Body basket. In later years, with some revival of the IWW in the area, they consoled themselves that whatever commendable distinctions Detroit unionism showed could be attributed to the unflagging propaganda efforts of 1933-4.

Meanwhile preliminary spadework for an organization campaign had been done in Cleveland with much leaflet passing and noon-day speaking by Jim Corrigan, old anarchist who never let a dogma interfere with his sense of humor. (During the Sacco-Vanzetti protest of 1927 when a scheduled demonstration was forbidden, he had loaded all the banners and signs on a wagon, hitched up the most decrepit nag he could find, and meandered down Euclid Avenue, tying up traffic, explaining in extenso and loudly to all interfering policemen that since the demonstration was forbidden he had to take the signs away to hide them.) The Bermunkas office on Buckeye Road was near a number of small plants and for a while the IWW concentrated on these smaller units, keeping that office continuously open for those who called in response to meetings in front of shops or leaflets. The Cedervalls and other organizers gradually shifted from Detroit and a wide campaign was on again for I.U. 440. A total of twenty plants got organized in the process, most of them medium size, some of them lost soon after organizing, but out of it continuous bargaining through the IWW continued at most of them from 1934 to 1950 when the union still lived on—and does to this day—but felt obliged under Taft-Hartley requirements and IWW refusal to sign affidavits, to disaffiliate.

First in the series (omitting a victory at Ferro Foundry in 1933 that resulted in no permanent union) was the enameling division of Ohio Foundry in April 1934. Next Accurate Parts with a two hour strike on April 28. At Draper Steel Barrel a few enthusisast for the new union got alarmed at the formation of an inside union, struck and got a promise of no company promotion and recognition of the committee to process grievances of union members. Two small metal container plants, Perfection Metal Container and Permold, followed. On

June 7 collision with the company union at Draper led to a strike that lasted to Sept. 10. During it word came that orders were shifted to a plant at Niles near Youngstown; a caravan of strikers went there, found it organized in AFL and got the men to demand of management that no struck work be accepted. AFL officials in Cleveland were not so union minded and took the company union under their wing. The Regional Labor Board offered a no discrimination settlement; I.U. 440 proposed return to work on promise that Labor Board election would be held and winner would get 100% union shop; the IWW won by a narrow majority of 93-75. Unionism grew solid in the plant, even after it was taken over by Jones & Laughlin, and members there brought in additional plants later.

While the three month strike was in process at Draper, noon-day talks continued at two of the city's larger plants, American Stove, maker of Magic Chef ranges, and National Screw, a major auto industry supplier. June 14 the committee was recognized to act for its members at American Stove. Organization grew at Cleveland Wire Spring. On October 1 a three day strike won recognition at Republic Brass. (All these victories were accompanied by wage increases, considered at the moment more important than recognition.) At Cleveland Wire Spring there was trouble with the company union and a strike was voted October 23 against the best judgment of the organizers. This became the first in a series of concurrent bitter fights that almost wrecked the new union; hired thugs attacked pickets and injunctions restrained the number of pickets; many were arrested for telling scabs what they thought of them; fights developed near the homes of scabs, and the strike dragged on through the winter. Before it was over the IWW was involved in two larger strikes, that of the charwomen at a group of the largest downtown buildings, including Terminal Tower, and at National Screw.

The charwomen's strike required a picket line long enough to circle the several blocks the buildings occupied, and members off shift helped fill it out. Their banners asked if $2.50 was too much to ask for scrubbing floors at night. Public sympathy was with them, and the antics of Captain Savage of the police force led all papers to deride his frequent arrest of the charwomen. The manager was a Regional Labor Board member, and one picket sign read:

"Snead is on the NRA.
He hauls scabs here everyday."

Mysterious cars intimidated the women by following them home; the Cedervall brothers were waylaid New Years Eve as they left the hall where they stacked the picket signs, and badly beaten. The AFL attempted to make a settlement without asking strikers or union. About the same time papers carried a scare headline about dynamite being found in the ventilating system of the Terminal Tower, the first of a series eventually depicting the IWW as terrorists. The strike dragged on through the winter.

On February 8, 1935 the men at the most recently and only partially organized plant, National Screw, struck also, though the charwomen's strike and that at Cleveland Wire Spring was more than the union could handle. It had been encouraging in January to add more small brass shops to the union list, Cochran and Holland Trolley, recognition at Dill Manufacturing, maker of most of the nation's tire valves, and recognition at National Screw with the promise of a 10% boost for its 1350 employees. Later National Screw claimed it had made no such promise and the men struck. When they had been out a few days and collected their pay, it contained a five cent boost. It was suggested to strike committee that they consider accepting this as a temporary settlement, go back with their more than doubled membership, and look for more later; but the committee felt it should hold out for the whole dime. Former bootleg gangsters now that prohibition was over were on hand to beat pickets and break picket lines; the strike grew weaker with increasing violence. Stench bombs were thrown in the IWW office; one that didn't break there was returned through the head gangster's window the same way, and the gangsters were out to get the IWW. The hall was now protected, and organizers at night moved with others a distance behind them; but papers began carrying stories of bomb outrages at loyal workers' homes. Mystified IWW officers checked and found repeatedly that those living at these addresses were not involved in any dispute. A member arrested for a picket line altercation got thrown in with a character who evidently believed the papers and started discussing rates for various window breakings and bombings, and indicating that plate glass suppliers, some building trades officials and those interested in what brand beer certain taverns served, all had a pool for such services. Anyway there was extensive vandalism and the IWW got the blame. Police raided the home of Mike Lindway, master mechanic at National Screw, and an enthusiastic unionist, without a search warrant or witnesses, and claimed to discover an arsenal there. Lindway was convicted. To sustain the conviction the Ohio Supreme Court had to overrule both the Appellate Court and its own previous decisions, to deny that federal search and seizure provisions applied to Ohio. Frank Cedervall was arrested on the charge of threatening the secretary of the company union. The prosecution had a large number of witnesses to the alleged threat. Attorney Wolfe moved that they be separated. Thus they could not hear the cross examination of their predecessors. One after the other repeated their story letter perfect in a singsong but all disagreed on cross examination about the weather, whether they were standing and the defendant sitting, or vice versa and all other relevant circumstances. Soon the jury was smiling and tapping a rhythm to their sing song, and acquitted the organizer. Over 200 were arrested during the strike, with many jury trials, but the only convictions were Lindway and Bart Dudek, who had escorted his fiancee through the thugs with a revolver in his car.

But legal victories did not win strikes. All three had to be called off, the AFL accepting the Cleveland Wire Spring. The blow would have knocked out the IWW as the Murray strike did in Detroit, had it not been for solid organization in various other shops. Within a year it was as effective as before, winning new shops and new gains in old ones. But meanwhile the IWW spotlight shifted to the woods of Idaho and elsewhere.

The Lumber Workers had been hit hardest of all industrial unions by the 1924 split. It recovered slowly to a peak in 1936 and declined again. It helped in the unorganized Grays Harbor strike of 1932 and acquired a few members afterwards there, but when the AFL Timberworkers campaigned and struck in 1935, it could play only second fiddle in the long log region of its greatest historic triumphs. It staged a serious campaign in the short log country east of the hump. Organizers went through camp after camp in the white pine country, getting meetings going after supper before the office force could prevent it, talking union and distributing a straw ballot to determine what demands the men favored and whether they wanted IWW to represent them. During the traditional July 4 shutdown meetings were held in all central towns, and by September 70 delegates or voluntary organizers on the job, were recruiting a sizeable membership in Idaho. The 120 "covered wagon," actually a truck used by part of the organization crew carried a mimeograph to issue bulletins, and headed through Oregon to Klamath Falls, then, after the AFL strike, up the coast to the Seattle District, where it found many wishing it·had been the IWW in the woods instead of this non-benefit wing of the Carpenters.

In March 1936 near Pierce, Idaho, where the flume system is used to get the logs down, the movie "Come and Get It" was being shot, and the Wobs used the occasion to raise the pay a dollar a day. A strike at Elk River raised the rate for the drive to $5 and another in May wound it up with $6.00. On June 29, when logging was in full swing, a complete walkout cleared the Weyerhaeuser and other camps. Along the St. Maries small employers settled promptly, but the big fight continued. Early in August as a truckload of 15 unarmed pickets went near Fromelt camp, plug-uglies opened fire, wounding several so badly they were crippled for the rest of their lives, and three died within two years. (Later the 10 thugs were tried and fined at the rate of $500 each.) Martial law was declared August 3. The situation became quiet; the Guard at one side of the road near each camp, the seven permitted pickets at the other, listening to the sounds of saws and hammers improving camp facilities. The strike was called off without seeking recognition, but a 10% boost was obtained. In a few years it was CIO territory, with an IWW organizing crew carrying on from camp to camp just the same as in 1932.

In Michigan the IWW had built almost complete organization in several camps. When the AFL struck the area, demanding union shop, the IWW's all struck too, with no effort to protect their hold on their own camps. NLRB action to do this was suggested, but they didn't want to mess around with politicians. There and in the west despite hard organization and fighting and propaganda, even using Tacoma station KNO, the Lumber Workers ended the decade as they had entered it.

Two railroad campaigns occurred in the thirties. In Detroit those involved were train crews. They were content to build slowly while maintaining their old unions, but quit their active grievance work in the Brotherhoods. Thus when they were accused of the inevitable infraction of the multitude of rules, the grievance machinery was in the hands of those who would be glad to see them fired. They retained their jobs by legal pressure, but the campaign was strangled. During 1937 to 1939 a campaign among the hundred extra gangs surfacing approximately 2000 miles of track on the Northern Pacific and Milwaukee roads was attempted. Conditions were improved, but wages would have taken system strikes, and adequate strength for this was never achieved at any one time.

Among WPA workers in the late thirties I.U. 310 built many branches. The strongest was in Oakland where the branch was recognized for processing all grievances in Contra Costa and Alameda Counties. In Missoula a 310 branch was built, and toward Christmas of 1937 the women on a WPA sewing project staged a sympathetic sitdown. Students leaving Work Peoples College in 1937 started several branches in Minnesota. In April 1938 the WPA workers around Watsonville, Calif., organized, won free transportation which was the current irritant, and the branch soon had a fruit pickers strike to handle. The 150 Filipino workers involved first asked CIO then AFL to do it for them, but both wanted cash on the line, so the IWW arranged their picketing and relief, won their strike, but retained no members from it, though the Watsonville branch was active to late in the forties. In Detroit in 1938 where IWW was campaigning on Great Lakes and organizing restaurant workers, a WPA branch won recognition of a committee to represent all workers though elected in IWW hall, also the right to make up for time lost due to weather or sickness. At Bloomfield, N.J. a 310 WPA local won pay for hours the men were required on job but not assigned to work. At Olympia Washington they won a dispute so they could build a fire to keep warm.

In the later thirties the revived I.U. 440 in Cleveland won new plants as American Brass, Superior Carbon, Globe Steel Barrel and Independent Register. It was anxious to get a number of the drum plants organized as its best chance to apply industrial rather than shop structure unionism; for organizers were already noticing that the shop-wide union, like the company union, led to the use of "we" to mean management and men, when even a craft union used it to mean those engaged in the same work. American Stove gave it two major issues: the need to organize in Lorain where one division had been moved during the National Screw strike, and the first occasion for a signed contract. This latter need grew from the fact that the company union which 440 had been steadily battling, joined the CIO, and sought recognition. Though the IWW constitution still forbade time agreements, the Cleveland union signed one, containing the provision that no struck work would be accepted. This stirred up hostilities between jobbites and radicals throughout the IWW; in 1938 the constitution was amended to permit the practice.

In the Lorain campaign the company signed with CIO over IWW protests; I.U. 440 struck to enforce an election; it was a draw; the run-off was moved up and the CIO squeaked through. During the campaign the Wobs got members at Steel Stamping in Lorain. The company lawyer, a son-in-law of William Green, induced the AFL, over the protests of members of the Trades Council, to sign a contract even though AFL had no members in the plant. IWW demanded NLRB election and won two to one. But hard battles in an unfriendly town eventually lost the plant.

As Europe went to war and the New Deal went in for peace time military training, the IWW was among the first to negotiate accumulation of seniority during this enforced service. In November 1940 an 11 day strike at American Stove ended with the trading of a demand for closed shop, for the settlement of an accumulation of grievances. This was what the bargaining committee wanted, for they saw a closed shop (unless accompanied by hiring through the union) ends up in the company personnel office eventually selecting the membership for the union. Instead they preferred a sieve system through which those who didn't care for the union got dropped by not fighting for them when they got into trouble.

This record is one of industrial action; but the chief efforts of the IWW was largely propagandist. Even much of its job conditioning was done through minorities on jobs where other unions had a check-off. The prime IWW concern was the large problem of a misemployed society drifting toward totalitarianism and war. It noted how government intervention was centralizing union functions in Washington, and unions becoming dependent on government props. It held up the ideal of job democracy, invulnerable to any such arrests as those with which Hitler had cracked the highly centralized German labor movement. Internationally it felt drawn toward the anarchist International Workingmen's Association. In 1934 a referendum carried to affiliate with it, then it was pointed out that this would commit the IWW to declaring for its members their religious and political attitudes which it had always left to the individual, and a new referendum reversed the decision, so the IWW did not affiliate. During the Spanish Civil War it had an assessment for the support of the CNT, and friendly relations with IWMA persist.

In Canada the IWW through the thirties had a similar history on a smaller scale. Because of customs difficulties, a separate Canadian Administration was established in 1931. Extensive unemployed agitation in the early years led to the imprisonment of organizer George McAdams and others at Sioux Lookout. In the later thirties organization work was undertaken in Newfoundland and the Maritime provinces. Dairy Workers at Ritchies Dairy in Toronto won a boost and a union work stabilization plan. A Fishermen's local was established at McDiarmid, Ontario in June 1939 and the 1939 Canadian Convention got considerable newspaper publicity with pictures of the eastern delegation detraining from boxcars. The Chilean Administration of the IWW, long repressed, came to life again in the mid-thirties. The world over serious labor journals discussed the IWW as a solution to problems otherwise insoluble.

Looking back in 1940 at the commemoration of its first 35 years, the Industrial Worker observed: "Today we see government agencies certifying the IWW as the collective bargaining agency for those workers logical enough to demand it. In post-war years we saw the same government sending hundreds of our members to jail for insisting upon the IWW as their bargaining agency. The IWW has proven itself able to carry on equally well in either circumstance."

Most material for this chapter from IWW press of the time and personal knowledge of events. Following notes are for further information rather than documentation.

1. Pamphlet: "The Shame that is Kentucky's"; also extensive reports in *New York Times* and other periodicals; also in Perlman & Taft, or Gambs' book previously cited. IWW among Colorado coal miners elected pit committees and checkweighman into January 1933.

2. New York situation described, without IWW angle, in Lens' "Right, Left and Center."

3. For more on Rossoni see "Black International" series in *Industrial Worker,* March 4, 1950. Another IWW turned fascist was Harold Lloyd Varney. Fascism has been described as a synthesis of syndicalism and nationalism.

4. Best account of maritime affairs through thirties is Taft in *Political Science Quarterly* for June 1939. Accounts also in Madison's "American Labor Leaders" (Harpers, 1950), Yellen's "Labor Struggles" and similar books.

XIII. World War and Cold War (1941-'55)

During World War II the IWW carried on its organization activities undisturbed, and expanded its policy of gaining bargaining rights by winning NLRB elections in the maritime and metal mining industries. Peace was followed by a period of manufactured hysteria—parallel to the reaction to the great French Revolution of 1789. In this period the IWW late in 1949, largely as the victim of the cold war, the subversive list and Taft-Hartley Act, lost much of its membership, and wound up a period of expanding influence. It observed its fiftieth anniversary unable to engage in collective bargaining anywhere. It persists because its members have no doubts that the working class needs the sort of organization it has been striving these many years to build, today more urgently than ever.

The story of U. S. Vanadium's operations at Bishop, California, typifies the period. During the summer of 1941 job delegates for Metal Mine Workers Industrial Union 210 of the IWW by old-fashioned recruiting, organized this camp high in the mountains solidly, and directly negotiated a 13% pay boost. In December a meeting in Bishop pondered what to do if someone wouldn't join. As reported in Industrial Worker of Dec. 6, "After some discussion it was decided that anyone refusing to line up will be told to state his reasons in a speech before the membership, now a body of 300 workers. The membership will then weigh the reasons given and decide the status of such new worker. The members are anxiously waiting to hear the speech of Objector No. 1." This union security program worked well.

Soon the union had a discriminatory discharge case to handle. Clarence Dahl, of its Organization Committee, working at the Bishop mine took a trip to Darwin, 125 miles away, where the same union

was involved in a strike at a mine. Returning over
mountain roads in winter, he was late for his shift
and was fired. Management refused to discuss his
reinstatement. The next evening at the mess hall
top management for this U.S. Steel subsidiary announced a wage increase but warned that any strike
would be dealt with by law and order. The union
took the case to NLRB and Dahl was reinstated with
back pay, in January. Next month a hearing was
held to arrange for an NLRB election. So far I.U.
210 was the only union concerned. It had been concerned only with the mine, but now that the question of bargaining unit shaped up, it decided March
12 the mill should be in same unit. This led AFL
Operating Engineers to hold a meeting at the Legion
Hall and seek members, but got none. Immediately
the company's eastern legal staff filed a brief with
NLRB asking for dismissal of the election on the
grounds that the IWW was not a union within the
meaning of the Act. In May the NLRB held further
hearings on the company contention and the desire
of AFL to carve out a unit of 75 men. A new election was scheduled and postponed on request of the
company. Meanwhile the IWW organized workers
in local taverns and restaurants and soon Foodstuff
Workers I.U. 640 and I.U. 210 opened a joint hall.
On August 7 the local Inyo Register carried a story,
"Angry citizens voice protest against IWW with
talk of vigilante action." The two unions issued a
leaflet explaining their aims to the community, and
nothing adverse occurred. In the election the IWW
won 231 votes to 55 in Group A, the mine, and 35
IWW to 41 Operating Engineers, with 6 no union
votes in Group B. In the run-off the AFL won
Group B.

The wartime wage and manpower freeze transferred much collective bargaining away from the
job. I.U. 210 demanded an increase and argued that
to require men to stay permanently at this high alti-
tude warranted pay above what the War Labor Board
permitted. The argument dragged on and in October 1943 the local accepted a 50 cent compromise to

clear the way for new demands, for the "gumpets," as the the Industrial Worker called the growing host of government functionaries, would not process new demands until the old case could be marked settled, tied up in red tape and stored away. The same request was made by UMWA for a similarly situated mine of the same company at Rifle, Colorado, but appears to have been settled for a checkoff instead.[1]

In 1944 the company wanted a tunnel and contracted the work to Morrison Knudsen. The contractor hired 37 local men of whom 30 had IWW cards, then contended that under his area-wide agreement with AFL they must all take out AFL cards. IWW insisted to NLRB that 7-a gave these men the right to choose their union and did not permit the contractor to choose their union in advance for them—but the NLRB didn't see it that way. I.U. 210 decided to sign a contract covering the mine, the first contract outside of those made by Metal & Machinery Workers. Soon operations died down and toward the close of the contract no union crew was on the spot to administer it with effectiveness. Work opened up and Mine, Mill & Smelter Workers won an election. Later in June 1952 the UMWA won over Mine-Mill by getting workers to vote "No Union," since UMWA had not signed the non-communist affidavits that had been signed by Mine-Mill, commonly considered "communist dominated."

Marine Transport Workers I.U. 510 carried on with increased effectiveness. Its activities in the Gulf centered from desirable facilities in a new building in Houston technically owned by a seamen's club, because the IWW ever since its printing plant fiasco in the twenties had avoided real estate. It held on to its straight principles during the ideological and jurisdictional fights of the maritime unions, and during the about faces of the "gumpet's" from drinking vodka with the Muscovites to wanting to bomb them. During the Finno-Russian war, the MTW backed the SUP proposal of an em-

bargo on material for Russia, but refused to join
it in whooping it up for war. War and post war
experiences made many seamen favorable toward
IWW views: tanker crews knew of oil transhipped
to Germany by way of Franco at the Canary Islands; all whose work took them to the waterfront
knew that top brass blaming the disaster of the
Battle of the Bulge on union action in American
plants, were frauds for they knew that the docks
were always fully loaded with materiel; others saw
food dumped in the Pireaus while Greeks were
starving within sight of it, so as to save free enterprise in its distribution; others saw the same in
Shanghai and the black market in operation; still
others brought home troops from Italy and Germany who had seen fascist cliques restored to power
in town after town, and the insurgent administrations ousted. IWW views on world affairs no longer
shocked such men.

In 1941 a new attempt was made to deport
Bridges. A new law provided for deportation for
previous membership in organizations seeking to
overthrow the government or alter it by unconstitutional means. In his 1939 case Bridges had recalled a short membership in the MTW about 1920.
The Department of Justice now contended that his
membership in the IWW was membership in an organization that sought by strikes and economic and
industrial pressures to alter the form of government
to One Big Union. The IWW provided witnesses for
Bridges defense and its attorney filed a brief as
"friend of the court." Judge Sears eventually issued
his decision that Bridges was deportable, but made
it plain that this was not on account of his past IWW
membership, for his examination of the record and
literature of the organization showed that the IWW
was not such an organization as the Department of
Justice contended. The case went up through the
courts and eventually in 1945 the United States
Supreme Court decided that Bridges was not deportable, incidentally thereby affirming the view
that the IWW was not engaged in the alleged activ-

ities. The previous Supreme Court decision in the
Fiske case, finding the purposes of the IWW lawful,
had been based on the preamble only; this decision
was based on all that the prosecution could gather
to give the IWW a bad name.[2]

The increasing activity of IWW on waterfronts
and elsewhere toward close of war led the observant
Business Week to note in a feature on IWW in its
issue of January 6, 1945: "The IWW shows signs of
life. In the metal shops of Cleveland, the vanadium
mines of California, the copper diggings of Butte,
on the waterfront of San Diego, New Orleans and
New York, the dead past is stirring and men are
carrying red cards." [3]

With war over, the quarrels between right and
left waterfront unions were intensified in reflection
of the growing cold war. Through the big maritime
strikes of 1946, embittered with jurisdictional disputes, MTW secured observance of its slogan "Respect All Picket Lines." When the 510 conference
met in Houston on Sept. 16 it received telegraphic
and other greetings from unions on all sides thank-
ing the IWW for its willing cooperation in a strike
that won $27.50 per month on all coasts.[4]

In 1946 the IWW had chartered a British Administration which was also active along its waterfront,
and during the 1947 "outlaw" British seamen's
strike, it backed the rebels. Here the MTW circulated the information the British Administration
provided about this fight against an Establishment
Scheme that benefited a few but left most worse
off. In 1948 when the SUP sent its members through
Bridges' picket lines, solidarity in the maritime industry deteriorated. In 1949 any MTW enthusiasm
for the SUP cooled further when the SUPSIU flew
scabs to break the strike of the Canadian seamen
on the grounds that their union was communist-
dominated. The IWW did not dispute this allegation, but held both here and in Britain that scabbery
was no way to undermine communist influence.
Even the staid Canadian Trades and Labor Congress

took the same stand and informed the SIU that though it had expelled the Canadian Seamen, it could not invite the SIU to affiliate on account of its policy of "replacements" i.e. scabs, in this strike. The MTW did endorse the repeatedly proposed boycott of Panamanian vessels, actually American vessels flying the Panama flag to escape American unions, wages, manning scales and safety inspection. These repeated attempts were always fouled by union contracts and Taft-Hartley.

The MTW'S own organizing activities were confined to the towing industry through the extensive inland channels on Gulf Coast, first in 1946 among crews working for the Galveston & Houston Towing Co. In 1947 it won an NLRB election on the Gulf Barge and Towing, with MTW getting all the votes, and in November on the Pasadena and Lynchberg ferries. It incidentally did a service to the "ancient mariners" of Snug Harbor, a foundation kept up by income from an old farm now in the center of New York's highest priced real estate. Late in 1948 the aged seamen there had been required to turn over to the institution all assets and claims so that they had no spending money. An account of this petty meanness in Industrial Worker Jan. 22, 1949, and later examination of the terms on which the foundation rested, resulted in rescinding these impositions.[5]

Several of the smaller shops organized by Metal & Machinery Workers I.U. 440 in Cleveland went out of business during the war and others were lost to the union through sudden changes of plant personnel. It acquired one "war-baby," Federal Aircraft where the contract had the unusual provision that no worker could be fired without the approval of the shop committee. The American Stove plant was largely converted to aircraft production, and the union changed from a departmental to a plant wide seniority system. It wanted rates as high as paid in aircraft plants elsewhere, but War Labor Board insisted that area rates applied. A slowdown developed, followed by a walkout in May 1943. The War Labor Board, finding a union that boasted it had given no "no strike pledge," considered the union viewpoint and allowed readjustments retroactive to Jan. 18. The expanding work brought many new people into the plant, usually from CIO plants. Most found the IWW a welcome difference, but a few wondered if it was patriotic. All new members were given the regular IWW dues book, with the Preamble up front, and some of these new workers questioned the propriety of its language. A pressure developed in the Cleveland branch to change the preamble or even sever IWW connections. Explanations of the meaning of the preamble and improved personal relations between the general organization and the branch soon led the branch to hearty participation in IWW affairs.

The members in these shops relished job action tactics. As American Stove expanded its work force, more timeclocks were needed, but the company said it was difficult to obtain them in wartime. One night all went home without punching. The additional clocks needed were installed the next day. A canteen service supplied coffee, sandwiches etc., and workers could get a pickup there whenever they wanted one. Management figured this led to a waste of time and ruled that this service would be available only during the 10 minute rest period. Committee induced them to try it out first in one department. When the experiment was made all maintenance, repair and other crews who had an excuse for coming there were on hand, and those who ordinarily brought a lunch and thermos bottle left them home that day. The committee and management had an appointment to examine the safety conditions in another department that morning, but the committee led the way through the new experiment just at rest period. Management saw a line at the canteen, went on to investigate the safety complaint, returned and the line was still there. It quit its attempt to confine coffee-and to the rest period. Such methods proved effective for many grievances and were thoroughly enjoyed. Freedom to engage in such methods was one of their strong ties to the IWW.

In a nearby plant of American Steel & Wire, the United Steel Workers had their customary multiple step grievance procedure. Under it grievances were regularly shoved up one step until they finally accumulated at the end where they were to be settled far away by legal minds who knew nothing of the conditions that produced the grievance. Local 1519 USW stopped work to demand a settlement of these grievances. The United Seelworkers removed the elected officials of the local and appointed in their place men who had been snowed under in the preceding election as the workers look-on them as "company men." The International representatives also told the custodian of the hall not to let the rebels use it. Men in the plant asked I.U. 440 for advice. The IWW rented the hall for the rebels to use and told the men that this combination. of check-off and rule by those they had defeated in an election was the same issue of taxation without representation as led to the American revolution. It was pointed out that the law in 7-a definitely assured them to the right of representatives of their own choosing; but that the Board had taken this to mean that they had chosen the Steelworkers as an international along with any such impositions it might order. I.U. 440 recommended that they raise this issue to NLRB, pointing out that the basic provision of 7-a outweighed any procedure the NLRB had set up under other sections. The IWW local prepared such an argument on their behalf, avoiding making it an inter-union dispute. No answer was given but the locally elected officials were restored to office. Very soon after, however, the leading militants were given new draft status and had to leave the plant for the armed forces.[6]

The IWW shop committees had found it desirable to take charge of the "share-the-ride" system for the transport of the expanded working forces. The streetcar system of Cleveland was municipally owned. The streetcar workers wanted a boost and were confident from a comparison with rates in other cities that if the City would submit the issue to arbitration, this comparison would get them a boost. But the City held that it was beneath its dignity to submit its labor relations to arbitration. Thus the streetcar men threatened to strike in May 1944. This created an embarrassment for the IWW shop committees, for to handle the "share-the-ride" might impair the effectiveness of the strike. I.U. 440 wrote a letter to the streetcar union expressing this reason for its concern, supporting the men's bid for arbitration, and suggesting that they put the responsibility for any break of streetcar service squarely where it belonged by offering to work during the dispute but collect no fares. A copy of the letter was given to the newspapers and Cleveland Press frontpaged it in an early noon edition. At barns and elsewhere streetcar workers discussed the idea and supported it, even with telegrams. That afternoon the City Council decided that after all it could submit to arbitration. It did and the men got their boost. (After the war this same tactic was developed in Japan.)

It was an era of endless regulations, interpretations thereof, executive orders and a growing body of case decisions that had to be digested by unionists if they were to administer contracts effectively in their members' best interests. Most unions had legal staffs for this, and a lawyers' view percolated to top officers who advised field representatives how to explain to shop committees what little they could do under this heap of regulations. The IWW could afford no legal staff, so it studied these papers with a workman's eyes to figure how either to use them or get around them. Summaries were given to shop committees and as these men met with committees in CIO and AFL plants quite often, more copies were wanted. Thus a "Labor Newsletter" was issued monthly by the Cleveland Branch, digesting new angles in labor law, and giv-

ing tips what could be done about it. It got about
a two thousand circulation chiefly among shop
committee members of different unions around the
country, and tended to make them much less dependent upon their International and its representatives for advice. It was an IWW bid to build
more organized self-reliance at shop level, rather
than to recruit members.

The IWW was much concerned with the developing pattern of unionism and alarmed at its tolerance
of government trespass and its solicitation of such
intervention. During the manpower freeze the Industrial Worker ridiculed the Statements of Avail-
ability required for a change of jobs as "Certificates
of Manumission." (In non-IWW shops they were
frequently obtained by wearing a large IWW button to work.) When Sewell Avery was carried out
of Montgomery Ward offices, the Industrial Worker
did not join in the general glee of the labor press,
but pointed out that it was part of the drift to give
unions the status of public institutions, and thus
deprive them of their rights as voluntary associa-
tions. The fate of the Roman guilds under like circumstances was pointed out. The growth of fringe
benefits under the wage freeze was noted also as a
means of tying workers to one employer, generating
a new industrial serfdom with virtual adscription
to the job, as our ancestors had been adscripted to
the soil. (For this reason it approved any such effort
as that of UAW in Toledo to pool pension funds on
an area basis.) The IWW was probably the only
union to welcome the U.S. Supreme Court decision
in the Elgin Joliet and Eastern Railway case. Employees whose claims for premium pay had been
sacrificed by the Brotherhoods in a general settlement of many grievances had gone to court as individuals and won their case; the company defense
was that it had settled these claims with the Brotherhoods. The top court decision was that the Brotherhoods were free to contract for more than the
worker could claim, but not for less than he could

claim as a contractual right from his employer. The IWW thought this a good one-way valve protection against the frequent complaints of "being sold down the river," but CIO and AFL sought a re-hearing on the ground that this upset all their bargaining functions; the decision was re-affirmed but with the additional dodge added that if application for membership forms contained an agreement to accept the settlements the International made, the workers signing these applications could not avail themselves of this decision. The IWW urged its members in other unions to resist the adoption of this dodge. When the Supreme Court ruled that the UMWA must not even by beck or nod approve a strike, the IWW press said this decision offered up the workingclass to the employing class on the terms of a forced sale, and observed that this, like all anti-labor decisions, was premised on the extensive "rights" given to unions, confirming Gompers' dictum that when the government gives, it can take away, and take away even more than it has given.

Though the 1946 General Convention was expected to provide a collision over contract policy, it turned out quite amicably. It was settled there that "No agreement made by any part of the IWW shall provide for a check-off of union dues by the employer, or obligate the members of the union to do work that would aid in breaking any strike." The opposition to the check-off was stated in another resolution: "It transfers to management an important function of the union. It takes from the hands of the dues payers their control over their own organization. It tends to make union officials more concerned with the good will of the company than with the good will of the members." On the developing cold war it took this position: "That we look upon the Communist Party and its fledglings as a major menace to the working class, and that the interests of world peace can best be served by labor movements that clearly represent the interests of labor and not the interests of any political state; and that we consider that the foolishness of the communists can best be exposed by assuring them complete civil liberty."

Though the Cleveland branch was the largest local organization of the IWW it was not so important as a financial prop as it was as evidence that the IWW ideals of on-the-job militancy and industrial solidarity could actually work. In this way it contributed appreciably to the growing influence of the IWW in early post-war years. With a stoppage that the IWW insisted was a lockout at the Jones & Laughlin barrel plant in 1946 and negotiations in other plants during these reconversion days, it kept rates at least "ahead of the neighbors." It encouraged the formation of inter-union bodies, such as stove worker councils, and copper and brass councils, and participated in them actively. In 1946 it organized the Schrimer-Dornbirer pump company; was sued under the War Labor Disputes Act for striking, but won a 45 cents boost and dismissal of the suit. In February 1950 it organized the Coleman-Peterson wire plant, but in November of that year the entire branch withdrew from the IWW over the Taft-Hartley affidavit issue.

This loss of its largest local organization is best understood from a consideration of IWW propaganda through this period and the reaction to it in various quarters. The IWW felt that the labor movement was veering in a disastrous direction, growing into a big business of labor brokerage, suppressing the organized self-reliance that is the yeast of unionism, and becoming increasingly a pawn of government in both internal and world relations. The Industrial Worker during this time pointed to many evidences of the inadequacy of this large labor movement: Since a strike is most readily won when supplies of material and orders for finished products are both large, strikes got in each other's road for lack of coordination; for example creating a steel shortage reduces incentive to

settle with auto workers. It was plain top management manuevered the timing of bargaining to set
a pattern for all with the union in the weakest
bargaining position—often weakened by attacks
from other unions in labor's reflection of the cold
war. If there were to be patterns for all, there
should either be a union for all, or means of joint
strategy judiciously selecting the order in which
different industries went to battle, and supporting
those so engaged. It was an era of shortages, and
full employment, and thus if more green paper was
given to workers, but no workers switched over
to producing the extra goods that workers wanted
to buy with their increases, the effect was simply
to offer more green paper for the same quantity of
goods. The IWW pointed out that a wage demand
if stated in physical terms is a demand that either
unemployed workers be hired to produce these
extra goods, or that employed workers be allocated
to their production. It urged therefore that a coordinated labor movement, maintaining full employment, would find it necessary to bargain for
increases in these terms demanding a voice in the
allocation of resources and the decision what is to
be produced. These IWW arguments were frequently reflected in other labor papers, for example
as "economic union" versus "organic union" by the
AFL Butcher Workman.[7]

This painful lack of co-ordination was plainest
in the acceptance of the Taft-Hartley Act which
all unions denounced. The IWW objected to the
act chiefly on the grounds that it initiated a system
of unionism by permit, such that the terms of permit
could be made into terms that guaranteed harm-
less and useless unions (as recent developments in
South Africa could prove); that it is up to unions
to keep free from political domination, not a job
for the politicians themselves; that the ban on sympathetic strikes and secondary boycotts, constituted
an order to scab. Otherwise the act provided much
amusement for the IWW, particularly the prospects,

when an employer did not want to deal with the union, of arranging for each individual worker to insist upon processing the collective grievance on company time, though it might take days and weeks to do so. The IWW held that all that was necessary to defeat Taft-Hartley was for no union to sign its affivadits or seek NLRB service under its terms. This was the general sentiment of the labor movement, but first the Machinists then one union after another, each claiming it needed NLRB service because some union threatening to raid it, signed up, until only the UMWA, the ITU and the IWW were outside the Taft-Hartley pale.

The IWW felt that this acceptance of Taft-Hartley was due to the decreasing democracy of the unions, and that the officers accepting it were not as actually opposed to it as they purported to be. For remedy the IWW sought to stimulate on local levels both inter-union solidarity and the demand for democracy.

A comparison of newspaper situations in Chicago and Seattle illustrates what can be done by insistence on inter-union solidarity. In Chicago when the ITU struck the newspapers, they published regularly for many months of strike from photoengravings of copy set up in Varitype. Newspaper trucks carried banners screaming: "21 Loyal AFL Unions Bring You Today's Paper." In Seattle a Labor Defense Council of active unionists, including many with IWW cards, told newspaper publishers when they made similar plans that Seattle labor would not sink to the Chicago level and the papers would be faced with the same picket lines of lumberjacks and longshoremen and other workers as won the Guild strike in the 30's. The publishers backed down. Later in 1950 in New York where there was some IWW influence among the trades involved, interunion solidarity had a similar effect. The IWW "two-card" members have been able to avert many obnoxious jurisdictional disputes and to secure local union cooperation.

The Industrial Worker devoted considerable space to supporting the contentions of local unions against the usurpations of their Internationals, as the San Francisco Machinists, the St. Louis Distribution Workers and the Roofers of Baltimore, but particularly Local 104 of the Boilermakers in Seattle, where a technical side-issue, the local paper, seemed to be an actual major concern. The issue was over whether the local could set its own salaries, technically, but actually the entire issue of union democracy was involved. Eventually the courts gave decisions substantially the same as the IWW contentions. The Local was happy but the AFL was so alarmed that it had its general counsel Joseph Padway seek a reconsideration of the case as impairing the capacities of the Internationals.

It was at this time that Tom Clark put the IWW on the "subversive list" as the newspapers customarily call the entire long list of organizations compiled originally as a guide to suitability for federal employment. The long list is divided into groups which Clark described as being "mutually exclusive" and only one of these is headed "subversive." The IWW was not placed under this heading but in the category of organizations seeking to alter the form of government by unconstitutional means. The IWW at once protested this classification both on the grounds that it was contrary to fact and that it was reached without the due process of enabling the IWW to confront its accusers or present argument or evidence. It has been pointed out that this listing conflicts with judicial determinations of the IWW aims and character, both in the Fiske and Bridges cases already mentioned. The Department has repeatedly been asked, what are the grounds, what form of government is the IWW alleged to prefer, and why refuse to tell it what the government believes it does or aims to do that is unlawful; but the answer is regularly that 'Executive Order 9835 contains no authority for a hearing or a disclosing of the bases upon which a designation is made." This irresponsible attitude has increasingly alarmed many conservatives and even awakened some "gliberals" to the constitutional dangers involved. The IWW is in, the dark as to why it is listed. It notes that to list it the Department must either overrule court decisions as to its character as late as 1945, or base its case on some novel policy instituted between 1945 and May 1949 when it was listed; and it can detect no such novel policy. Opinion in IWW circles runs that if it had been listed simply on the basis of newspaper bogyman repute, it would have been listed at the beginning of this practice; thus the time of the listing leads to the suspicion that it was listed as a favor to some labor skate on whose toes the IWW had stepped in its efforts for greater union democracy. As a result the IWW has the distinction of being the only union which must pay an income tax and whose members cannot occupy federal housing projects. This, it contends, is penalizing it and its members without due process, but it has found no way to make the government obey the law.*

A New York law relating to public schools provided a sort of hearing before the Board of Regents of New York University in, July 1949. When the IWW was notified to present its case, it requested the Regents to try to have Tom Clark there to defend his listing, or at least to tell them on what grounds he had listed the IWW, so that it would have something more or less specific to answer. According to the Ithaca Journal of July 8, 1949, Clark told the Regents that of the seven or more score organizations he had listed, there were five that he "was sure were subversive." Tom Clark did not appear to defend himself. The IWW pointed out that his statement about being sure of only five after listing over 150 indicated a gross carelessness with the reputation of others and would make him an incredible witness if he appeared. (The statement was also in contradiction of Clark's own statement about the six categories being "mutually exclusive.")

*These results and list itself dissolved by 1976.

The IWW went ahead with its class-struggle program. In Cleveland it succeeded in winning two new shops. When the city observed its Sesquicentennial, the unions and management of many plants staged a big labor-management celebration in the Municipal Auditorium. The IWW was approached and agreed to participate, if it was free to put up its own display. The result was that it had the only booth with a union rather than a brotherly-love motif. Typical IWW slogans decorated the booth; it distributed its newly revised One Big Union pamphlet and a special issue of the Industrial Worker telling the history of the working class of Cleveland. (This seems to be the first instance of the labor history of a city.) In the railroad industry, somewhat neglected by the IWW since its Detroit campaigns in the mid-thirties and the extra gang efforts somewhat later, the IWW made renewed efforts in 1944, issuing a monthly Railroad Worker, widely distributed through railroad yards across the country, and again in 1948 to 1950 concentrating on Southern Pacific and Western Pacific crews with activities centered in Oakland. For this campaign it issued several leaflets, a railroad workers' pamphlet, and the Industrial Worker ran a series of articles from July 3, 1948 to November 6, giving the most complete account of the history of railroad labor so far available.

The 1950 General Convention was stormy. Indignation at Clark's listing expressed itself in a resolution that the organization should refuse to pay any income tax so as to force a court review of Clark's irresponsible action. The Cleveland members wanted the issue of signing Taft-Hartley affidavits put to referendum. They had some support from other delegates who aimed at job control unionism, but most of the delegates were opposed to signing. The NLRB had ruled that since the IWW was One Big Union, its Industrial Unions could not sign effectively unless its general officers also signed. The decision was to submit it to referendum.

Shortly after the convention, while the referendum was still being voted upon, efforts were made by other unions to raid the IWW shops in Cleveland. It was suggested that in such a raid they ask the members to vote "No Union"; but it was felt that with considerable change of personnel, some of them very friendly to organizers in the competing unions, and with the disadvantages that competitors could allege came from being on the subversive list, it would be unusually difficult to hold their union, together. The Cleveland Branch was confident that the referendum would carry to sign up, and that submission of the affidavits would require a review of the subversive listing, so what it needed was time until these events happened. It decided to withdraw from IWW until such time as the IWW branches could avail themselves of NLRB service. It took this action November 5, 1950 and adopted a lengthy resolution explaining why it felt compelled to do so, and ending up that it would pay all per capita to that date, but withhold it thereafter. Only this conclusion was transmitted to membership, and much indignation was expressed that the Cleveland branch was attempting to coerce the rest of the organization. Outside of Cleveland, the vote on the Taft-Hartley issue was two to one against signing, but if the Cleveland votes were counted, it would have swung the decision to require signing. The ballot committee contended that since they had withdrawn, their votes could not be counted. Those taking the opposite view contended that if the members were in good standing when they voted, the votes must be counted, the same as a dead man's vote would be counted. The concensus of branch minutes around the country was not to count the votes. Thus the Cleveland branch was lost. In May 1955 it joined the MESA with which the IWW and it had been friendly especially as it took a critical attitude toward capitalism, and later MESA joined CIO. With the

1955 merger of CIO and AFL this Cleveland body will have boxed the compass of collective bargaining agencies.

The loss of the Cleveland membership also checked a possible reorganization of class struggle unionism. There were a number of industries in which either Communists or fellow travelers had taken a leading hand, and had twisted unionism to suit party purposes. They had been tolerated by the rank and file, not out of sympathy for Communism, but because in most instances the alternative was to back bootlickers. The Mine, Mill and Smelter Workers offered such an example; a communist hard-rock miner is a rare bird indeed, but even such a hostile compilation of the evidence as Jensen's "Nonferrous Metal Industry Unionism 1932-1954" makes it plain that the metal miners choice was militancy and progressive policies associated with the Moscow-tainted candidates, or a meekness that spelled disaster. In the United Electrical Workers and various other unions, this situation existed either in locals or generally. The IWW had been building increasing contact in such unions with active members who wanted a militant, anti-capitalist program, free from Communist or other political domination. Their pending ouster from CIO made them consider new organizational possibilities. Many such delegates to the ousting CIO Convention in Cleveland discussed possiblities with IWW members there, and a considerable correspondence was developing at the time that the Cleveland branch felt it necessary to secure access to NLRB. All plans to rescue these militants from the communists were voided by the IWW decision not to count the Cleveland ballot.

Since that time the IWW has had to confine its efforts substantially to local instances of promoting inter-union solidarity and its educational work. The latter is no small chore. Its general arguments have been indicated already. A resolution adopted at its 1950 convention shows its slant on the major current world problems: 'Kremlinism is a social tendency, an institutional development . . . it cannot be shot with bullets or devastated with A-bombs. Reliance on these inappropriate means has permitted Kremlinism to stretch from where it engulfed only a sixth of the world's population to where it now engulfs a third. . . . It grows only because the labor movement of the rest of the world is not effectively serving the interests and needs of labor. This is the indispensble condition for the growth of Kremlinism. The only escape from it is for the labor movement to act independently of governments and capitalists and proceed to serve the interests of labor. To do so it must advance to a social system in which essential production, is carried on for use under the direction of organized labor, for the good of mankind. Doing this will stop Kremlin expansion. Further it will topple Kremlinism in the areas it has already engulfed."

The occasional picket lines of the fifties have been joint protests with other groups as at Spanish consulates in New York and Chicago, or the "Third Camp" poster walk in the Chicago loop during the Christmas rush of 1953. There leaflets consistent with foregoing resolution were passed out to the crowds while posters proclaimed "Against Both War Camps" or "Capitalism — No! — Stalinism — Never ! !" The protest picketing that attracted most attention however was that at the New Republic in April 1948. Its January 6th issue had carried a piece by Wallace Stegner depicting Joe Hill as a stick-up man. The Friends of Joe Hill formed and asked that corrective information be published; the picket line won the point. The committee engaged in extensive research and wrote too lengthy a study for the magazine; the New Republic ran a synopsis of the study and the whole document was published in the Industrial Worker for Nov. 13, 1948.

Under the circumstances it has focused its attention on maintaining its own press and occasional leafleteering. Its most noted columnist T-Bone Slim (Matt Valentine Huhta, an Ashtabula Finn) died in October 1942. Another columnist, John Forbes, was put in the penitentiary for refusing to register, but he kept up his column of satiric verse from behind bars. His conviction was protested even by an American Legion group as he was a veteran, not subject to draft, but he could not square his conscience and concede the right of the politicians to register him. Of current union issues the Industrial Worker had been particularly concerned with the longshore situation on the New York waterfront, and has not been without influence in it.

The IWW observed its 50th aniversary with its 1955 General Convention, representative of a scattered membership chiefly along Atlantic, Gulf and West Coasts. It was the first convention since 1950, and the first since the early thirties which the "no contract, dyed-in-the-wool" Wobs completely dominated; the few who disagreed with their views felt that to bring up any such proposal as signing Taft-Hartley affidavits, would only constitute a futile gesture, and provoke disunity where unity was necessary for survival. Thus it was a harmonious gathering, and a remarkable one as a bridge across history: one delegate could readily recall the depression of 1893, or compare the difficulties currently faced by the IWW with those encountered by the Knights of Labor about that time; the convention installed as editor of its official organ, a spry octogenarian, C. E. Payne, who had edited that paper in earlier years and had attended the first convention in 1905. These delegates had no idea of "giving up the ghost." They had read premature obituaries of the IWW as long as they could remember—some as early as July 1906. They knew that the IWW had the stamina not only to withstand militia, prisons and plain plug-uglies, but what is harder: fond hopes shattered, sudden reverses, and repeated losses of substantial memberships. The IWW had been near to extinction and pronounced dead many times before, but had always come to life again. Why give up in a world that plainly needed the sort of unionism the IWW had been championing these fifty years?

Accordingly the 1955 Convention attended to routine chores, passed a resolution clarifying its concept of revolutionary unionism, another aimed at the age-group blacklist confronting those over 45, and approved the publication of this record, on the understanding that it be not the history of the IWW, but the history of its first fifty years.

1. *Industrial Worker,* Aug. 23, 1943.

2. Bridges' account of leaving MTW was much along the line of Furuseth's attack on J. Vance Thompson. Sears decision was summarized in press at the time, most fully in San Francisco papers.

3. The *Business Week* account of IWW was reprinted with editorial comment in *Industrial Worker* on Feb. 27, 1945.

4. The maritime situation through 1946 was summarized in *Industrial Worker* of Sept. 28, 1946 and in end of year labor summary. The *Industrial Worker* of that period is an exceptionally full source of waterfront news.

5. *Industrial Worker,* July 10, 1949.

6. *Industrial Worker* carried full account of this including the document I.U. 440 submitted to NLRB—Apr. 8, 1944.

7. *Butcher Workman,* May 1950.

Work Peoples College, Duluth, 1939 summer school
for workers' children. See pages 101 and 175.

Cleveland I.U. 440 Baseball Team, 1943. See page 185.

Australian IWW leader Viola Wilkins speaking at mass meeting in Perth August or September, 1939.

General Headquarters in 1946. Left to right: Alice Westman, Walter Westman, Charles Velsek, Jennie Velsek, Fred Thompson and John Russell.

Sam Oberman and Claude Erwin, Oakland, 1950. See page 195.

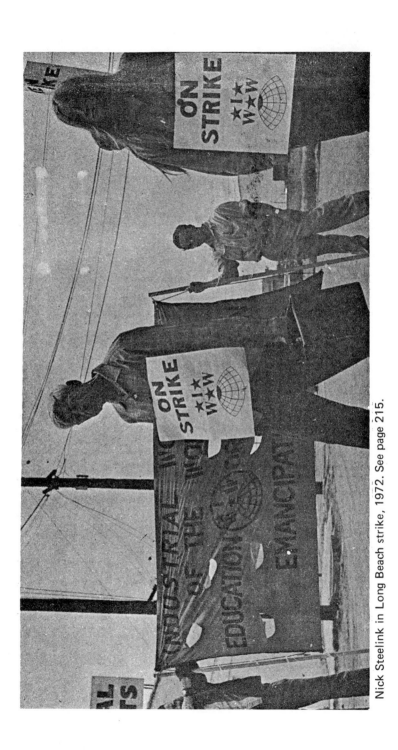

Nick Steelink in Long Beach strike, 1972. See page 215.

XIV. The IWW 1955-1975

by Patrick Murfin

During the last half of the fifth decade of this century the IWW experienced its lowest point in membership. According to Leland Robinson's study of General Organization financial statements, membership declined through most of the Fifties until 1961 when he counted only 115 fully dues-paid members. This estimate may be a bit low due to the method of computation—dividing the total dues stamps reported sold in the year by 12 to reach an average—but it sums up the condition of the organization during most of those years. Death had thinned the ranks of those active in early years and efforts to recruit younger workers were met by minimal success.

Even during this bleak period, however, there were the early signs of the resurgence to come in the Sixties. In 1957, Chuck Doehrer, the young editor of the *Industrial Worker,* was instrumental in launching a "Chicago Committee for a Young Workers' Union" with little success. The December 8, 1958 issue of the *Industrial Worker* carried the following report on activities undertaken by the New York branch by Alan Graham: peace marches in New York and Washington partially organized by IWW members, picketing of the Russian embassy to protest the execution of Hungarian workers, picketing of the French tourist agency in protest of the Algerian War, and joining with the Congress of Racial Equality to protest racist hiring practices by the airlines. In addition, Graham reported that the branch had distributed thousands of pieces of IWW literature "at home, factories and street corners throughout New York." A number of young members had been recruited in that year in New York. Most were members of the Libertarian League, a discussion and propaganda group which included some old time IWWs like Sam (Wiener) Dolgoff who encouraged many of the League's student or student-age members to join. A few others came from the extreme left of the Socialist Party's Young People's Socialist League. Some were previously unaffiliated but identified with the then flourishing Beat culture. Whatever their backgrounds the new members threw themselves into activity with genuine enthusiasm.

Pleased with the level of involvement they had been able to sustain in 1958, the Branch decided to undertake an ambitious organizing project in 1959. The target was to be the city's restaurant employment agencies, which were then charging fees of $25 to $40 for jobs that often paid below the minimum wage. The selection of employment agencies was more than just an echo of the famous "job shark" battles of the Pacific Northwest decades earlier; it was a reiteration of the IWW's consistent commitment to workers at the very lowest levels of society—the workers ignored by the prosperous business unions.

In May, a well-coordinated campaign began with picketing of the employment agencies and a call for a boycott. As an alternative to the job shark system, the Branch tried to organize its own hiring hall and got agreements from some restaurants to hire only from the hall.

In the June General Organization Bulletin a member of the boycott committee reported that two months of picketing had been effective despite continued harassment by police and by thugs hired by the agencies and the intimidation of the workers. Over 300,000 leaflets had been passed out and the writer estimated that he had personally spoken to more than 3,000 people. Forty restaurant workers had already taken out cards and hundreds of others supported the drive. Special educational and social events were held for the new and potential members to better acquaint them with the aims and structures of the union. Workers who filled out cards requesting information were receiving home visitations by members of the boycott committee.

Interest in the IWW in the New York area as a result of publicity about the restaurant drive produced an unexpected request for the branch to help organize greenhouse workers on Long Island. New York members did lend a hand and one Suffolk County greenhouse was apparently organized in August of 1959 with plans being laid to contact others.

But by September the New York restaurant drive was sputtering. Continued police harassment of pickets and intimidation of workers had taken its toll. Although the union had developed a core of support in the industry, additional recruits were no longer lining up. The hiring hall faced legal difficulties due to licensing laws and failed to come up with enough jobs. Workers not already committed were reluctant to take a chance that there would be jobs for them through the IWW.

The eventual failure of the restaurant drive was a bitter experience for the branch. Members had put an enormous amount of energy into the project. Disappointment caused branch activity to fall off dramatically and contact was lost with the greenhouse workers. Membership again began to drop off in New York. But most members of the boycott committee stayed with the union and some would be at the center of resurgent activities in the 1960s.

Branches in the San Francisco Bay area had also shown some activity in the late Fifties. Students from the University of California at Berkeley and other young people had been attracted to educationals and socials offered by the Oakland Branch at their hall. Activity in the area was further sparked when several of the young veterans of the New York campaign moved to the area in 1959. Although the Oakland hall was closed in 1961 because local members had come to view it as more a drain on resources than a serviceable facility, the branch remained active and there were enough additional members across the bay to charter a new San Francisco Branch. With two active branches on the bay, membership began to grow steadily until by 1965 Bay area membership comprised a healthy majority of the total IWW dues-paying members.

Initial IWW activity in the area was mostly educational as members tried to spread the One Big Union idea. Besides much leafletting, members were very active in the still infant peace movement. In December 1959 members protesting the construction of missile launching pads at Vandenberg Air Force base were blasted with fire hoses. On Hiroshima Day, Wobblies picketed the Atomic Energy Commission in Berkeley.

The new Bay area members were also interested in trying to define what sort of role a revolutionary labor union could play in a rapidly changing society. With membership concentrated in one of the early crucibles of the movement of the Sixties, the local branches were naturally influenced by events around them and in turn influenced events. As had been the case earlier in New York, there was a close relationship between IWW members and groups on the political and anti-political libertarian left. Several recruits came from the Libertarian Tendency (a caucus) of the Young People's Socialist League. One of the results of this was that activity of the two branches was often a somewhat incongruous combination of traditional IWW labor concerns and early counter cultural fights. Along with such traditional activities as leafletting unemployment offices, street meetings, and attempting to organize craft-divided railroad workers, branch members organized a poets' union with well-known members like Alan Ginsberg. They also planted a "hunger garden" on unused redevelopment land and became directly involved in student activity for the first time.

In 1963 the IWW began to leaflet campuses. Activity centered on the University of California at Berkeley, which had already firmly established a reputation as a radical campus. Early leaflets urged students to look upon revolutionary industrial unionism as an outlet for a vague militancy that often, in the words of one leaflet, ". . . is twirled around cans of cheap beer at 'discussion groups'." To this rather altruistic call for student support for a radical labor movement was quickly added a call for students to use union forms and tactics to better their own lives. Out of this grew a more formalized notion of "student syndicalism," which aroused considerable interest on campuses and through which the IWW influenced significantly the emerging student movement. When the Berkeley Free

Speech Fight erupted in September of 1964, it was heavily influenced by the general IWW notion of direct action and by the example fo the IWW free speech fights of the teens and Twenties. IWW members were actively involved in the fight.

Despite this the Bay area members still thought of the organization as a union primarily concerned with job conditions. In October of 1964, the San Francisco Branch organized and took out on strike the workers at a popular "beat" coffee house, Cedar Alley. Despite considerable community support, the owner was intransigent and there were arrests on the line. The strike dragged on until the owner filed for bankruptcy and closed the place in mid-1965.

As the earlier failure in New York did, the Cedar Alley incident was a bitter and frustrating experience for the members involved. Some members believed they had not received enough support from General Headquarters in Chicago, especially in regard to court and defense costs. Resentment broke out in fighting over issues not directly related to the strike.

Feathers had been ruffled even before the strike over a snafu in issuing a new edition of the IWW songbook. Young Bay area members of the General Executive Board, including the Chairperson of the Board, had issued a General Organization Bulletin on their own authority that was highly critical of Secretary-Treasurer Walter Westman, who had held that post for the better part of twenty years. Older members regarded the special GOB as the illegal product of a "rump" session of the board and came strongly to Westman's defense. Unwilling to stir up a possible divisive organizational controversy, Westman declined to stand for re-election.

In the fall balloting, Robert Rush of Berkeley was the only serious candidate on the ballot and most Californians assumed he would win the General Secretary's position. Older members countered the Rush candidacy with a write-in campaign for Carl Keller, editor of the *Industrial Worker.* Keller won the contested election, but Bay area members complained that some of their ballots had been ruled ineligible by the ballot committee for the relatively minor infraction of not having paid one or more press assessments.

This episode represented the first and last time the organization divided along issues that could be interpreted as "old vs. young." It might have caused a disastrous split, but most Bay area members, including Rush, remained active in the organization. Many ruffled feathers were smoothed by Keller's diplomatic handling of his new job. On the whole, despite some differences, younger members had tremendous respect for the seasoned labor veterans like Keller and Westman and they in turn were eager for younger members to join and take an active role in the organization.

Meanwhile the Chicago Branch itself was becoming more active and from 1964 on rapidly picked up new members. Much of this early activity centered at Roosevelt University which, unlike the University of California, was a commuter college heavily attended by working class students. An IWW "club" was formed there to gain access to University meeting rooms and a series of educational meetings there attracted good-sized audiences and worried the administration. When anarcho-pacifist poet Joffre Stewart (not an IWW member) was invited to address one of these meetings, he burned a United States flag and the club was outlawed on campus. A brief free speech campaign ensued.

But out of the Roosevelt meetings and Branch peace activity came a committed core of members. Again there were some who had been attracted from the left of YPSL while others were influenced by the Surrealists. These new members helped put out a mimeographed branch magazine, *Rebel Worker,* which contained a mixture of classic IWW reprints, articles on the contemporary meaning of the union and surrealist illustrations. Most of these young members were more interested in job than campus organizing activity and in 1964 launched two ambitious organizing projects.

The branch decided to organize a union of the unemployed in Chicago. Leaflets, *Industrial Workers* and *Rebel Workers* were regularly distributed to unemployment offices. Outdoor and indoor public meetings were held. The project at first looked encouraging. Then the Students for a Democratic Society (SDS), financed and supplied the organizers to a pilot community organizing project, Jobs or Income Now (JOIN), in the Uptown area where the branch had also concentrated its efforts. With neither full-time organizers nor much money the IWW effort was soon eclipsed by JOIN.

Many of the older members of the Chicago Branch had been active in the IWW agricultural drives of earlier years. They looked upon migrant farm workers as the last remaining part of the IWW's traditionally mobile constituency and believed such activity to be the most natural starting point for a resurgence of IWW activity. On their urging younger members planned a drive in the Michigan berry fields. Enthusiastic young members were able to organize a strike at Hodgman's Blueberry Farm in the summer of 1964. The issue was largely living conditions in the camps. A major demand called for installation of clean shower baths. Employer intimidation caused some workers to abandon the strike but a picket was kept up. Eventually enough scabs were brought in to harvest the crop and the strike was broken. But the union did have a significant effect in that its presence in the field brought wage increases in the area and resulted in cleaner camps in some instances.

In 1965 and '66 the Chicago Branch responded to appeals from fellow workers in the Yakima Valley to send organizers for the apple harvest season. In those years a small team of Chicago members joined local delegate George Underwood in the persistent missionary effort he and other local members had been putting in for years. They focused on practical issues like the dimension of boxes, the unit by which pickers were paid. Their activity no doubt helped stop the cheating that had been done in this way. A few scattered job actions resulted from this activity, but no long-run inroads were made.

Although membership was still concentrated in the three centers of New York, Chicago and the Bay area, membership was on the upswing in a half dozen other places in the mid-Sixties. More and more young people became attracted to the IWW because of its tradition of direct action, its libertarian stance and its long-standing anti-war position. In 1967, for instance, the whole of the Boston Resistance, one of the first organized anti-draft groups, joined the IWW and became the nucleus of the newly-chartered Boston Branch.

In 1967 the Union voted in referendum for the first time to allow students not currently employed to join the IWW's Education Workers Industrial Union 620. The referendum that year endorsed the convention view that students should be considered as apprentices for the occupations they expected to fill. They became eligible to join IU 620 along with wage workers in the educational industry. This gave rise to campus-based branches and groups. The first of these to exceed a hundred members was formed at the University of Waterloo, Ontario, Canada.

The Waterloo branch formed quickly in 1968 and came to exert a large measure of student control over that institution. Waterloo members, impressed by the student-worker alliances in France in May 1968, also did extensive strike support work in Ontario. Their activity began the revival of the IWW in eastern Canada.

Other campus branches like those at Madison, Wisconsin and Ann Arbor, Michigan were soon in operation. Campus branches became involved in a variety of activities. Besides presenting educational programs and conducting general recruiting activity, they often came to the support of local labor struggles. They took the demand for student and worker control of the institutions into the demonstrations and occupations that marked that peak of the student movement. IWW members also were regular contributors to the student and underground press. Several student branches spawned print cooperatives, as well as housing and buying cooperatives.

The emerging counter-culture had given birth to small workers' cooperatives not only in university towns, but in many cities in the United States and Canada. Most of these shops were organized on a shoestring to provide printing facilities for the peace and related movements or to provide some other service at a low cost by eliminating the profit motivation of conventional business. Many were organized collectively with all workers sharing in the decision-making process and dividing the revenues equally among themselves. Workers in these shops were naturally drawn to the IWW. The union began chartering such shops as job shops on the grounds that their experiments with worker self-management constituted an attempt to "build the new society in the shell of the old." Most of these shops came under Printing and Publishing Workers Industrial Union 450, but others engaged in construction, food distribution and other activities. By 1970 there were more than two dozen such shops in the IWW. The IWW union label had become a fameral movement literature circulated in North America. IWW forbids use of its label to undermine union conditions.

Some of the 440 shops came under attack for their activities. The French language *La Presse Populaire du Montreal* was shut down by a raid of police and the army during the Federal occupation of Quebec under the War Measures Act in October 1970. One member was arrested, denied due process for one month along with 500 others suspected of supporting the French Separatist FLQ. Other shops suffered lesser degrees of harassment.

In 1967 and '68 the IWW began its period of rapid growth. In part the organization was the beneficiary of the rising tide of radicalism among the young and rapidly expanding peace movement. But more directly, as Leland Robinson pointed out in his study, the union reaped the harvest of the dismemberment of the SDS. Like the IWW, SDS had drawn large numbers from the Libertarian Tendency of YPSL. Through the mid-Sixties there was in fact a considerable overlap of membership between IWW and SDS. At some schools virtually the entire membership was IWW or anarchist allied with the union. IWW members were delegates to the SDS conventions of 1967, '68 and the disastrous '69 gathering. They played a leading role in the large libertarian caucuses at these meetings.

In 1969 the three authoritarian factions of SDS—Progressive Labor, Weatherman, and Revolutionary Youth Movement—plotted to gain control of the national organization and each packed the convention with as many of their adherents as possible. Outnumbered on the convention floor if not in overall membership, the libertarian caucus gathered at the IWW hall in Chicago during the convention. But there was little they could do to keep the SDS from tearing itself apart. With the majority of the membership outside the three contesting authoritarian factions, SDS promptly collapsed on most campuses. That left only the IWW representing libertarian labor action on the campuses and former SDSers flocked to the organization. The general trend toward authoritarianism on the left also affected many who were not students. As a result, according to Robinson's figures, IWW membership grew 28% in 1968 and 44% in '69.

Interestingly enough, many of these new members were instrumental in turning the union away from campus activity and towards on-the-job and community work. Although general recruitment continued on campuses through speaking tours by veteran IWW soapboxer Frank Cedervall, the thrust became recruiting people willing to bring the union to the job. Even actions on campuses became directed at job conditions. Typical of these was an IU 620 strike of part-time workers at the University of Wisconsin at Milwaukee in 1972.

But by 1975 students made up a small minority of members in the IWW, although many who joined as students in the late Sixties and early Seventies remained active as members on the job.

IWW branches became involved in community affairs both because the branches tended to include members of community service cooperatives such as the print shops and newspapers and because many of the new members had come from SDS community organizing backgrounds. The IWW experience in San Diego in 1970–71 is an example.

The branch in San Diego began when street vendors

of the local radical newspaper, *Street Journal,* began organizing because they felt they were being unfairly treated by the staff of the paper and because they were being regularly harassed and jailed by the San Diego police. A major issue was a *Street Journal* rule that restricted vendors from selling other papers, but the IWW members also demanded a voice in the editorial policy of the paper. This demand for self-management first got them a page or two per issue. When some of the staff members also joined the union, the job shop assumed editorial control of the paper. Half of the paper was in English under the name *Street Journal,* the other half in Spanish under the name *El Bario.*

Fighting the police and the strong reactionary element in navy-dominated San Diego, however, proved more difficult. Vendors continued to be arrested on petty charges. Several were assaulted and their papers destroyed. The Branch then called for and conducted a free speech campaign with the support of more than a dozen community organizations. Repression mounted. A house occupied by IWW members was firebombed twice and one young woman member was shot in the arm through a window of the house.

In 1971 IWW member Ricardo Gonsalves was indicted with two members of the Chicano Brown Beret organization on charges of criminal syndicalism. They were accused of printing a diagram of a molotov cocktail on the cover of *El Bario* despite evidence that the diagram was planted by Jesus Lopez, a police undercover agent. The charges stood against the men who became known as "Los Tres de San Diego."

Criminal Syndicalism was the law under which hundreds of IWW members were sentenced to prison in the 1920s, but had laid largely unused for almost 40 years. Defense funds for "Los Tres" were raised through the pages of the *Industrial Worker* and the General Organization Bulletin. The charges were finally dropped after another case involving criminal syndicalism in Sacramento resulted in the law being declared unconstitutional.

It was in Chicago where IWW community participation reached its peak in 1969–70. In December, 1968 the Chicago Branch, demoralized by the futile efforts at agricultural organizing, failed for the third consecutive month to come up with the required quorum of seven members to conduct business. By August 1969, however, there was standing room only at the regular business meeting at headquarters on North Halsted Street. In between those two meetings the Chicago Branch rapidly absorbed many members disgruntled by the authoritarian left. It had also benefited from an accident of geography—the Halsted Hall, occupied by the IWW for almost 40 years, just happened to be in the center of the Lincoln Park neighborhood which had become a center of radical community activity in Chicago. Urban renewal, which was tearing out enormous swaths of the old working class neighborhood, was the rallying issue which brought disparate segments of the community together. Several IWW members had been working with the Young Lords, originally a Puerto Rican street gang which had become politicized by the urban renewal effort. The Young Lords, with support from Lionel Bottari and other IWW members, had succeeded in stopping the widespread gang wars that had plagued the area in previous years. This helped unite neighborhood opposition to the city's urban renewal plans.

Up until August of 1969, anti-urban renewal efforts had largely been confined to picketing, street demonstrations, leafletting and attempts to get the floor at planning agency meetings. Then the city announced it was turning over a vacant parcel of land in the middle of the Puerto Rican community to developers who planned to erect an exclusive tennis club. Outraged, the Chicago branch joined the Young Lords and other community groups in taking over the land and declaring it "Chicago Peoples' Park." Hundreds of community residents turned out to begin the task of turning the rubble-strewn lot into a real park with grass and playground equipment.

IWW members arranged to get the use of a bulldozer and obtained eight truckloads of top soil. Other members constructed creatively designed playground equipment. In the end, faced with massive opposition, the city abandoned the tennis court plans and transferred the land to a nearby grade school for "recreational use" but leaving actual control of the park to the community. The success of the Peoples' Park project also put an end to urban renewal by bulldozer in Lincoln Park.

In 1971 the Branch moved with the General Administration from the Halsted Street address to an old bowling alley on nearby Lincoln Ave. Soon dozens of organizations were holding fund raising events in the large hall. This tied the branch and the community closer together. As in San Diego, street vendors of the radical paper *Seed* joined the IWW and the collective staff soon followed suit. Workers at a radical community center, "Alice's Revisited," also joined as did workers from a number of stores and restaurants in the Lincoln Avenue community. There were also volunteer workers at community medical clinics, food cooperatives, print shops and radical book stores. In the absence of an umbrella community organization, IWW membership became one of the bonds that held these people together. The branch was frequently called upon to mediate disputes within the community. This led to holding weekly community meetings at the hall that were often attended by more than two hundred people and were run town-meeting style.

The Chicago Branch did not, however, ignore job organizing. In 1971, warehouse workers at Hip Products, a division of Mafia-dominated Arts and Leisure Corporation, came into the union. The young men involved had been working in classic sweatshop conditions. When the company refused to negotiate and moved its warehouse to a ghetto area to avoid dealing with their troublesome workers, a strike was called. The strike began during the worst sub-zero cold snap in Chicago for years. Pickets were maintained for weeks and members tried to recruit the young jobless blacks that the boss was using for strike breakers. Sympathetic office workers provided the addresses of retail outlets of Hip Products merchandise and branches in several cities picketed those stores in support of the strikers. Striking workers were fired and the IWW filed charges of unfair labor practices with the National Labor Relations Board. The charges were upheld and the company was forced to pay a cash settlement to the workers: It refused to rehire some of the workers, however, and the rest refused to go back without them. The strike financially crippled Hip Products which reported a quarter of a million dollar loss in 1971 after several years of large profits. The following year the company was dissolved by its parent.

In the fall of 1971 the employees at the Three Penny Cinema came to the branch and asked to affiliate. At first the boss refused to negotiate and a strike was called. Virtually no one crossed the IWW picket lines and the strike was quickly won. For the first time since Cleveland the IWW had a shop under contract.

The following spring the owner leased the theater to a pair of exhibitors who refused to honor the IWW contract. When they began firing IWW members, a second strike was called. This dragged out for three months in the summer of 1972. The lessees eventually skipped town and the original owner refused to honor the contract. Again a cash settlement and reinstatement were won, but the theater changed its policy to show pornographic films and the workers did not take their jobs back.

Since the early Seventies the IWW has concentrated on job organizing. Members continue to be involved in certain community activities, such as tenants' unions in Massachusetts, but most activity has been concentrated on the job. Job activity did not confine itself to established branches. Silver miners in Ward, Colorado established a job branch in 1971. The same year a small group of members opened a hall in a working class district in Sioux City, Iowa and began organizing activities. This promising drive was scuttled when Progressive Labor Party sympathizers in the local group substituted PL for IWW literature at factory gates, which killed off growing support.

In April of 1972, Mark Warrior and other members organized a construction job crew in Gastown, Vancouver. The British Columbia provincial Labour Board refused to certify the IWW as a union under provincial law and the job shop was lost by June. The Vancouver activity did spark a rapid growth in IWW membership in Western Canada.

Workers at Park International and International Wood Products, related companies with plants in Long Beach, California voted unanimously to join the IWW in the spring of 1972. The workers, angry over conditions and pay, went out on strike within three days of joining the union. The strike rallied support from the organization. Branches, groups and individual members responded generously to calls to build a strike fund. Three Chicago members agreed to go to Long Beach to help with the strike, but could not arrive on the scene until almost two weeks into the strike. After a few weeks and some picket line arrests the workers voted to return to the shops until an NLRB representation election could be held. Scabs hired during the strike were allowed to vote and ordinary turnover cost the union enough sure votes that the IWW lost the election when it was held.

Shortly after the end of the Long Beach strike, the Portland Branch requested assistance for their on-going organizing activities. The three members who had gone to Long Beach agreed to go to Portland. A drive, had been going on at a wooden box factory for more than a year. Even though that drive proved unsuccessful, local members felt they had learned enough to form an organizing team with the new arrivals. They chose Winter Products, a firm employing about 200 workers engaged in brass plating household hardware. In September and October 1972 seven IWWs got jobs at the plant and began the organizing attempt. They steadily gained supporters throughout the plant. But they may have moved too quickly and exposed themselves too early. Rumors of organizing attempts had reached the boss's ears and he found excuses to fire the IWW "trouble makers." The second week in November the organizers found themselves on the outside looking in and the other workers badly frightened.

Because the IWW had filed unfair labor charges or

participated in National Labor Relations Board elections in a number of local instances, General Headquarters was required to file an annual report with Reporting and Disclosure section of the Department of Labor in accordance with the Landrum-Griffin Act. General Secretary-Treasurer Michael Brown routinely filed the report when it was requested in 1973. This began a serious controversy within the organization which in some ways was reminiscent of the Taft-Hartley split twenty years before. Some members felt that submitting the reporting form would amount to an agreement to abide by other obnoxious provisions of the Landrum-Griffin Act such as those that forbid the secondary boycott, the hot cargo bans, and restrictions on who can hold union office. These members came to the 1973 General Convention but failed in their attempt to get the convention to agree not to submit the forms in the future.

Feeling strongly about the issue, dissenting members got enough signatures on a referendum petition to have the question put to the general membership in referendum. A lively debate ensued in the pages of the General Organization Bulletin and at local branch meetings. The results of the referendum sustained the convention decision to continue submitting the annual reporting form.

In Portland organizing activities continued. In 1974 the Portland Branch organized the staff and parents of a day care center in a predominantly Black neighborhood. The issue was worker and community control. The union succeeded in winning several of its demands, including the dismissal of the center's director. Other Portland attempts of the period, however, were not so successful. These included attempts to organize bean harvest workers and the employees of a small hospital.

In the early Seventies the IWW conducted a number of organizing campaigns in high turnover industries. These included Shopright, a grocery store in Milwaukee in 1973; a Boston nursing home in 1975; and a number of fast food outlets over a period of time from 1973–75. Fast food drives were conducted at

Winchell's Doughnuts in Portland; McDonalds in Chicago; Kentucky Fried Chicken and Roy Rogers in State College, Pennsylvania; and Pizza Hut in Arkadelphia, Arkansas. In most of these locations local organizers had little difficulty initially organizing a majority of the workers and filing for NLRB elections. But in each case, legal maneuvering by the bosses before the NLRB meant many months of delay before the election was finally held. In Milwaukee and Pittsburg other unions also filed in the elections. Meanwhile the employers counted on regular turnover and harassment of union workers to bring in new, anti-union workers. As a result each of these elections was lost. Most IWW organizers now have learned that in small, high turnover shops it is necessary to organize the workers and demand immediate recognition without an election, if possible.

Among the more active of recent IWW organizing efforts has been Guam. Although there had been a core of members on the island since 1970, it took until 1974 to get into job activity. 1974 marked a drive among workers in the island's tour bus industry into Transportation Workers Industrial Union 540. The campaign ultimately failed, however, and no further action was taken. Valuable lessons learned were applied in an organizing drive in a related industry, which is still in progress as of this writing. The Guamanian group remains among the most ethnically mixed in the organization and includes Filipinos, Guamanians, North American whites, and workers from some of the islands in the U.S. Pacific Trust Territories.

Other branches throughout the U.S. and Canada have conducted a variety of organizing campaigns over the past two years. As an example, IWW workers in a Chicago metal and machinery plant have been carefully building strength over the past two years and at this writing are well established within the factory. This effort helped spark a Metal and Machinery Workers Industrial Union 440 organizing drive in the city which has attracted members from other parts of the U.S. to come and participate as organizers. This committee recently expanded its focus to include other

general production shops in Chicago. This and similar
activities have helped the union develop a group of
experienced organizers who can avoid earlier pitfalls.
As the depression of the Seventies closes around us,
most members are confident that the union is once
again in a position to become a force on the job,
where the IWW has always belonged. This may be a
bit the easier since on June 11, 1974 Nixon by executive order abolished the subversive list and so terminated the IWW's continuing demand to be removed
from it.

Side by side with these organizing activities, the
IWW has seen a steady rise in two-card members in recent years. The often hopeless bureaucracy of the established business unions has driven many into taking
out IWW cards. Unlike other labor-oriented radical organizations, IWW members on jobs controlled by other
unions do not usually undertake caucus style activity
aimed at seizing political power within the business
union. IWW members tend to believe that in most
instances caucus activity diverts the attention of
workers from the boss to the union bureaucrat. IWW
two-carders have generally refrained from caucus activity except where the existing bureaucracy presents
an otherwise insurmountable obstacle to job action.
Instead, two-card members have encouraged the use of
direct action on the shop floor to force the bosses to
slow down, to provide safer working conditions, and
to be responsive to workers' demands. They have encouraged the formation of shop committees which,
unlike most caucuses, can bring direct pressure on the
bosses. In general, two-card members have tried to act
as an example to their fellow workers of what class
conscious militant unionism is all about.

As the IWW has grown in the United States in recent years, it has also grown elsewhere in the world.
Canadian membership grew through most of the period. Spurred on by the activity in Western Canada and
by the establishment of a Toronto Branch, the Canadian Administration was reconstituted in 1972 with
headquarters in Vancouver, British Columbia. However in 1973 a split grew between Canadian Admini-

stration officers and members in eastern Canada. At
issue was the stress placed by the CA on Canadian nationalism and the handling of dues money. The issue
was brought before the General Convention which ordered a referendum on discontinuing national administrations. The referendum carried, resulting in the re-
signation of some Western Canadian members. Many
have since rejoined. In the place of national administrations, autonomous Regional Organizing Committees were established under the general authority of
the General Executive Board. The Board is now open
to international membership and members from Australia, Canada, Sweden, and Great Britain have served.

IWW activity continues in Canada with most
strength concentrated in Ontario and Quebec, but
with a growing membership in the western provinces.
The Toronto Branch was especially active in strike
support work, including one very bitter dispute, the
Artistic Woodwork strike, in which several IWW members were arrested in 1974. Toronto members have
also become active in international defense work. Toronto General Defense Committee Local No. 2 publishes a regular newsletter and has raised considerable
sums for both IWW members facing trial in the U.S.
and Canada and for embattled class war prisoners in
Spain, Italy, France and Germany.

Defense activity by the Toronto GDC is symbolic
of the relationship that has long existed between the
IWW and the revolutionary union movement the
world over. IWW picket lines have regularly appeared
around Spanish tourist offices in defense of the militants of the Confederacion National de Trabajo (CNT).
Likewise, branches and groups have offered support
to Portuguese workers, particularly the Conferacao
General Trajabalo (CGT) in Portugal. In the summer
of 1975, Carlos Cortez, former editor of the *Industrial Worker,* attended an international conference of
revolutionary unions sponsored by the Sveriges Arbe-
tares Central organization (SAC) in Stockholm, Sweden. These and other revolutionary unions throughout
the world share a mutual respect with the IWW. Together they are all part of an international struggle to

win more than just more money—a struggle to win true workers' self-management.

At least one IWW member has died in reactionary violence abroad. Frank Terrugi, a student member, was machinegunned to death by the Chilean fascists after the 1973 coup that overthrew the Marxist government there. Terrugi was in Chile studying worker movements when he was arrested by rightist troops. He was found machinegunned after he had been "released" from a soccer stadium-prison. A year later IWW journalist Frank Gould disappeared in the Philippines while covering the Moslem rebellion in Mindanao. At first he was presumed killed in a government attack on a rebel training camp in October of 1974, but evidence has recently emerged that he may have escaped and be in hiding on one of the remote islands.

The IWW has also grown in Sweden. For years there had been a Scandinavian administration headquartered in Stockholm which was made up mostly of retired workers who had returned to their homeland from the United States. Then in 1971 a job branch was formed in the Malmö shipyards. Now branches in Malmö and Stockholm along with small groups in other towns are part of the Swedish Regional Organizing Committee. The Swedes have also established a General Defense local and were active in bringing the United Farm Workers' grape and lettuce boycotts to Sweden, with continued cooperation of Swedish union SAC.

British members formed a Regional Organizing Committee in 1973 which was reformed into the British Section in 1975. The British Section, with membership concentrated in the heavily industrialized Northwest of England, now publishes its own magazine, *The Industrial Unionist,* and operates a workers' center in Oldham, Lancashire.

That brings us pretty much up to date. Twenty years after the 1955 convention the IWW is both larger and more active than there was any reasonable chance to hope. The IWW not only lives, it is beginning to thrive in the energy, dedication, and activity of its membership. We look forward to the next 70 years with enthusiasm

SOURCES FOR IWW HISTORY

In 1955 when this book was first published there was little reading on the IWW readily available. The books by Brissenden, by Dowell and by Gambs cited in it were out of print. Growing interest in the IWW since then has led to their being reprinted (in 1957, 1970 and 1971 respectively) and to the publication of most of the forty articles in academic journals and seventeen books on specific aspects of the IWW listed further along as up-dated chapter notes. Several doctoral dissertations on the IWW have been written since then, its periodicals have been made available on microfilm, and its recoverable records carefully archived. Also since 1955 five general accounts of the IWW have been published, all with such extensive bibliographies and documentation that these chapter notes avoid duplication of the less readily accessible sources that they cite. These five are:

Rebel Voices, An IWW Anthology, by Joyce L. Kornbluh, University of Michigan Press, 1964, 418 pages, original edition 8 x 12, later issued as a reduced size paperback. It includes photos, cartoons, poems and articles from six decades of IWW periodicals, each chapter starting with an historical essay. It includes data on authors quoted.

Rebels of the Woods, by Robert L. Tyler, University of Oregon Books, 1967, 230 pages. Focus is on northwest lumber industry to midtwenties, but includes a general background; develops author's 1953 dissertation and articles cited in following chapter notes.

The Industrial Workers of the World, by Philip Foner, being Volume IV of his *History of the Labor Movement in USA;* International Publishers, 1966; 558 pages plus 50 pages of notes and index; covers period 1905-1916; makes extensive use of local, labor and socialist press and of AFL correspondence regarding IWW.

We Shall Be All, by Melvyn Dubofsky, Quadrangle

Books, 1969; 484 pages plus 70 pages of index and notes; 1974 paperback edition corrects earlier premature obituary of IWW. It covers period 1905-1924, omitting Philadelphia; makes extensive disclosures from National Archives and from lumber company and AFL correspondence.

The Wobblies, by Patrick Renshaw, Doubleday, 1967; 312 pages. Later paperback edition includes some corrections; translated into Italian and Japanese. Focus is on IWW as part of world syndicalist movement and has more coverage than other books of its transnational activities.

In the following chapter notes, reference will be made to these five books simply by author's name and page or chapter number. Two other general works on IWW are Irving Werstein's *Pie in the Sky* (Delacourte Press, 1969), written for a youth audience, and Joseph Conlin's collection of essays, *Bread and Roses Too.*

Archives: The chief earlier archives of IWW materials were those built up at Wisconsin Historical Society and in the Labadie Collection at University of Michigan, Ann Arbor. Most records seized by federal government in 1917 were burned July 13, 1925 on an earlier federal court order. Cornell has five boxes of IWW correspondence of the 1920's. There is an extensive largely regional collection at the university library at Thunder Bay, Ontario, and the Ministry of Labour at Ottawa has extensive microfilm and printed material. The University of Washington in Seattle has an extensive collection of documents and printed materials, and the Mark Litchman papers, some of these on Yakima strike, 1933. The Mary Gallagher papers at Bancroft Library, U. of C., Berkeley, have materials on San Pedro, 1923–1924 and on Colorado strike 1927–1928. At the Immigration History Research Center, University of Minnesota, St. Paul, files of *Il Proletario* (1899–1946) are available, and the extensive Finnish collection includes *Industrialisti* and other Finnish IWW publications and the records of Work Peoples College.

In 1965 the IWW made the Archives of Labor and Urban History at Wayne State University, Detroit, its official depository. Records from 1930 were placed there and what could be found of earlier records, including a transcript of the big Chicago trial, 1918, and an extensive collection of printed materials. Subsequent deposits have kept these archives up to date. Other holders of such material have been urged to make this collection as complete as possible, and students writing research papers on IWW using sources not readily accessible have been requested to provide copies for this collection. Since much of the material at Wayne State (as these archives will be called for brevity in these notes) exists in one copy only, access to it is restricted by archival rules to "persons with serious scholarly interest." This includes non-academic researchers, but all prospective users are told they "should write to the Archives in advance to establish their credentials for using the collection." This procedure is recommended in regard to all archives.

At the National Archives there is extensive material cited by William Preston in his *Aliens and Dissenters,* and by Joan Jensen in her *Price of Vigilance,* though and by Joan Jensen in her *Price of Vigilance,* though some of this material was withdrawn later by FBI from public accessibility. Data on disputes is mostly in Conciliation files, arranged geographically. Considerable material gathered for Commission on Industrial Relations before WWI on migratory workers but not published is available. In general government files are to be made public within 25 years, but in 1974 when IWW under that rule sought access to Department of Justice papers possibly explaining why it had been put on subversive list in 1949, it was told this information will not be made public until 2024.

Dissertations

These are some of the master theses and doctoral dissertations that have been prepared on the IWW. University Microfilm number added in some instances.

Barnes, Donald: "Ideology of the IWW," Ph.D. Hist.

Washington State 1962 (U.M. 67-06332).

Brown, Myland Rudolph: "The IWW and the Negro Worker," Ph.D., Ball State, 1968 (69-4186).

Burns, John J.: "IWW in Illinois during WW I," M.A. Hist., Western Illinois Univ., 1972.

Calvert, Jerry: "A Changing Radical Political Organization: The Wobblies Today," Ph.D., Washington State University, 1972.

Crow, John: "Ideology and Organization," M.A. Pol. Sc. Univ. of Chicago 1958.

Conlin, J.R.: "The Wobblies: A Study of IWW before WW I," Ph.D. Univ. of Wisconsin, 1966 (66-05901).

Evans, Robt. E.: "Montana's Role in Enactment of Legislation to Suppress the IWW," M.A. Univ. of Minnesota, 1964.

Faigin, Henry: "The IWW in Detroit and Michigan, 1905 to WW I," M.A. Hist., Wayne State, 1937.

Herrin, Robt. A.: "Great Lumber Strikes in Northern Idaho," M.A., Northern Illinois, 1967.

Jokinen, Walfrid: "The Finns In Minnesota," M.A. Louisiana State, 1953. "The Finns In USA: A Sociological Interpretation," Ph.D. Louisiana State, 1955.

Lynch, Patrick: "Pennsylvania Anthracite," M.A. Bloomsburg State, 1974.

McEnroe, Thomas: "IWW Theories, Organization Problems and Appeals as Revealed in *Industrial Worker,*" Ph.D., Univ. of Minnesota, 1960.

Robinson, Leland W.: "Social Movement Organizations in Decline: A Case Study of the IWW," Ph.D., Northwestern, 1974 (74-7808).

Schmidt, Dorothy B.: "Sedition in State of Washington, 1917–1919," M.A., Hist. Washington State, 1940.

Van Tine, Warren E.: "Ben Williams, Wobbly Editor," M.A. Northern Illinois 1967.

Wortman, Roy T.: "The IWW in Ohio, 1905–1950," Ph.D., University of Ohio 1972 (72-4695).

NOTE: The IWW expects to issue occasional bulletins listing new books, articles, dissertations, etc. dealing with it. It welcomes copies or notice of publication and frequently lists such information in its monthly journal.

Supplemental References Arranged by Chapter

Chapter 1. The Industrial Union Manifesto calling for the 1905 convention is the first document in Kornbluh. The most complete account of Father Haggerty is that by Robert E. Doherty in *Labor History*, Winter, 1962. *The One Big Union Monthly* of 1919-1920 is now available in Greenwood reprints and includes Harold Lord Varney's series on history of IWW. The circumstances motivating the various participants in the founding convention have so far been given only superficial study, the most extensive being Brissenden's 1913 monograph, *The Launching of the IWW*, Dubofsky, first 87 pages, and essay, "Origins of Western Working Class Radicalism" in *Labor History*, Spring, 1966.

Chapter II (1905-1908). On Boise trial see Joseph Conlin's *Big Bill Haywood and the Radical Labor Movement*, Syracuse University Press 1968, or same author in *Pacific Northwest Quarterly*, 1969, pp. 22-32; Stephen Scheinberg in *Idaho Yesterdays*, Fall 1960, shows Pres. Roosevelt had spy on Haywood defense committee.

Schenectady: paper by David Goodall filed at Wayne State details IWW as outgrowth of earlier local militance.

Goldfield: Russell Elliot in *Pacific Historical Review*, 1950, pp. ·369-384; Brissenden, *IWW*, pp. 191-212.

Bridgeport: Foner pp. 84-86 adds details from local press; Hungarian radical press of time said to have fullest account.

De Leon: Don McKee in *Labor History*, Winter 1962, and Glen Seretan in same, Spring 1973 and subsequent issues.

Spokane and IWW song cards: see memoir by Richard Brazier in *Labor History*, Winter 1968.

General Executive Board Minutes 1906 to 1910 at
Wayne State show situation following the 1906 convention and give much space to the Connolly-De Leon
dispute.

Chapter III (1909-1911). McKees Rocks: Foner, 281-
295; Dubofsky, 202-209; most complete account is by
John Ingham in *Pennsylvania Magazine of History,*
1966 (XV, pp. 353-377), who cites related investigation into charge of peonage.

Free speech fights: Kornbluh 94-104; Foner, 172-
189; Dubofsky, 173-197. Brazier wrote his recollections of the Spokane fight in *Industrial Worker,* January and February, 1967, and E.G. Flynn gives her recollections in memoirs variously published as *I Speak
My Piece* or *Rebel Girl.* On Fresno, Ted Lehman's
paper filed at Wayne State explores role of Frank
Little and his elder brother; Charles P. LeWarne published recently discovered lengthy account by E.M.
Clyde of the trip to Fresno in *Labor History,* Spring
1973; also Ronald Genini in *California Historical
Quarterly* 53 (1974) 100-128. On Aberdeen: "The
Aberdeen, Washington, Free Speech Fight of 1911–
1912" by Charles Pierce LeWarne in *Pacific Northwest Quarterly,* January 1975. Vol. 66. On San Diego:
to observe 60th anniversary, IWW branch there in
1972 reprinted as pamphlet *New York Call's* summary
of that fight; McKay's participant recollections run in
Industrial Worker July 26 to August 9, 1947. Theodore Schroeder, *Free Speech for Radicals,* Riverside,
Conn. 1916.

On IWW and Mexico: Lowell L. Blaisdell, *The Desert Revolution,* Madison, 1962; Rey Davis' series on
Magon in *Industrial Worker,* May through August,
1974.

On Foster's "boring from within," his case is stated
in Foner, 415-434. See Conlin, *Bread and Roses Too*
for critique of Foster's position.

Chapter IV (Textiles 1910-1913). Lawrence background in Donald R. Cole, *Immigrant City,* Chapel
Hill, 1963; *Readers' Guide* for period indexes many

current accounts; all the listed histories have extensive accounts, Foner, 329-350 giving most detail on the Breen dynamite affair.

Paterson: Far more has been written about this lost strike than about any of the IWW's successful union activities, one example of the quantitative distortion of IWW story by even its sympathetic historians; Foner, 351-372; Dubofsky, 263-283; Kornbluh, 197-226; Graham Adams' chapter on Paterson in his *Age of Industrial Violence* (Columbia University Press, 1966) has focus on Scott and Quinlan trials; *Art in America* for May-June 1974 has illustrated article on Paterson Pageant; Mel Most in the regional *Sunday Record* for Nov. 11, 1973 and Sept. 1, 1974, interviews participants in Paterson strike on both sides and concludes local industry was ruined as boomerang effect of employer lies about violence. The Botto home in Haledon, site for free speech, now a National landmark. The Henry McGuckin memoirs at Wayne State show effort to bring out competitive plants. Little has been written on IWW activity in other textile plants. Generally ignored IWW silk strike in Hazelton, Pa. Feb. 5 to April 2, 1913 detailed in Patrick M. Lynch's M.A. thesis, "Pennsylvania Anthracite," Bloomsburg State, 1974.

Chapter V. British Columbia strike: Foner, 228-231; Agnes Laut has good pictures but distorted account in *Illustrated Technical News,* Oct., 1912. Good footage in CBC film on Joe Hill, Other Voices series; details of strike and Hill's involvement in Louis Moreau's recollections filed at Wayne State.

Southern Lumber: James R. Green, "The Brotherhood of Timber Workers, 1910-1913," in *Past and Present* No. 50, August, 1973; Merl Reed, "IWW and Individual Freedom in Western Louisiana 1913," in *Louisiana History,* Winter 1969, and also Reed's "Lumberjacks and Longshoremen" in *Labor History,* Winter, 1972. Covington Hall's manuscript history is on file at Wayne State. Grady McWhiney's article on area socialists in *Journal of Southern History,* August 1954 gives that part of background. M.R. Brown's Ph.D.

dissertation, "The IWW and the Negro Worker" (University microfilms No. 69-4186) studies this and other situations involving blacks.

Aberdeen: McGuckin typescript at Wayne State adds much detail on Aberdeen, B.C. and Paterson.

Akron: Harold S. Roberts' *The Rubber Workers* is major printed source; Foner, 373-390; Journal, Ohio 80th General Assembly 1913. Appendix of Reports of Committee investigating Akron Rubber Industries; Roy T. Wortman, Ph.D. dissertation "The IWW in Ohio 1905-1950" (University Microfilms 72-469), pp. 23-50, also source on Toledo Wheel and other Ohio strikes; Wortman's interview with Paul Sebastyan, participant, in Labadie Collection.

Studebaker strike: Henry Faigin, "The IWW in Detroit and Michigan, 1905-1919," MA thesis, Wayne State 1937, also describes other IWW activities in area.

Wheatland Hops: Richard H. Frost, *The Mooney Case,* Stanford, 1968, describes prosecution pressure and California power structure; Kornbluh, 236-239; Foner 258-280. P.W. Eldridge "The Wheatland Hop Riot and the Ford and Suhr Case" in *Industrial and Labor Relations Forum* 10 (May 1974) 165-195.

Philadelphia: Irwin Marcus in *Negro History Bulletin,* October, 1972; Foner, 126 and article in *Journal of Negro History,* January 1970; Spero and Harris book already cited remains chief account in this important but little written-about phase of IWW history. Myland Rudolph Brown's dissertation in "IWW and the Negro Worker," University Microfilm No. 69-4186.

Chapter VI. Kornbluh, 35-64, includes survey and samples of sabotage argument from the years 1911-1917. Most extensive study is by Joseph Conlin in *Bread and Roses Too* and essays "IWW and Question of Violence" in *Wisconsin Magazine of History,* Summer 1968 and "Case of the Very American Militants" in *American West* March 1970. Marc Karson, *American Labor and Politics,* Southern Illinois University Press, 1958, pp. 150-211, gives sketch of IWW 1905-1917 in terms of ideological disputes in it and S.P., assuming it anti-parliamentary rather than non-political. Extensive treatment in Foner chapters 5, 6 and 17, and in Dubofsky, chapter 7.

Chapter VII (1914-1915). Michael S. Sideman "The Agricultural Labor Market and the Organizing Activities of the IWW 1910-1935," MS thesis, University of Illinois, 1965. Philip Taft, "IWW in the Grain Belt," in *Labor History,* Winter 1960. On Joe Hill, the definitive work is Gibbs Smith's *Joe Hill,* University of Utah Press, 1970, re-issued as Grosset & Dunlap paperback under title *Labor's Martyr, Joe Hill.* On film there is a very good CBC documentary on Joe Hill in its Other Voices series, in which Hill's songs are well sung by Don Francks, and a lengthier film directed by Bo Widerborg that IWWs found disappointing.

Chapter VIII (Events of 1916). Mesaba Range strike: Donald G. Sofchalk, "Organized Labor and the Iron Ore Miners of Minnesota, 1907-1936," in *Labor History,* Spring 1971, probes AFL abstention from organizing these miners in hopes of freedom to organize other trades, and details 1916 strike; also Neil Betten, "Iron Range Strike of 1916," in *Minnesota History,* 1968, pp. 89-94. Foner, 486-517 and Dubofsky, 319-333 include opposing views of E.G. Flynn's defense strategy. On Finnish involvement, "The Finns of Minnesota," by Walfrid Jokinen, MA thesis, Louisiana State 1953; paper by Prof. Douglas J. Ollila, "Emergence of Left Labor Radicalism among Finnish Workers on Mesaba Range, 1911-1919," copy filed at Wayne State. "Pennsylvania Anthracite: A Forgotten IWW Venture, 1906-1916," MA thesis by Patrick M. Lynch, Bloomsburg State College, 1974, 165 pages, is only detailed study of IWW in anthracite.

AWO and NPL: Agricultural references of Chapter VII, also Robt. L. Morlan, *Political Prairie Fire,* Univ. of Minnesota Press, 1955, p. 135 etc.; Joel Watne ties changed outlook to dollar wheat in "Public Opinion Toward Non-Conformists," in *North Dakota History,* Winter 1967; Charles J. Haug, "IWW in North Dakota, 1913-1917," *North Dakota Quarterly,* Winter 1971-72.

Everett: Norman H. Clark's *Milltown* (Univ. of

Washington Press, 1970) probes social history background, and his "Everett, 1916 and After," in *Pacific Northwest Quarterly*, 1966, pp. 57-64; Walker C. Smith's *The Everett Massacre*, IWW 1918; Robert Tyler, *Rebels of the Woods* (1967) and "The Everett Free Speech Fight," *Pacific Historical Quarterly*, 1954, pp. 19-30; Kornbluh, 105-126, includes contemporary and participant accounts; Dubofsky, 333-343; Foner, 518-548.

Minnesota Lumber 1916-1917: John Haynes' "Revolt of the Timberbeasts," in *Minnesota History*, Spring 1971, summarizes 1500 page typescript report by Governor's investigating committee.

Australia: Renshaw, 279-287; Ian Turner, *Sydney's Burning* (Alpha Books, Sydney, 1969) is chief account; also his *Industrial Labour and Politics*, Cambridge University Press, 1965; Bertha Walker, *Solidarity Forever!* (Melbourne, 1972), pp. 102-134; Joe Harris, *The Bitter Fight*, 1970.

Chapter IX (1917-1918). Great wartime profits provide essential background for period, noted in Nye Committee Report, Report 944, Senate, 74th Congress, 1st Session, and in Congressional debate on Chamberlain bill regarding lumber, *NYT* April 6, 1918 and June 30.

Basic study of effort to suppress IWW is William Preston's *Aliens and Dissenters* (Harvard University Press, 1963, later Harper Torchback paperback) based on study of government correspondence, etc.; p. 129 for proof IWW membership lists given Gompers for blacklist; Joan Jensen's *The Price of Vigilance*, Rand McNally, 1968, describes some of the unofficial terrorism against IWW; Eldridge F. Dowell, *History of Criminal Syndicalism Legislation*, John Hopkins 1939 and Da Capo reprint 1970 has focus on state action. Robert C. Sims, "Idaho Criminal Syndicalism Act," in *Labor History*, 1974, explores motivations and its surviving ban on slowdowns; Dorothy B. Schmidt, "Sedition in the State of Washington," MA thesis, history, Washington State College, 1940; Woodrow Whitten, "Criminal Syndicalism and the Law in California,'' *American Philosophical Transactions,* 1969, pp. 1-73.

IWW attitude toward War: Foner, 554-558; Kornbluh, 316-348; Dubofsky, 349-358; James O'Brien, "Wobblies and Draftees: the IWW's Wartime Dilemma, 1917-1918," in *Radical America,* Sept.-Oct. issue, 1967. For Rockford draft resistance, see John J. Burns, "IWW in Illinois During WWI," MA thesis, history, Western Illinois University, 1972.

Agriculture: Carl F. Reuss, "The Farm Labor Problem in Washington 1917-1918," in *Pacific Northwest Quarterly,* October 1943; Thorstein Veblen, "Using the IWW to Harvest Grain," *Journal of Political Economy,* December 1932; and agricultural references given to chapters 7 and 8.

Lumber: Tyler; Dubofsky, 358-365; Benjamin G. Rader, "The Montana Lumber Strike of 1917," in *Pacific Northwest Quarterly,* May 1967 draws on District Forester reports to acquit IWW of sabotage; Robert Herrin, "Great Lumber Strikes in Northern Idaho," MA thesis, history, Northern Illinois, 1967.

Copper: John H. Lindquist and James Fraser, "A Sociological Interpretation of the Bisbee Deportation," in *Pacific Historical Review,* November 1968; *American West,* May and November 1972, for procompany account of Bisbee and insider rejoinder; Philip Taft, in *Labor History,* Winter 1972, includes Bisbee aftermath and whitewash trials; *Arizona and the West,* Autumn 1969, Lindquist account of Jerome deportation; Arnon Gutfield, "The Speculator Disaster," in *Arizona and the West,* Spring 1969, and "Murder of Frank Little," in *Labor History,* Spring 1969, implying Anaconda used IWW to hamper AFL organizing, a notion discredited by Brissenden's evidence on rustling card in *American Economic Review,* December 1920.

Big Trials: Chicago indictment is quoted complete in *Labor History,* Fall 1970; Philip Taft's summary of the trial in issue of Winter 1972; Michael Johnson, "IWW and Wilsonian Democracy," in *Science and Society,* Summer 1964; there is out-of-print pamphlet, *The Silent Defense,* on Sacramento trial; on Wichita indictment, Clayton R. Koppes, "The Kansas Trial of the IWW, 1917–1919" in *Labor History,* Summer, 1975, and "The IWW and County Jail Reform 1915–1920" in *Kansas Historical Quarterly,* Spring 1975; the most extensive research on Wichita case is by Bruce White for dissertation still in preparation (1976) at Sterling College, Kansas.

Chapter X (1919-1921). Harvey O'Connor's *Revolution in Seattle,* Monthly Review Press, 1964, gives details of Seattle strike and movement people involved. *Butte Daily Bulletin* of the time (one filed in Wayne State) is repository of both local history and all news that cheered leftists, gives extensive space to left organizations for veterans; for anti-labor purposes in launching American Legion see series in *Nation,* July 7 through 28, 1921 and William Gellerman's *American Legion as Educator,* 1937. Ford strike, Toledo (Rossford) detailed in Wortman dissertation, pp. 101-109. For Sioux City see Taft, "Mayor Short and the AWO," in *Labor History,* Spring 1966.

Centralia: Kornbluh has Anna Louise Strong's biographies of the four defendants, pp 271-274; *Pacific Northwest Quarterly,* October, 1954 for Robert Tyler article, April 1966 for McLelland summary of literature on case, and April 1968 for Ray Gunn's article on Ray Becker; *Industrial Worker,* March 17, 1950 for obituary of Becker, buried as Rev. Burgdorf, and February 1973 for research by Tom Copeland on Elmer Smith. There is 1973 reprint of Chaplin's *Centralia Conspiracy* with updating foreword by Eugene Nelson available from IWW.

Winnipeg: See *Canadian Historical Review,* June 1970, for David J. Bercuson's account of Winnipeg strike prolonged out of bureaucratic fear of radical implications of industrial union structure, 1969, pp. 381-399 for Richard Allen's essay on "The Social Gospel," or his 1971 book, *The Social Passion,* Toronto University Press.

Latin America: Peter De Shazzo (Dept. of History, University of Wisconsin, Madison) and Robert J. Halstead (Dept. of History, University of Massachusetts,

Boston) have made the only extensive study of the
IWW in Latin America. Their as yet unpublished paper
traces IWW in Mexico from WFM support for strikers
at Cananea 1906 through the 1911 fight against Diaz,
activities via Casa del Obrero Mundial, and 1917–1929
efforts in Tampico despite opposition of Mexican government and U.S. Navy. The Chile account notes successes among marine transport and construction workers 1918–1924, repeated repressions, temporary revival 1931 after fall of Ibanez, and merger into CGT. It
includes some account of IWW efforts in Peru, Ecua-
dor and Argentina, and of its Spanish-language publications here and abroad. The manuscript, which may
be quoted with their permission, is available only from
them.

Chapter XI (1922-1929). Maritime: *Pacific Historical
Review,* 1950, pp 385-396, for Giles T. Brown, "West
Coast Phase of the Maritime Strike of 1921"; also
November 1969 for article, "Politics of Confronta-
tion," for free speech angle of San Pedro 1923 strike.
On this strike, Louis B. Perry and Richard S. Perry
give 25 pages in their *History of the Los Angeles Labor Movement 1911-1941* (University of California
Press, 1963), treating the strike as a disturbance of
the labor movement. Dublin Dan's verses, "The Portland Revolution," in various editions of IWW songbook 1933 to date, depict IWW enthusiasm over 1922
events in Portland.

Agriculture: Don D. Lescohier, "IWW in Wheat Harvest," *Harpers,* August 1923, reports 1922 trip by this
economist and his staff living the life of the harvester.

Lumber: On IWW job conditioning activities see
E.B. Mittleman's articles in *Quarterly Journal of Economics,* June and December 1923.

Trials: Re Attorney Harold Mulkes (page 148), see
NYT, Jan. 15, 1922; on Criminal Syndicalism cases in
California, see Woodrow Whitten, *American Philoso-
phical Transactions,* 1969, pp. 1-73.

1924 split: Gambs' book is the only readily available one, otherwise Thomas McEnroe, "IWW Theories,
Organization Problems and Appeals as revealed in *In-*

dustrial Worker," University of Minnesota dissertation 1960, and chief study of the IWW, 1924 to 1973, a Ph.D. dissertation in Sociology by Leland W. Robinson, Northwestern University, 1974, unfortunately entitled "Social Movement Organizations in Decline: A Case Study of the IWW," 442 pages, available in three forms from University Microfilms, order No. 74-7808.

Colorado Coal: Gambs; Charles J. Bayard, "The 1927-1928 Colorado Coal Strike," in *Pacific Historical Review,* 1963, pp. 235-250; or Donald J. McClurg, "The Colorado Coal Strike of 1927—Tactical Leadership of the IWW," in *Labor History,* Winter 1963, pp. 68-92. An opera dealing with the shooting of six strikers Nov. 21, 1927, titled *Columbine,* with music by Mary Davis, libretto by Joanna Sampson, was produced at Boulder, Colorado Civic Opera April 1973.

Chapter XII (1930-1940). On Harlan, Ky.: Gambs gives some description of IWW involvement. In 1972 Appalachian Movement Press, Huntington, W.Va., reprinted E.J. Costello's 1931 pamphlet, "The Shame That Is Kentucky's." Herbert Mahler's papers re defense of these miners at Tamiment Institute. On Yakima, 1933, Litchman papers at University of Washington, Seattle; article by Cletus Daniel in *Pacific Northwest Quarterly,* October 1974.

Metal and Machinery Workers: Chief study is Roy T. Wortman's dissertation, "The IWW in Ohio," University Microfilms, Order no. 72-4695; extensive discussion of contract question in Robinson's dissertation, no. 74-7808, cited in regard to preceding chapter.

On IWW in Canada: Gary Jewell's account appeared as supplement to *Industrial Worker,* May, 1975.

On Hormel stay-in 1933 see article by Larry D. Engelmann in *Labor History,* Fall 1974.

Chapter XIII (1941-1955). *Industrial Worker* for period, Wortman's and Robinson's dissertations; see notes on archival sources.

Chapter XIV (1955–1975). For membership figures: Leland W. Robinson did much of the basic work in this area in his doctoral dissertation, "Social Movement Organizations in Decline: A Case Study of the IWW," available from University Microfilms. Jerry Calvert's less comprehensive study, "A Changing Radical Political Organization: the Wobblies," although unpublished, was still useful. It was submitted as a Ph.D. thesis to Washington State University in 1972.

Other important sources include Gary Jewell's "IWW in Canada," which first appeared as a supplement to the *Industrial Worker* in May, 1976, and is now available through the IWW General Headquarters as a pamphlet; *Industrial Worker* for the period; *General Organization Bulletin;* General Headquarters correspondence files, and personal interviews with several participants.

Many towns are listed under Strikes only if an IWW strike occurred there. Check also notes in appendix for relevant chapter.

238   INDEX